THE ODD THING ABOUT THE COLONEL

& other pieces

COLIN WELCH

The Odd Thing About the Colonel

& other pieces

Edited by
Craig Brown & Frances Welch

Bellew · London
in association with
The Daily Telegraph

First published in Great Britain in 1997
by Bellew Publishing Company Limited
8 Balham Hill, London SW12 9EA

A catalogue record for this title is available
from the British Library.

ISBN 1 85725 122 9

Typeset by Antony Gray
Printed and bound in Great Britain by
Hartnolls Ltd, Bodmin, Cornwall

CONTENTS

MUSIC

WAY OF THE WORLD

HOME AND ABROAD

BOOKS

SOCIALISM

Preface

Colin Welch wrote his first article, for the *Glasgow Herald*, in 1949. He wrote his last – on Richard Neville and *Oz* – for *The Times*, in 1995. In between, he wrote many thousands of articles, only a handful of which we have been able to include in this book. Even when anonymous, as in many editorials for the *Daily Telegraph*, his style was instantly recognisable, his thoughts entirely his own. This has made our task of editing both richly enjoyable and desperately tricky. We have had to exclude articles which many of his friends will have remembered with fondness. Notable among these are his parliamentary sketches, both for the *Daily Telegraph*, from 1950 to 1964, and for the *Daily Mail*, from 1984 to 1992. Linked so closely – and often brilliantly – to the comings and goings at Westminster, these now seem to us of less permanent worth than his other pieces.

We would like to thank those who have helped us in collecting and choosing the contents: Sybil Welch, Charles Moore, Mel Lasky, Peregrine Worsthorne, Michael Wharton, Nick Welch, Nicholas Garland, Edward Pearce, Frank Johnson, Kit Wharton and Tony Robinson. Also, special thanks to Colin's agents, Andrew and Margaret Hewson, for their faith in the project.

CRAIG BROWN
FRANCES WELCH

Dedication

In April 1995 my father suffered a stroke from which he never recovered. He was unconscious for nearly two years, a long-term patient at three NHS hospitals – the Princess Margaret Hospital in Swindon, the Royal National Hospital for Rheumatic Diseases in Bath and the Savernake Hospital in Marlborough and lastly a nursing home, Brendoncare in Froxfield.

Over those two years, he was looked after by many different nurses and members of staff. Their kindness, both to him and to those who visited him, made what should have been an unbearable situation bearable.

They carried out their nursing duties with dedication, but added much more of their own, always calling him by name ('Colin' or even 'Col'), playing him his favourite pieces of classical music on a cassette, and lending him a dignity that his stroke might otherwise have robbed him of. For Christmas '95 they gave him a Gilbert and Sullivan tape and for his 72nd birthday a large cake, which we distributed amongst his fellow patients.

The cheer and comfort they offered us, his visitors, was often the difference between hope and despair. My father was never able to express his gratitude so I'd like to say thank you from him as well as from us, his family. We dedicate this book to these kind people, his last friends.

F. W.

Introduction by Peregrine Worsthorne

It is right and proper – as well as generous – for the *Daily Telegraph* to be associated with the publishing of this collection of Colin Welch's journalism. Working for that newspaper from 1949–80, eventually as deputy editor, he pretty well *gave* – so exiguous were the salaries in those pre-Black days – the best years of his working life to that paper, which he read avidly and enthusiastically until his reading days were over. He differed from those of his Cambridge contemporaries contemplating a career in journalism, including myself, in that the *Daily Telegraph* was the paper he actually wanted to work for; his first choice. Whereas most of us in the late 1940s were attracted by the classier, more prestigious reputations of *The Times* or, depending on our political bent, the *Guardian*, the *Observer*, the *New Statesman* or *The Spectator*, he had always been impressed by the dullness, the lack of smartness, the bourgeois respectability of the *Telegraph*, for whose bank-manager readers he had not only great respect but also – even more peculiar in a senior scholar at Cambridge – boundless affection.

It most certainly was not that he identified with the *Daily Telegraph* or its readers. On the contrary, he was bohemian to a fault, drawn most irresistibly to wine, women and song, late hours and a rackety private life. It was more, if you like, an attraction of opposites. It was because he was so vulnerable to the attractions of wildness, dissipation, disorder and idleness that he saw the need for steadiness, sobriety, order and hard work. Somebody had to keep the show on the road and since he was all too aware of his own shortcomings in this respect, the last thing he was inclined to do was to disparage those better at it. So instead of wanting to *épater les bourgeois*, as was the general preference among writers in those days – *vide* the young

Kingsley Amis in *Lucky Jim* – he wanted nothing more than to be allowed to defend them, and the more he saw of life in general, and the more he lived his own in particular, the fiercer this determination grew.

In an article, one of his finest, recalling the Normandy campaign, he describes how his own experiences then of the cruel chaos of war made him even more aware than before of how mistaken it was to risk cracking the crust of civilisation. *Epater les bourgeois* indeed. He had seen where German radical romanticism could lead and, like another dream turning into a nightmare in the Soviet Union, it didn't work. Both as a result of looking inward and sensing how easily and fatally an individual life might collapse into ruin, and by looking outwards and observing how easily the same fate could befall a whole civilisation, he had developed a horror of those who stir things up, of those who despise the conventions, of those who mock the pieties, and of those, above all, who subvert the established order.

In Colin, however, unlike in Evelyn Waugh, this dread of chaos, as much personal as collective, induced no warm nostalgic feelings for the old upper class, whose disorderly and hedonistic habits, and seductively stylish way of life, seemed to him more part of the illness than part of the cure. For Colin the cure lay with the middle class, with the bourgeoisie, about whom he waxed not one jot less lyrical than did Evelyn Waugh about the aristocracy, the only difference being that whereas Waugh actually wanted to join the upper class – dress like it, behave like it – Colin never went quite that far with the middle class, not at any rate in his chosen method of transport, a high-powered motorcycle, or in his favourite clothing, a black leather jacket or, least of all, in his hopelessness about money. As someone who preached so eloquently about capitalism, Colin was sadly incapable of putting it into practice – in this respect he was not unlike Evelyn Waugh with his Catholicism.

With the war won, Colin returned to Peterhouse, Cambridge, as did I, and it was then that I remember him first enthusing about the bourgeois virtues of Soames in the *Forsyte Saga* – the subject of another fine essay – just when the rest of us were falling hook, line and sinker for the aristocratic charms of Sebastian Flyte in *Brideshead Revisited*. This again was typical. Colin always preferred the unsmart to the smart. He preferred Stowe (where our paths first crossed) to Eton, Peterhouse to King's College or Trinity, the Royal Warwicks to the Coldstream Guards – for which we were both found unsuitable – Galsworthy to Waugh and, most significant of all, the *Telegraph* to *The Times*.

How the *Daily Telegraph* came to hear of Colin or, once they had heard of him, to offer him a job, history does not relate. Sent down from Cambridge without a degree for threatening to blow up the bursar – a retired air vice-marshal and, as it happened, loyal reader of the *Daily Telegraph* – quite penniless, having foolishly entrusted his patrimony to a crooked accountant, he cannot have seemed, on the face of it, a very promising leader writer for that bible of the bourgeoisie. But somehow or other, once again proving that God does move in mysterious ways his wonders to perform, the *Daily Telegraph* did offer him a job. Never before or since – except possibly on the day when Sybil accepted his hand in marriage – was he so over the moon. He took me out that night to celebrate his appointment – needless to say not at the Ritz, or at a gentlemen's club, or at some legendary Soho or Fitzrovian joint – all of which he religiously steered clear of – but, characteristically, at some unstylish Earl's Court eating house, popular with Australians, which nobody but he had heard of before or has ever heard of since. Being then already smugly ensconced as a leader writer on *The Times*, I rather pitied my friend, and found his extreme excitement – almost on a par with Churchill's on the night in 1940 when he first became prime minister – grotesquely disproportionate.

As it turned out he was entirely justified in feeling that his life work, indeed his destiny, was about to begin. For although Colin sadly never became editor of the *Daily Telegraph* – as he deserved to do – his influence on the paper for twenty years was far greater than that of the men who did, two of whom regarded the *Telegraph* as little more than a *salon des refusés*, having come there only after being turned down for the editorship of *The*

Times. For Colin, as I have said, it was the culmination of an ambition, if not the consummation of a passion, and this strange combination of man and paper came to play a crucial role in nourishing the intellectual and moral soil out of which Thatcherism grew, a role equalled only by the dedicated groundwork of the Institute of Economic Affairs, and surpassed only by the inspirational preaching of Enoch Powell.

This dimension of his achievement is worth celebrating, I think, because his greatness as a journalist lay not just in his own writing – of which there are many examples in this book – but also in the general influence he exerted over many years on the *Daily Telegraph* and through the *Telegraph* on the course of British politics generally. Before he arrived the paper had little ideological cutting edge. About the only article of any real political impact it had carried was the famous one by Donald McLachlan, then deputy editor, calling for 'the smack of firm Government'. Since this article was credited with galvanising the prime minister, Anthony Eden, into the disaster of the Suez expedition, which precipitated his downfall, the less said about it the better. But except on that occasion in 1956 the paper had been content to rest on its 1930s laurels earned when, unlike *The Times*, the *Mail* and the *Express*, it did *not* support Neville Chamberlain in his policy of appeasement. Colin, by devotedly following the precepts of Adam Smith – brought up to date by Hayek and Milton Friedman – transformed it into the mostly widely read organ of what came to be known, many years later, as the Thatcherite social and economic counter-revolution.

If this transformation had been brought about with the proprietor's blessing it would have been remarkable enough. But in fact the proprietor, of those days, Michael Berry (later Lord Hartwell), very much a benevolent despot whose slightest word a largely sycophantic executive staff soon hardened into iron law, was a committed Keynesian, having been taught economics at Oxford in the 1930s by Keynes's biographer and disciple, Roy Harrod. So to begin with, at any rate, monetarist doctrine had to be introduced between the lines, almost in code, so as to avoid incurring the proprietor's blue pencil. The editor at that time, Maurice Green – a former city editor of *The Times* – whom Colin loved and admired, shared many of his heretical free-market views but much of the burden of arguing with, and incurring the irritation of, the proprietor fell on Colin's shoulders, as it did even more onerously and perilously when Bill Deedes, a delightful man entirely without ideological convictions, followed Green into the editorial chair.

For Colin this was a high risk crusade. To be a free-market enthusiast, or rather fanatic, in the Macmillan–Heath era was not the best way to earn a reputation for a safe pair of hands, either within the office or outside – particularly if you travelled to work, as Colin did, dressed in black leather on a motorcycle. In fact it was the best way to be laughed out of court, as I remember happening to Colin at a Bow Group dinner where Heath, then the leader of the party, was guest of honour. The subject of Heath's talk was state education and in the question session afterwards Colin's advocacy of the voucher system got short shrift. 'Not only impractical but retrograde,' Mr Heath snorted, with the coldest of glares.

The transformation of the *Daily Telegraph* from a paper of the middle way to a paper of the Thatcherite right was not, of course, Colin's work alone, but it was very much his doing that over the years its opinion-writing staff began to share his views. For as deputy editor he helped choose the new recruits, and if they were not of his persuasion on arrival, they were very soon converted, not so much by the strength of his own arguments as by the devastating mockery he would level at those of his opponents. First to arrive, entirely due to Colin, was the Tory seer, Peter Utley, then the incomparable satirist, Michael Wharton – who took over the Peter Simple column which Colin had started – followed by Frank Johnson, now editor of *The Spectator*, and John O'Sullivan, now editor of America's leading journal of the right. Entryism was the name of the game. Without Lord Hartwell noticing it, a non-ideological leader-writing staff had been replaced by an intensely ideological one, of the highest quality, which Bill Deedes was powerless to control, even supposing he wanted to.

So Colin's career in journalism consisted of much more than his own writing. By his example and exertions he created a team of writers at the core of the paper who made it something which it had never been before. Always the leader in news-gathering, it now became as well the leader in opinion-forming as well. Nor was this done simply by the strength of Colin's intellect. Just as important was the charm of his most unusual character. For he was immensely funny as well as wise. It was this combination that made writing for the leader page and feature pages of the *Daily Telegraph* so special when he was still around. Unlike run-of-the-mill Thatcherite think-tanks, this one had moral depths, rich cultural resonance, wide erudition and, most valuable of all, abundant wit. As the paper, under Lord Hartwell's mismanagement, sank ever deeper into the financial mire, its intellectual reputation, under the inspiration of Colin Welch, began to rise. Even the chattering classes began to take notice, as did their gossip sheet, *Private Eye.* Writers and pundits from all over the world, instead of limiting their Fleet Street visits to the legendary El Vino's or Dr Johnson's Cheshire Cheese, began to call in also at the Kings and Keys where the *Daily Telegraph* staff were known to hang out at all times of the day and night. Perish the thought, the *Daily Telegraph* had started to become, much to Colin's amused dismay, smart and fashionable, the kind of place he had always shunned.

AUTOBIOGRAPHY

❦

The Dreadful Fate of Smethwick Two

'I say, Squelchy,' my informant's voice dropped to a theatrical whisper: 'do you know why old Whatters was chucked out of the army?' 'No.' A conspiratorial glance both ways. 'Keep it dark. Don't tell a soul. For swearing.' My informant was assured, if not of his own precise veracity, at least of the receptive credulity of his audience. At eight years old, confined in a prep school as remote as any penal colony, neither of us had that rich experience of life which might have leapt immediately to the possibility that graver misdemeanours might have caused Mr Whatfield's downfall. Of the hated maths master we were prepared to believe any atrocity we could imagine. He would call us up in class to stand beside him. His pencil stabbing with jerky menace at our stomachs, the snarled threats and reek of stout and fags which belched forth from under his bristling moustache, his dandruff and blue-black five o'clock shadow all awoke in us supernatural terrors.

He drove with ferocious *panache* a bull-nosed Morris tourer with many essential parts missing. Through gaps in the scanty floor boards you could see the road whizzing past and exposed cogs whirring. Into these, his seat collapsing, Mr Whatfield at last fell backwards, his legs waving impotently in the air like those of an overturned beetle. The seat of his light grey, sharply-pressed flannels was remorselessly chewed up in the machinery till the speeding, driverless motor was arrested by a tree. Mr Whatfield's curses on this occasion spectacularly supported the cashiering tale: they would have astonished the broadest-minded

RSM. His mishap, I'm afraid, gave widespread pleasure. Had Childline existed fifty-five years ago, we'd have denounced him at once, innocent as he was of anything normally called molestation. Have Miss Rantzen and her friends, irresponsibly soliciting delation by telephone, forgotten how mischievous, vengeful or even ruthlessly wicked children can be?

At eight we were incapable of judging our school, its good points or its bad. We knew no other and wrongly thought that all schools were like this. We were blind to the beauties of the house, a noble neo-Grecian edifice *à la* Smirke or Dobson, and its rolling beech and rhododendron infested park. I came across it recently, pictured in a book about stately homes now demolished. I realised with a pang that I too had dwelt in Arcadia and never knew it.

As for the school, hindsight places it unhesitatingly in the last of the four grades established by Church and Gargoyle, the scholastic agents in Evelyn Waugh's *Decline and Fall*: 'Leading School, First-rate School, Good School and School.' With Llanabba Castle, Strutley Hall was School, *tout court*, though with pathetic traces remaining of better days as 'Good School' or even 'First-rate'. The scholarship boards were impressive, though less was added to them every year. Classics were taught, in an accent which even Porson might have thought old-fashioned, by a distinguished scholar, himself fallen on evil times. Tall, grey, old and vague, he was found by us exquisitely witty. 'Smith,' he would enquire with pain of a boy fooling about in prep, 'do you really like yourself?' And we would squirm with delight.

To adapt Tolstoy's remark about families, all good and happy schools resemble each other while bad and unhappy schools are all bad and unhappy in their own way. Strutley Hall was richly idiosyncratic.

My informant about Whatters' sacking was always called the Sabre Tooth Tiger. This did him an injustice. His teeth, though prominent and ill-restrained by a complex plate, were as perfectly regular as tombstones in a military cemetery, more like those of an amiable horse than of any carnivore. Indeed, it was as a starch-eater that he won fame, if you assume sago to be a starch rather than proteinous frogs' eggs as we then supposed. At a price of one peardrop per plate, he would rapidly eat thirty or forty plates of sago pudding for those who couldn't stomach the obligatory slime. He was an indomitably cheerful, clever, inventive and resourceful boy, an expert civil engineer – a McAlpine or Manzoni of his day – who built deep in the rhododendrons a network of cambered cement roads for Dinky Toys, complete with drains, pavements, bridges, cuttings, roundabouts and garages. The STT was also a prodigious source of wizard japes and wheezes, always first, too, with 'the latest', as often with verses appropriate to the occasion. In this joyous figure were embodied aspects of the later constructive Faust, the Last Minstrel and Blowitz.

As in prisons and Fleet Street pubs of yore, rumours abounded at Strutley Hall, fantastic seeming yet often hardly more so than whatever truth lay behind and might have prompted them. 'I say, Squelchy, heard the latest? It's awful! Smethwick Two's *dead*.' 'What, *dead*?' 'Yes, of *starvation*!' 'Of *starvation*!' 'Yes. Keep it dark.'

This rumour was at least half true. Smethwick Two, alas, was dead all right, though perhaps not of starvation. We were all known only by surnames, with numbers added if necessary. Christian names were rigorously repressed, used only if unusual for choral ridicule: 'Dear little Egbert – wah, wah, wah'. Family ties were also suppressed so far as possible. Dehumanised as 'mops', 'pops' and 'sops', relations turned up rarely and furtively, to be subjected to hostile scrutiny and often to bring shame on their loved ones. 'Barber's sop's a skivvy!' 'Fowler's mop gets her false teeth at Woollies.' 'Goldsmith's pop's an oiky Jew.'

The full reality of life at Strutley Hall eluded not only us inmates but also my mother, who assumed control of my destiny after my father's early death when I was eight. This was partly because I told her little. Our letters were censored, and sneaking was a fearful crime, condignly punished by various irregular but powerful courts of honour, as terrifying as any *Freikorps Femgericht*. In her innocent ignorance my mother must have found the week's howling which preceded my third term almost inexplicable, as well as deeply distressing to such a kind parent.

No one fully in the picture would have sent me back in dark grey cord shorts with so much room for growth (room almost for two to grow) or in a jersey of the wrong colour with a turned over collar and *buttons*(!) at the neck, like a little boy's. She thought the jersey 'nice': other boys would envy it. Nice! As if anything could be nice which differed in the slightest from the Harrods' regulation kit! Any variation led only to a vicious hue and cry, to persecution and pogroms, to 'rumbles' or 'lammings', as brutal bullying was locally known. Tolerated or even admired were only the grey *Lederhosen* permitted to a boy of German extraction, who, however, was soundly lammed for having sunk the *Lusitania* and murdered Nurse Cavell. What history we knew we turned, as in Ireland and Germany itself, to dark purposes.

Admittedly, growth did take place, gradually reducing my shorts to normal proportions: but the penalties of unorthodoxy are most feared by the smallest. The most favoured shorts were old, short, fairly tight and washed out to a near white. They were, of course, a mark of seniority, of successful survival. Did they also make oblique references, unrecognised at the time, to sex? In retrospect one can see that all-mastering instinct already slyly at work on us, even at nine years old, rattling and snuffling under doors still tight closed, trying to force an entry, assuming in the process, like Proteus, all sorts of weird, vague and tentative forms, some of them perverse and shameful, to be kept private.

Even the steel-rimmed spectacles I was supposed to wear always, but didn't, must have had furtive sexual connotations for me. They were necessary all right. The cheery history master used to write notes on the blackboard. Prominently figuring in these, especially during the Reformation period, were mysterious zealots he briskly called the RCs. Unable to see the blackboard, I transcribed these as Arsees. My long held impression was thus that our country was entirely dominated till the sixteenth century by an exotic sect like the Parsees (familiar to me from seafaring forebears) who, then expelled, continued to give much trouble, especially in the reign of James II, himself an Arsee.

* * *

I loathed my specs and was fascinated by them. Did I discern in them elements of the mask, so often a potent erotic accessory? Were they also a mark of dependence, of inferiority and humiliation, of weakness and vulnerability, of imperfect manhood (my father had had perfect sight), appealing thus to undreamt-of masochistic tendencies? Even the velvet-lined case they came in smelt of some interesting organic glue. Men, we know, seldom make passes at girls who wear glasses. I was an exception, for reasons perhaps buried in that distant past.

More obviously sexual was the manifest relish with which fifty-five years ago a senior boy, a 'pre' no less and with a distinguished career ahead, buried his face in his own used bed-clothes, sniffing greedily. More obviously sexual still was the rude and precocious boy who, in the sickroom of which we two were the sole occupants, masturbated publicly, presumably for my edification as well his own. Aged nine, I witnessed this 'explicit' or 'adult' entertainment with total and genuine bafflement, as if at a Pinter play: don't call us, we'll call you. Yet it sticks in the memory, while manifestations which made more sense at the time do not.

The lammings were directed specially at boys with some sad weakness, boys inclined to 'blub', boys who stammered or, worse, wetted their beds or dirtied their knickers. Unsurprisingly in the circumstances, there were many of these. Their shame was the mark, the cause and effect, of their utter misery. The cruel retribution it brought on them exacerbated their condition. Unkind sobriquets were pinned to them, like tin cans to a dog's tail, and jeeringly repeated by circles of dancing persecutors in rhythmic chorus – 'Fishy' for a boy whose knickers smelt of stale urine, 'Cowpat' for a boy whose lapses were all too solid: 'Oh dear, oh dear, Nannie's forgotten Cowpat's nappies – goo, goo, goo. Baby Cowpat!' Blushing stammerers were surrounded by mobs derisively intoning d-d-d-or p-p-p-or mocking the tongue-tied apopletic hum which Patrick Campbell made famous.

Yet the most rewarding target for lammings was always a boy called the Maniac, or the Animal, who more or less literally went mad under pressures applied with malign skill. He would dance about; his hands would wave wildly and claw at the air, striving to scratch his tormentors; he would aim vicious kicks, only to have his foot seized and to be tipped back violently on to his head. Hoarse, meaningless screams, real foam, would issue from his mouth, distorted like a Greek mask into an agonised square. Never did the lenses of his battered steel spectacles fully coincide with his eyes: one lens was always too low, the other too high. During these contretemps, the specs would usually fly off altogether, fantastically bent, striking with a tinkle some distant radiator or hurtling clean through the window, leaving the Maniac blind as well as mad, a fearsome embodiment of impotent rage.

And what did I do during these disgraceful proceedings? The question might be put to me as to various 'good Germans' emerging shamefaced from the Nazi time, and might be answered in the same shabby and evasive way. I was not myself a prime target for lammings. I got my share, no more. For the rest, like good Germans appalled by the excesses of the *Kristallnacht*, I stood aside and kept my distance, not knowing or wishing to know too much, too small, apprehensive and apparently solitary – though others were in fact shocked too – to court danger by protest.

The terror was in fact roughly organised in two rival gangs, fighting for street supremacy much as Communists and Nazis had fought in pre-Hitler Germany. They were both led by big, superannuated boys, too wild and irresponsible to be made pre's and too thick to pass common entrance into even the dimmest public school, staying on therefore till aged fifteen or more. One warlord was a brutally benevolent despot, humorous, unscrupulous, popular and lazy, a sort of Danton, ferocious but by no means without attractive characteristics. His father was rumoured to be in prison for fraud, though presumably his fees were paid. The other seemed coldly vicious, a real turd. In the centrifugal strife which preceded Hitler, many Germans took refuge in Nazism or Communism who were not strongly attracted to either. At Strutley Hall, too, you had to join or be associated with one mob or the other and put yourself within its sphere of influence. You couldn't survive on your own. Only innate wickedness or abject terror could lead you into the turd's mob, though it lack recruits. I established friendly feudal relations with Danton, acknowledged his suzerainty, enjoyed his rough protection and inevitably shared some of his guilt.

Danton's problem was to get rid of the turd, to 'rub him out'. His plan was simple and effective. He stole a rifle from the school armoury, wrapped it in a scarf and other clothes marked with the turd's nametapes and hid it under the stage. Even sneaking being permitted to a warlord, he reported the turd as having been seen leaving the armoury with the rifle and hiding it where it would be found. The turd was expelled, leaving Danton supreme, perhaps even till called up or till the school foundered. The turd, I think, came to a sticky end, and I can't help wondering still what part was played in his downfall by the early injustice done to him by a Night of the Long Knives which I knew about but had neither exactly abetted nor deplored nor denounced. Not much, I hope: he seemed damned already. Sinful so to judge him, true, but sinful too to harbour excessive guilt, so they say. Ho hum.

There are no bad soldiers, so they also say, only bad officers. By the same token, a school as dreadful as Strutley Hall looked at from below must have postulated a truly dreadful staff. This was not altogether so. Inadequate it must have been, but in a negative rather than a positive sense, negligent and frivolous rather than evil, more Pennyfeather than Squeers.

Then there was the headmaster's French wife. Rumour of course had it that he had married her for economic reasons, to have at his disposal free of charge someone to teach French, which she did, gracefully, to the little ones. Her gentle melancholy supported the economic theory. Her 'fragrant' beauty and mysterious, shadowy elegance hinted at more romantic possibilities. My first sight of a picture by Helleu reminded me of her. When my father died during termtime, I was entrusted to her charge. Together we cut flowers and walked slowly, hand in hand, through the park. In her presence you could talk quietly, remain silent, weep, hug and be hugged – all activities otherwise proscribed in a world probably as alien and incomprehensible to her as to us. To the bereaved she dispensed French chocolate – exotic to me, to her, perhaps, a comforting reminder of home. Were we both exiles, consoling each other?

There was the headmaster himself whose murderous smile made us clench our buttocks and walk self-consciously. Did it portend a beating? It often did. There was his son, too, by a previous marriage: a vast, indistinctly spoken, loose-lipped hulk, like his father an amateur heavyweight boxer. What he taught I can't remember, but his methods remain in the mind. Roaring with incoherent rage, he would violently throw whatever lay to hand: chalk, metal waste-paper bin, most usually the blackboard duster which was not a mere cloth but a heavy bit of wood faced with felt. It would hit the skull of some luckless victim, usually the wrong one, with a crack like a mallet on a croquet ball, often sailing thereafter upwards, right through the window, leaving behind clouds of chalk in the astonished air. These frequent outbursts were in fact more comic than tragic, to be eagerly anticipated rather than deplored. They could be heard and enjoyed three or four classrooms away – 'Listen, the Bruiser's gone off again.'

The rest of the staff seem in retrospect amiable if remote. A green baize door separated their quarters from us. Through it seeped distant laughter, the occasional tinkle of a glass, jazz from a wind-up gramophone. This was prudently stuffed with socks (note for the young: origin of the expression put a sock in it') to avoid paining the classics master or infuriating the head. Sometimes the socks would be drawn inexorably into the clockwork. The jazz would slow to a profound, Brucknerian *adagio* and Jessie Matthews would sound like Chaliapin.

Two of the masters were actually famous – or seemed so to us – though not for any academic attainment. One batted gracefully for a minor county. Another played the piano in night clubs and composed with equal facility pieces for Hutch and rousing sub-Elgarian hymn-tunes, one of which I can hum to this day. To pin any vast burden of guilt on to such harmless innocents would be plainly absurd. One thing at least they did teach me: that as much misery, or more, can spring from tolerated disorder as from the harshest discipline. This last, indeed, was present too, but only intermittently and capriciously, not to suppress anarchy but savagely to mark its borders. The old Ottoman empire was, I fancy, governed rather similarly: the prevalent *laissez faire* punctuated by rare but memorably effective atrocities.

Strutley Hall was, I suppose, in its way character-building, a preparation for life – for life at its worst. Kindness and justice were not wholly absent. But they were rare luxuries, treats like jam *and* butter on your bread. We were not to expect them, or to blub at their absence.

Finally my mother cottoned on – I think it was the death of Smethwick Two that alerted her – and transferred me to a prep school of a very different sort. Here I was greeted by a mild, plump, blinking boy, who explained to me some of the prevailing *mores*. 'You see, Colin – it is Colin, isn't it? – we're all specially kind to Charles Blewett, because he's – it's hard to know how to put it – because he's, well, a bit weak in the head.'

I blinked in my turn, as might the reluctant SS man who wakes up suddenly to find he's been transferred to a Quaker ambulance unit. I did not then know the prisoners' chorus from *Fidelio*. A pity. No other music could suffice. My eyes filled with tears as I thought of the poor Maniac left behind. His lot may have improved under Danton. I hope so.

The Spectator, 23 September 1989

*The Trouble with Welch**

You will understand how difficult it is for me to do impartial justice to this book. In the house the Berrys built I spent some thirty years, three-quarters of my working life. To its prosperity I devoted such talent and industry as I had, with results mixed, half successful and appreciated, half not. All, I suppose, was in the outcome ephemeral, swept away to Hastings in the Black Knight, though Perry Worsthorne – bless him – maintains on the *Sunday Telegraph* a shadowy existence, waxing and waning amidst the chaos. They were years crowded mostly with happiness, interest and struggle, mirth and friendship, though ending in frustration and despair. For this I blame in large part myself, about whom I belatedly learnt much, not all creditable.

I was on the *Daily Telegraph* in succession a leader writer, the first – though never the complete or best – Peter Simple, a parliamentary sketch writer (which I am now again for the blessed *Daily Mail*), then deputy editor, then, well, still deputy editor, the road ahead blocked, then nothing. Ideally qualified then by experience at least, the very chap to review this book? Well, yes and no. Knows a lot, true, perhaps too much, especially about matters which directly concerned him. Chip on his shoulder? Can't see the wood for the trees? You'll inevitably get more I, I and I than is proper about a book in which he, Duff, tells us about them, the Berrys. I can't do it any other way, and I hope that something about him and them will emerge *en route*.

I know too about scandalous matters – drink problems, adulteries and so on – which Duff has prudently or charitably

* Review of *The House the Berrys Built: Inside the* Telegraph *1928–1986* by Duff Hart-Davis.

suppressed or shrouded in nameless generalities. He was trying, he explains, to write a public chronicle, not a long gossipy column emanating from behind the bar curtains or from under the bed. Fair enough, and well in the *Telegraph* tradition of public propriety and private peccancy. But who on earth, for instance, was the leader writer who was once dead drunk in the gutter outside the Kings and Keys at 2.45 p.m.? Editor Sir Colin Coote did indeed make some weird appointments and his great successor, Maurice Green, was not always lucky. But wasn't 2.45 a bit early or late, with the leader writers' conference due in an hour?

Within his chosen limits, Duff has done an absolutely first-class reporter's job – fair, comprehensive, thorough, to me fascinating. Don't get any idea that humour has been austerely excluded – the book is full of good and illuminating stories. And don't get the idea that the book told me nothing, that I knew it already. On the contrary, it told me lots, explained much that was obscure or hidden from me, much that happened before I came or after I went, much in particular about the deeds and misdeeds of the heroic and intelligent 'sycophants' – not my word – of the paper's management. These harassed men we respected, at times pitied, liked and trusted, but did not know as well as we should have done. They had little time for journalists. It was all spent in hopeless wrestling with the print unions. What a shock it was when the final catastrophe mercilessly revealed among them some clay feet! Why, even Michael Berry, Lord Hartwell, that is, the proprietor, was shown up, inadequate where we had least expected it. We might grumble and quarrel with him about journalistic matters, but at least we thought that the money side of the show was in safe hands. As journalists often are, we were wrong.

Michael Berry was, according to Duff, 'honest, decent, fair and self-effacing – and about how many other Fleet Street proprietors could that be said?' Duff is dead right there. Michael was indeed one of the straightest men I've ever met, and I'd like this to be remembered throughout whatever I have to say about him.

Towards the close of my *Telegraph* days, I laboured foolishly under grievances imposed upon me by this man, more wounding precisely because he was liked, respected and fatherly. I felt like, say, a child-molester sent down for embezzlement, or vice versa. Resentful, nothing much really to grumble about, but wasn't there something wrong? Weren't my real crimes and shortcomings quite different from what Michael thought or, alternatively, I concede, quite different from what he for charitable or other reasons ever said? Upon this long and baffling misunderstanding Duff throws much light, presumably derived mostly from Michael Berry himself – who else?

'The trouble with Welch,' Duff reveals, 'was that he was far too funny.' Instead of soberly dealing with facts *à la Telegraph*, 'his mind piled castles of fantasy high into the air'. 'A fount of merriment', he was apparently 'perplexed only by the problem of what joke to tell next'. Talent is not altogether denied to this odious creature but he had Michael worried. 'Marvellous' in descriptive writing (really?) his style was 'quite unsuitable for serious leaders'. Such misgivings engendered Peter Simple, not so much a device to keep Welch out of mischief as a small oasis in which mischief was licensed, smiled on.

This picture of the young Welch seems now to its ageing sitter a high-piled castle of fantasy. Others may hotly disagree; who after all knows himself perfectly? I was probably funnier then than now, and then as now I would defend humour's place in rational discourse. But I was also, like Matthew Arnold in the Beerbohm drawing, perfectly serious and solemn, po-faced or even pompous, didactic and theory-ridden, the respectful if unworthy follower of Burke, de Tocqueville, Hayek, and other seminal savants. Even what I wrote for Peter Simple, before it acquired that Whartonian perfection, seems mostly now to err on the sententious rather than the frivolous side.

If this priggish youth seemed perplexed only about what joke to tell next, perhaps that is because of the acute difficulty of communicating with Michael Berry. Perry Worsthorne superbly describes the long chilly silences, luring the unwary further and further into error: 'Incapable of argument himself, he gives others enough rope to hang themselves', transforming 'his own inarticulateness into a dialectical skill'.

Without theory, said Hayek, the facts are dumb. Michael utterly disagreed. He was impatient of theory and ideas, though without them factual leaders are dumb. Facts he adored, nor was his appetite over-fastidious: he was hospitable enough to nonsense if it could be arrayed as hard news. Where philosophic discussion is perilous, or found boring and irritating, the temptation to take refuge in jokes is irresistible. Yes, Michael did have a marvellous sense of humour, which made good or even belied his philosophic Philistinism: for is not humour itself based on some theory or idea of what is normal and what is laughable? Anyway, we laughed often as all unknowing I dug my own grave.

The difficulties we had with leaders and the Berrys are well illustrated by an anecdote of my own which Duff gets slightly wrong: my fault doubtless. I wrote a leader attacking (no, not defending) Richard Neville and the hippy magazine *Oz*. Michael's wife Pamela did shriek at me before some outsiders at lunch, 'A *dreadful* leader, Colin – quite dreadful!' To suggest that she thought 'dreadful' a leader defending Neville, or that I could ever have written one, is to put us in the wrong boxes. She was more friendly to novel notoriety than I was. In self-defence, I mentioned that I'd had a record number of approving letters. 'Oh, yes,' she jeered, 'from retired colonels in *Cheltenham*!' – a class of persons dear to me and, I'd have thought, to the *Telegraph*.

Loyally silent during lunch, Michael attacked later. I had pointed out that some of the *Oz* gang, though noisily contemptuous of rational calculation and meticulous craftsmanship, wore spectacles, thus indicating their dependence on the humdrum world they despised. Michael was completely baffled. 'Why ridicule them for wearing specs? You wear specs. Robespierre and other revolutionaries probably wore specs. Why shouldn't *Oz* wear specs?' I can imagine him puzzling over my remark above about embezzlers and child-molesters, wondering to which crime I had confessed and kindly doubting whether I'd actually committed either.

I had never realised before reading Duff, I must admit, that my appointment as deputy editor to Maurice Green was made by the departing editor Coote without consulting anyone (what, not even Maurice Green?). It also much put out Michael Berry, who, however, did not feel he could countermand the appointment. Had I known all this, I might have refused, thus resolving the difficulty. It was Coote, too, who promised Perry Worsthorne the deputy editorship of the new *Sunday Telegraph*, which greatly annoyed the new editor, Donald McLachlan, whom Coote disliked. It is astonishing what a high and careless hand can achieve against seemingly immovable obstacles.

Already suspicious of me as 'too clever and too imaginative by half', Michael's reservations increased. I was 'incurably frivolous, incapable of keeping jokes and fantastical notions out of serious articles'. Worse was to follow. I had, it seems, 'a habit of changing [my] stance on important political matters', so that one leader was contradicted a few weeks later by another. Good gracious! 'A habit'? Did I *ever* do such a thing? I can't remember doing so; but then a chap who forgets a whole leader in a few weeks may forget everything else too. Yet the cautions and admonitions which Michael says he piled on me – to look back, to be consistent, to change slowly if at all – were precisely those which I piled on the leader writers and on myself. They were part of our *Weltanschauung*. The cast of my own mind, moreover, was also perhaps to a fault rigid, over-principled, even doctrinaire, inclined to apply stiff unchanging opinions to ever-changing new facts, changing results. These last may have offended Michael. On the other hand, he may have disliked the opinions which produced them. Perhaps what he really meant is that the opinions themselves ought to have changed, slowly, indeed, but more.

I must not give any vaunting impression that I alone incurred Michael's displeasure. 'Warning', wrote Peter Utley to Bill Deedes after I'd gone: 'Lord H thought Charles [Moore]'s leader on hereditary peers "perfectly frightful".' You and I may doubt whether it really was. Nor must I suggest that once a leader had appeared in the paper, for whatever reason, its sentiments became holy writ, never to be questioned or varied. Sir Colin Coote's anti-Americanism once tempted him into writing late at night what I and others thought disgraceful nonsense about Kennedy and Cuba. The consequent effective row did produce a marked and rapid change, which may of course have annoyed Michael Berry.

This abrupt change was really from the abnormal back to the norm. It was not achieved by any succession of jokes. Any perplexity I felt was about how to persuade Coote, a charming man to whom I owed so much, of the enormity, as it seemed then, of what he had hastily written – to persuade without discourtesy or disrespect. Nor was it only with jokes that, under Maurice Green's editorship, as Duff records, the late Peter

Utley and I and others 'sharpened the paper's traditional stance and – often to the considerable disquiet of the proprietor – set about redefining Tory ideas'. Did we achieve gradually a quiet conservative revolution? When Peter was around, indeed, humour was never far away; but it was either incidental or deployed purposefully to illuminate or clarify complex and difficult political and philosophical truths.

Over all the work of intellectual reconstruction Maurice presided benignly, protectively, cautiously, helpfully, indulgently, loyally, dare I say humorously? The responsibility after all was his. When Edward Heath executed his famous economic U-turn, we were all shocked. The paper, which had supported him till then loyally throughout, criticised him strongly. Mr Heath ('that horrible man', Maurice called him once, the worst I ever heard from this restrained source about Heath or anyone else) bitterly accused the paper of letting him down, though we saw it all exactly the other way round. Leaders, some written by me though all commissioned and approved by the cautious Maurice if he was there, drew mumbles of Keynesian disapproval from Michael. Yes, Keynesian, for Keynes' economic ideas had put down roots in Michael's youthful mind when he was a brilliant student, had survived there and had perhaps kept others out. But it was not, I suspect, the mind-blowing theorist Keynes who appealed to Michael. Rather was it the prestigious (old meaning) and beguiling man of affairs, effortlessly telling us all how to manage our country's business successfully without cost or thrift, without tears or pain.

On one particularly strained occasion, Maurice demanded of Michael, 'Are you asking for my resignation?' Startled, Michael stammered that er, yes, er, he supposed he was or rather, smiling, no, of course not. And an uneasy peace was restored.

My own position and prospects grew increasingly uncertain. In the end I asked Michael what his plans for me were. Was there a black ball, so to speak, against my succession to the editorship? If so, I ought to reconsider. Awkwardly honest as ever, hideously embarrassed, more than usually incoherent, Michael blurted out that there was indeed a black ball. He muttered something about 'lack of *gravitas*'. I swallowed this 'insult' (as a friend called it) as well as I could – not very well actually – and sloped off after a bit to do something unrewarding but rewarded for a Dutch oil tycoon – the *Mail* came later.

The fortunes and vicissitudes of the *Telegraph* remained inevitably my concern. I detected myself still editing it, applauding this, protesting at that, just as I had done for years while Maurice and later Bill Deedes were away. In their absences I wonder how Michael ever dared to commit his beloved paper to such frivolous and unworthy hands as my own. For he cannot have known how much I loved that paper too, and did not seem to notice that my editorial stints passed without any of the disasters he should logically have predicted.

Eventually, the dreadful crash came. Michael, according to Ivan Fallon, once city editor of the *Sunday Telegraph*, gave away 'nearly £900 million, and what he had worked for, [in] one of the great financial as well as personal tragedies of the age'.

After an interval I rallied round, offering sympathy, perhaps some sort of help, about as welcome perhaps as a man selling comic souvenir hats at the scene of an awful motorway pile-up. Michael wrote to me in terms familiar, flattering and defensive. I went to see him. I got the ghastly impression then – I hope by now totally misleading – that this great man, once so shrewd and illusion free, had no perfect idea of what had happened, of what had hit him and with what consequences. He seemed to be under at least two misapprehensions: one, that I still wanted or even expected to be editor of the transformed *Daily Telegraph* and, two, that he still had the power to prevent any such catastrophe. The consequent conversation was friendly and halting, confusing and negative. I left in perplexity, unable to summon up an appropriate joke.

About the new Conrad Black *Daily Telegraph* I can say little or nothing now from inside knowledge. It has jewels in its crown: Deedes, for instance, Mount, Heffer, Booker – until recently a different Peter Simple, but what a good one. Many of the new paper's opinions and stances, its appointments and dismissals have seemed to me alien, precipitate or inexplicable. Never mind: it is no longer in any sense my paper nor Michael's, alas, and financial success silences many doubts and reservations.

I must confess and you must believe that I read the last part of Duff's book with tears. Duff is not at all an over-emotional or lachrymose writer, yet deeply moving is his account of the simple and honourable functional creed which governed Michael's life's work, a creed indeed which I was always mindful of even when we disagreed. Deeply moving, too, is his account of Michael's final eclipse.

Still nominally editor-in-chief, he supposed (as I divined) that he still had the right to appoint or at least to approve of new editors. He still fired off memos, gave orders on the intercom. Subordinates asked the new bosses, should they obey them, and were told not to. Senior managers still reported to him as a matter of course. The new chief executive, Knight, told them to discuss nothing with Michael and to take no instructions. He and the Sunday city staff actually invaded the Berrys' sanctuary on the fifth floor. New editors, Max Hastings and Perry Worsthorne, were chosen behind Michael's back.

Michael 'blew his top' (his own words), unprecedently lost his self-control. 'Surely if I'm still editor-in-chief, I control these appointments?' he cried. 'Why didn't you tell me what you were doing?' 'Well,' replied Knight with cool effrontery, 'I didn't think you'd agree.'

Worse was to follow. It was Worsthorne whom Michael really couldn't stomach: 'He couldn't edit his school magazine, let alone a national newspaper! He's a brilliant writer but terrible with people. It would be a disaster. You're mad.' He brought up again Perry's fateful gaffe, when he blurted out 'f—' on television. Michael fought and fought, lost and finally capitulated with dignity. (Perry has since admitted that he was wrong to say 'f—'. Michael has since admitted that he was wrong about Perry's editorial abilities. When will the new regime admit it was wrong later to demote Perry?)

I read of Michael's final humiliations with appalled horror. Others too will do so. To their lips as to mine will spring unbidden questions. How could they have done it to him? How *could* they?

CW gives farewell speech. Hartwell and Deedes look on.

Why are we all so shocked? Michael had made some mistakes: we all have. He was struggling to make another, as I see it, at the very moment he went under. By some of these mistakes and misjudgements some of us had suffered, or thought we had, or thought the paper had. We are as shocked as any. Why?

Oh well, we remember many other things: Duff tells you all about them, triumphs as well as disasters, the losing struggle against the unions which, if not finally victorious (it nearly was), was at least resolute, courageous and honourable. We remember a great *bourgeois* institution, which justly commanded the loyalty of many intelligent and decent people, staff and readers alike. It commanded the absolute loyalty of one man in particular, a man whose actions and judgement might at rare times be open to question but whose motives and probity never were.

Most of us remember, too, little silly things which bring a lump to the throat. I recall Pamela and Michael at a modest supper party, not in their own house. She was an absolutely charming guest. I saw him sitting happily on a sofa, chatting, gargling, chuckling and chortling away to some lady who obviously mattered to her hosts but not perhaps to him at all. They were gassing away not about great public affairs but about some dear though relatively trivial pursuit which engrossed them both – trees and shrubs, perhaps, which he adored, or some interest of her own. On his lap, shedding white hairs all over his immaculate dark suit, reposed contentedly a little dog. He stroked it lovingly, chattering on regardless. I thought then, what a decent unaffected man. I think so still. He commanded not only respect and loyalty but deep affection.

The Spectator, 21 April 1990

Lost Friends

Still no news of my old mentors, off in my lost commonplace books to some unknown region. I try to commune with them, beseech them to get in touch: a smuggled note in Church Latin, say, from Cardinal Newman; a copy of Carlyle's essays, with the words 'white', 'city' and 'estate' ringed, and a page number; a bottle with a near illegible message from woozy old Coleridge in it. In vain. Pity Sir Oliver Lodge was not of the company, or others expert in paranormal perception.

I mentioned last week certain attitudes which most of them have in common and which may comfort them in their exile: conservatism, a love of order as of liberty, a sense of how the latter must be constrained to preserve both itself and the former.

They have for some reason in common too a shared epoch, roughly 1760 to 1914, an age in which they were at home, and I feel so. From before that time I recall La Rochefoucauld; from after it, Nadezhda Mandelstam, Hayek, von Mises, Bertrand de Jouvenel, Michael Polanyi, Irving Kristol and Michael Oakeshott on rationalism in politics. But all these last seven are surely rooted in the past, and view our own epoch with eyes trained in the last. It was an epoch of liberalism *and* conservatism, of liberty *and* order, transformed by three revolutions, French, American and Industrial; an age of reason *and* romanticism, of music and the bourgeoisie, of burgeoning socialism *and* nationalism. Plenty of tension here, plenty to quarrel about. I still hear in memory furious rows rising from those commonplace pages: old deaf Treitschke, for instance, roaring that nationalism was both a conservative and a liberating force, others, more truly conservative than he, demurring; Grillparzer predicting 'Humanity via nationality to bestiality', and Burckhardt (or was it Acton?) that any attempt to make the nation the mould and measure of the state would end in material and moral ruin.

Rows provoked by Hegel, Nietzsche (Treitschke thought the former a fake, the second mad) and Marx, whose errors of analysis and prophecy are usually held to have been revealed only by the passage of the social-democratic decades, but were all apparent in Marx's lifetime to that neglected liberal-conservative genius W. H. Mallock, whose loss I specially regret. Notebooks containing both Carlyle, say, and Cobden can hardly be a peaceable kingdom. But at least most of them were fascinated by the same problems that fascinate me still, just as pressing now as then or even more so, and they mostly bring to their debates a shared mode of thought and speech, a common *style*.

It may seem absurd to claim a common style for people writing in different languages, some of them read by me only in translation. But that style inspires also their translators, especially Henry Reeve, a *Times* leader-writer when those leaders really did lead, whose translations of de Tocqueville are in effect a rebirth.

To describe that style, first take away whatever has ruined the style of political and economic discourse in our own day: vague slang and neologisms, the intrusion of false science, especially social, of mathematics misapplied, of bogus or misleading quantification, of the hideous jargon which follows in their train, the habit of regarding life as so many 'problems', each in isolation. Then add some old-fashioned ingredients: a liberal education, still founded on the classics (no true classicist myself, I can see well enough and with anguish what has happened to language since it lost its classical foundations); a general respect for debating manners; a desire to enlighten and persuade rather than to blind with science, to include rather than exclude; a conviction that much wisdom lies in systematised experience and enriched common-sense, and that much true wit is what oft was thought but never so well expressed.

If we have done our addition and subtraction right, we should have an idea of that marvellous style, spacious, rich, elaborate, limpid, polite, which our European and American forefathers brought to the discussion of politics as of everything else. A style miraculously friendly to thought and feeling, which move within it as in a well-cut suit – an inadequate image, since style, thought and feeling are not separate, like body and clothes, but a unity. Are not thought and its expression one and the same thing? A style difficult for us now to reproduce and work in, because we have largely ceased to think and feel in the way it expressed. A style, alas, repulsive and impenetrable to many of the young, who, rootless and alienated from the great dead, seeing them as discredited or rendered less 'relevant' by recent 'advances' in their fields, survey their works with the uncomprehending bafflement of a savage at a learned society.

Unless memory errs, many of my quotations are about memory itself. The lines which Conrad and Ford Madox Ford placed at the head of *Romance*, '*O toi qui dors dans l'ombre, O sacré souvenir.*' Newman recalling how verses learnt by rote when we were children return to us in later life with a mournful poignancy. Pushkin –

> And reading with abhorrence my life's tale,
> I quake and curse,
> Complaining bitterly and shedding bitter tears,
> But the sad lines I'll not wash away.

Mrs Mandelstam – 'What can we expect to happen in a country with a disordered memory? What is a man worth who has lost his memory?' De Tocqueville emphasising the extreme importance, in understanding a society, of studying its inheritance laws, in which its memory resides. Young Otto Weininger, who regarded all forgetfulness as immoral and self-murder as world-murder, yet forgot all when he committed suicide on Beethoven's grave. Genius is for him, if not memory itself carried to extreme, then utterly dependent on memory, the staff of its life. There is the storing memory which in fact supplies all the materials for a masterwork, however forward-looking and original it may appear. There is too the shaping memory, which at the beginning of a great act of creation remembers its end, at the end its beginning. Strokes of genius:

what are these but the bold conjunction of what memory has given and was perhaps never joined before? Or do I traduce Weininger? I would look him up, but he too has been abducted along with the others, taking so much of my memory with them.

How shall I fare without it? 'Think for yourself,' you may crisply retort; 'learn to walk without crutches. I have a quotation for you, from Young:

> Some, for renown, on scraps of learning dote,
> And think they grow immortal as they quote.

A happy chance has delivered you from this folly. Make the most of it.'

Alas, how much 'thinking for oneself' is in fact a process of linking memories together to form new entities, of putting what someone thought on top of what someone else thought, adding whatever one can of one's own and seeing what happens.

Yet what indelible memories our wicked century has in fact conferred on us, memories inspiring as well as dreadful. We have seen crimes and destruction without precedent. Yet we have also seen peoples who have lost everything but courage, and have started all over again – the Jews (or such as survived), the uprooted eastern Germans, the Asians of East Africa. Beside such prodigious adversities confronted and overcome, to bewail the loss of keys, credit cards and commonplace books is truly shameful. It reminds me of the headlines in a Scottish newspaper: 'Train Smash in South: Many Feared Dead: Scot Loses Pudding' . And of course my lost friends and teachers may yet be restored to me: months sometimes elapse. What mountains of *sauerkraut* and sausages await them, what fatted calves, what beef roasted or *en daube*, what haggis and pumpkin pie, what wines, women and song, what masses or puritan thanksgivings as may be appropriate, what *pâté de foié gras* and trumpets! And what a speech I shall deliver, with what a wealth of apt quotation!

The Spectator, 24 and 31 March 1984

. . . *But by God They Frighten Me!*

Neighbours of ours in a quiet cul-de-sac were burgled so many times that at last they put up a notice on the door. 'Don't bother to break in – it's all gone.'

We've been much more fortunate, perhaps because our house is overlooked by an audience so vast and critical that only the most hardened and insensitive burglar could go about his business without embarrassment. When I get out of bed in the morning in my underpants I feel like an actor at curtain-up: should I bow, at the window, and recite a prologue by Dryden, perhaps, or sing a lively opening aria?

None the less, burgled we have been; and this, I am sorry to say, by an uncultivated person who took away the record player and some 'pop' records, leaving my rare and precious Pfitzner, Elgar, Goldmark, Cornelius and Nicolai discs intact. Glad as I am in a way, it is yet sad to note how little burglars have used their new and presumably unique wealth to broaden their horizons and cultivate their taste.

Inevitably since returning from holiday, I have been wondering whether our precautions are adequate. Apart from the usual locks, bolts, etc., I had already installed a somewhat unimaginative time-switch. By switching one light on and off twice a day this suggests that while we are away on holiday the house is occupied by a silent recluse, scholar or mystic of preternaturally regular habits, who enters the drawing-room at precisely 8.55 every evening, reads for 56 minutes, then sits in darkness either still in the drawing room or elsewhere in the house, till 10.37 when, tiring of meditation, he switches on the light for another 83 minutes of Thomas à Kempis, Rumi or Meister Eckehart.

How could any self-respecting burglar be dismayed or repelled by such a weedy figure? Something more dramatic and alarming is clearly required.

More lights, of course, for a start, switching themselves on and off according to a complex master-plan. But really, eight mystics gliding noiselessly about the house are hardly more terrifying than one: they might all be in trances, totally unresponsive to burglars or other worldly stimuli. *Son* is clearly required as well as *lumière*.

I am brooding on the possibility of a tape recording, or series of tapes, to be played at stentorian volume, clearly audible outside the house, and to last a whole fortnight, then to be repeated till our return. I have already started to prepare a suitable script.

The basic cast consists of a family, not particularly resembling our own, indeed in every way more formidable, untouched by mysticism or other unhealthy tendencies, noisy, extrovert, sociable, aggressive, even brutal folk.

As their conversation proceeds, conducted needless to say in a continual and repetitous bellow, it will be made clear to the prospective burglar that the father was till recently heavyweight boxing champion of the Metropolitan Police and rules his family now with an iron and frequently raised fist, not to mention clubs and shillelaghs. His wife, a German lady whom he met while serving in the army of occupation after the war, was acknowledged conqueror of all the immense women who wrestle in mud at clubs on and around Hamburg's Reeperbahn. Her brother, over on a visit, is none other than the notorious Professor Adolf Kaiser, terror of all other all-in wrestlers.

The children, now grown up, have inherited all their parents' skills and interests, adding some of their own.

The eldest son, a sergeant in the police, is a black-sash judo expert. The eldest daughter, also in the police, is a champion shot-putter who, at a recent unofficial international athletics meeting, astonished the spectators not merely by throwing the shot some hundreds of yards but throwing her gigantic Iron Curtain opponents the same distance for good measure.

'I could have eaten two of 'em for breakfast,' she roars with a laugh that shakes the house to its foundations.

Another son has unfortunately turned out a bit of a black

sheep, though still loyal to the family and living at home in the hope of redemption. From the bad company he keeps, he has learnt how to sever a wasp with a thrown flick-knife and how to slit a windpipe with a razor blade sewn into his cap-peak. A third son, on leave from the paratroops, is a Bisley champion; and indeed the principal hobby of the whole family is marksmanship, the house itself serving as a firing range.

'Let's have a go with that old Lueger of yours, Dad,' bellows Enid. Bang! 'Got it in one!'

'I'll larn yer,' thunders Dad, 'shooting yer uncle's Iron Cross off of the wall! Still, you 'it it in the middle without aiming bless yer!'

These menacing conversations are punctuated at suitable intervals by the sonorous baying and growlings of a mastiff or other gigantic hound, and also by the loud crunching of bones.

Every now and then the family will throw a party – and how! No chamber music for them, no minuets, no bows or hand-kissing, no whist or polished conversation. No, the banging of beer mugs hammering on the tables, the crash of broken glass, hoarse roars of pleasure and fury, old and obscene Artists' Rifles and rugger songs belted out *fortissimo*, the proceedings culminating in furious games of Up Jenkins (not Roy, presumably), Cardinal Puff, indoor rugger, with cushions, and high cockalorum.

Appalled by this fearsome revelry, would not the burglars fold up their tents like Arabs and as silently steal away?

One snag – the neighbours. Would they complain to the police – the real police, I mean? What then?

The police knock and ring: the mechanised uproar continues unabated. The police force an entry. What on earth would they make of these ghostly revels, a deserted house, all hell let loose in it, like Hogarth's sinister ball at Wanstead, or the spectres' party in *Ruddigore* at cockcrow? Have the police strong enough nerves. Or would they too flee, as from midnight on the Brocken or Pendle Hill, deeming the house to be the abode of djinns, ghouls, zombies and afreets?

NB: To all burglars who read the *Daily Telegraph* – we're back now; and it's all gone . . .

Daily Telegraph, 6 September 1976

Within Our Sausage Skins

A few weeks ago it was my sixtieth birthday. I sauntered past the milestone, kicking up the dust, eyes averted, whistling with assumed nonchalance Papageno's birdcatcher song, hoping to escape the notice of the Reaper, of the President of the Immortals, the proprietor of all earthly bumpers and boats for hire. I was born on 23 April, St George's Day, Shakespeare's birthday and the very day in 1924 when the Empire Exhibition opened at Wembley with the statue of the then Prince of Wales carved in New Zealand butter, near which Bingo Little – I think it was – rapturously rediscovered his mislaid fiancée. Gone Empire, statue, Prince; gone even St George (so the impious say). I live yet (DV) for a little spell, Shakespeare and Wodehouse for as long as English is spoken.

I had not thought of issuing a message to the world on this obscure and grim event, till I recalled how interested I had always been in the reflections of those who were travelling a few years ahead of me. The great and good Maurice Green, editor of the *Daily Telegraph* when I was entering *nel mezzo del cammin di nostra vita*, often reported back on what life was like at sixty. His dispatches were on the whole encouraging, so I pass them on. If you feel weary, out of sorts and a failure in your fifties, he said, no need to think it's going to be like that but getting worse all the time for the next twenty-five years. After the male menopause (I don't think he used such a modish expression), there are recoveries of lost health and powers. Some things indeed are lost forever, but the pain of losing them is mercifully abated. Unabated in Maurice's case was his joy in Wagner, fishing, shooting, porcelain, smoking cigarettes, sluicing and browsing, even editing. Logan Pearsall Smith said: 'There is more felicity on the far side of baldness than young men can possibly imagine.' I think dear bald Maurice would have agreed. Do I? For many or most, to be sure, for the lucky and the wise. For me? Yes, though of course there is sadness too: 'Who never ate his bread with sorrow, who never spent the midnight hours weeping and waiting for the morrow – he knows you not, ye heavenly powers.' That remains true. As for the risks of boring my contemporaries by writing about senescence, they exist, but grow less with every passing year till, after eighty, all contemporaries are friends.

I think that many of us at sixty are conscious, though it is fruitless to wail about it, of daily unavoidable injustices done to us. Try as I may, for instance, I cannot see my contemporaries in, say, the Press Gallery as they were when they were young, unless like George Lochhead I knew them then. To Auberon Waugh we look like walking sausages. So we do, as will he, DV. Yet within our sausage skins lurks and lives still, though invisible, all we ever were – children, youngsters, little rascals, bullies or bullied, swots or truants, young lovers, young journalists, young fathers, journalists in their prime: yet all that can be seen is old fools. And, of course, it is the most distant parts of our lives which seem to us old fools the nearest. The first time we encounter this, that or the other, it makes an indelible impression: we are bowled over with an amazement, joy, fear or love which we shall never forget. So long as we are still receiving these first impressions, life seems infinite, unfolding slowly with leisurely luxury. As we gain experience and lose the faculty of wonder, so do the telegraph poles fly past ever faster; the scenery in between is less memorable; and so at last I can better describe my young nanny's dress when I was two (very fashionable then and since – a short shift or cutty sark, with candy stripes of yellow, green, blue, orange, black and mauve) than a dress I admired last week.

Wilde's Lord Henry said that the tragedy of old age is not that one is old but that one is young – yes, and in great part very young indeed. The injustice is that we don't look or seem so. Behind the huge soup-stained beards of old Tennyson and Brahms were imprisoned the ardent handsome young men they had once been, just as in Keats and Shelley lay immanent, never to be achieved, the possibility of huge soup-stained beards.

Peter Simple regards photography as one of the most baneful fruits of progress. For once I can't agree with him. For what better than fading snaps in an album can bring back what we were and therefore still are, resurrect tracts of our own lives half forgotten, reveal passages of other people's half-forgotten or never known, raise the dead and forcibly remind their children that they too were young once? Snaps are a sort of higher court, to which we can appeal against the harsh verdicts of old age and failing memory.

Someone said that no one was ever in love who did not have a passionate interest in the loved one's childhood. And there, in snaps part of that childhood may be preserved, complete perhaps with spade, bucket, floppy hat, beaming aunts, picnic rug and cherished dogs. Vividly do I recall a yellowing photo of my mother, then still at convent, arrayed in a costume both absurd and touching to play St Pancras (saint not station) in some edifying entertainment, her proudly smiling face a much younger, sweeter and more innocent version of Gustav Mahler's. And when my mother died at a great age, I could not help thinking with anguish of that little girl going down within her, as in a shipwreck, piteously screaming and battering vainly on the bolted hatches for release as the water poured in.

Another inescapable injustice is done to the opinions of the old. These may have been with luck the product of long thought, reasoning, not all of it conscious, and debate, inner or outer, about experiences or things heard or read. Yet, when passed on to young people, without any possibility of reproducing, even if they could be recalled, the complex and tedious processes which produced and link them, they must seem mere arbitary prejudices, as hollow, empty and meaningless as broken bits of statues or pottery piled up in a scrapyard. And of course many of them have ossified into mere prejudices. A long life has taught us that this is the best way of doing or judging this or that. Often we can't easily remember why. What once may have been reasoned has become automatic, a reflex action. Challenged, why do we behave or speak so, our old jaws drop open: we haven't thought about it for years. Once we too debated with each other far into the night the nature, say, of the laws of property. Now we just say flatly, 'That's my coat'; we put it on and go.

A long life is like an old city, with many different layers on top of each other, with old buildings adapted, shored up or falling into decay, new buildings built within or on top of them. It appears inexplicable, incomprehensible, its message confused and muffled, its mysterious rationality (if any) accessible only to patient study, excavation and imagination.

Every generation, moreover, is doomed to be a sort of secret society, with special thoughts and interests which, like passwords, are well known to its contemporaries but cannot be communicated to its descendants. Our descendants. Our descendants begin to outnumber us and our friends. Our failure to communicate with them thus becomes ever more serious. For as we grow old we lose, as Goethe lamented, one of the greatest of human rights – the right to be judged by our peers. This loss did not daunt Goethe. Life was for him like the Sibylline books, the more precious the less of it is left. May our judges and descendants be merciful to us.

The Spectator, 26 May 1984

Goodbye for a Time *

When the composer Meyerbeer died, his nephew composed a funeral march in his honour. He showed it to Rossini, who said, 'Very fine, my boy, but what a pity it wasn't you who died and your uncle who wrote the funeral march'.

When Brigid and the Utley family asked me to compose a march in Peter's honour, they did me the greatest honour of my life and set me a daunting task. I feel inadequate. Why daunting? Well, think for a start how well Peter spoke on all occasions, grave and gay. *His* eloquence came naturally to him. Wit and paradox were his constant companions and faithful servants. He was in perfect command of his thoughts and feelings, his heart and mind, master always of that sonorous, clear, dignified and old-fashioned style, in which alone, I think, can profound and humane wisdom be expressed.

The least pompous of men, he was none the less a marvellous mocker of pomposity. One of his most irresistible comic ploys was to expound in richly Johnsonian terms the most trifling or base matters, the earthiest of advice, the raciest of gossip, the most ludicrous anecdotes, very often at his own expense.

Many fine writers are rotten speakers. The two modes of expression came alike to Peter, were indeed for him the same. All he wrote was first spoken – perhaps that's why it read so well – normally dictated to Brigid or to one of that succession of lovely secretaries who helped him so much and whom he helped tirelessly in return.

Many people, from the founding aunts who brought him up onwards, helped Peter in various ways. They rejoiced to do so,

* A memorial service address by Colin Welch for Peter Utley at St Martin's-in-the-Fields, Monday 24 October 1988.

and can have no regrets. They were richly rewarded, got more than they gave and can take pride in having helped to sustain an irreplaceable and bounteously creative life, by which we have all been enriched. Not only Peter and Brigid were in their debt, but all of us. As Peter's parish priest put it so movingly: 'In common with everyone who knew him, I was better for having known him.'

Peter of course spoke perforce without notes. Yet to say so is terribly misleading. No one in a sense had more notes, was better prepared. His speed of composition was prodigious. This was in his case the mark of a mind not shallow and facile but richly endowed and stocked. Kindly souls sometimes thought it cruel to ask a blind man to produce a five-hundred-word leader on a subject not specially his own in half an hour or, say, to report from Ulster. His handicap was in fact made good, not only by the eyes of Brigid and others, but by that superb organising and generalising intelligence which, presented with a few facts, could at once by insight, logic, imagination and experience, by the application of good principles firmly held, grasp a wealth of truths not readily accessible to the sighted.

Another factor obviously daunting to me was the number, nature and distinction of Peter's friends. Look around you here: *Si monumentum requiris, circumspice*. Among this throng could be found many more eloquent than I. Yet I must please emphasise that most of Peter's friends were not eminentoes. People who mattered a great deal sought his counsel and company. So did people who didn't in a worldly sense matter at all, except to him and God.

All were welcome at his feast of reason. I was about to say all except fools and bores, but they – or we – were gladly suffered and welcomed too. His court was catholic at what has been called that vile pub, the Kings and Keys. Bless me, it wasn't vile when Peter and his family and circle were there! It heard some of the best talk in London, not so much a saloon as a salon.

Another daunting factor for me was the flood of beautiful, sincere and moving tributes – often affectionately and appropriately amusing – which saluted Peter's death. Mrs

Thatcher spontaneously and most justly honoured his courtesy, rightly seeing in this no mere ornament but an expression of the great spiritual quality she discerned in him. From another angle, Frances Hill, one of the secretaries, lovingly recalled reading Evelyn Waugh's *Scoop* to Peter on the top of a bus, he helpless with mirth, soon the whole top deck helpless too. And so on: who could excel all these?

Peter must have been pleased to note how many of these tributes came from younger people who were grateful to him for teaching them, among much else, how to think and write. Yet in a sense he *taught* nothing. He was the least didactic of men, the least inclined to mould or reshape the young he loved. If we all learnt prodigiously in his company – and we did – it was from his presence and example, from the standards of intellectual rigour and lack of cant which he imposed upon himself rather than on others.

From Peter's *courage* too we learnt – learnt, for instance, not to complain about trifles – not anyway to do so without shame. This too he did not teach. Many people who have overcome great handicaps, who are in this sense self-made, become conceited and harsh, unsympathetic about the lesser misfortunes and struggles of others. Not Peter, on the contrary.

Peter's courage was exemplary and unfaltering in the face of, at times, disappointments, difficulties and seeming betrayals which would have sunk lesser men. He treated them all with a serene and gallant insouciance, confident that God would provide. One fine tribute to him spoke of his bitter disappointment at losing an election in Ulster. I hope it isn't nit-picking to assert that such a man could never have felt bitterness about any such earthly temporal setback. He met it with his invariable humorous fortitude.

Also exemplary and unfaltering was – indeed is – Brigid's courage, different I think from Peter's, not less, perhaps even more. It is of a more defiant and combative sort, perhaps more realistic and earthy, battling always to keep the family craft afloat no matter what waves broke over it, facing always the storm, determined always somehow to provide whatever God in his wisdom had withheld, and to provide it lavishly too, plenty for others. The bank manager might groan, but so did Brigid's hospitable board. To praise Peter is inescapably to praise Brigid too: every word adds to her glory. Without her the story would have surely been very different, and sadder.

Peter was a great family man. His family brought him comfort and just pride. Some family men find in the family all they need, become a bit narrow, content to restrict their affections to that circle. Not Peter. While lavishing warmth and interest on his own, he also went radiantly outward with warmth and interest for others, as if we were all his family.

May I end on a personal note? I went to see the old boy in hospital, where he was unconscious or supposedly so, a bit restless but not, I think, in pain. I cannot speak of the desolation I felt to see him thus, to miss the loved familiar inevitable admonition, 'Colin! Have a drink!' – though the family soon made good the want. Ollie Knox told an excellent joke. Peter's mouth opened, his feet twitched. Was he still with us? Was this for him his last earthly joke?

As I left, I kissed him on the forehead and said, 'Goodbye, my dear old friend. Goodbye for a time,' I added quickly, in hopeful respect for his hard unshaken Christian faith, the greatest faith one of his disciples thought he'd ever encountered.

Now, if a mind and soul of this quality has faith, who are we lesser mortals to doubt? Perhaps already in another place another voice has said to Peter, *'Well done!'*

WAR

❦

The Somme

Over the slow rivers of northern France shimmers in summertime a peculiar, soft, luminous and serene radiance. In their quiet glassy waters we now see reflected only peaceful things – fishermen, reeds and weeping willows, friendly inns, picnicking families with their tables spread in the shade, the children stripped to bathe. How hard it is to believe, sixty years later, what hell broke out on the Somme on July 1, 1916! The weather forecast, then as now, was fine and hot. Here was launched, against German positions all too well prepared, the very flower of British manhood, even of boyhood. In the sunshine they advanced, with a gaiety and confident patriotism never surpassed before or since. By the end of the first bay 60,000 were casualties, nearly 20,000 of them dead. The battle, or battles, ground on into the rain, mud and misery of the autumn. What was gained? In terms of territory or other advantage, precious little. What was lost? Dear and irreplaceable lives beyond doubt, the best of a generation.

British generalship may arguably have been discredited; but this was not wholly loss if later leaders learnt anything from their predecessors' dire if well-intentioned mistakes. The hierarchy from which those 1916 generals sprang, the ordered society which they represented, also came under bitter questioning; this may be gain or loss as you think it. Yet the Somme and subsequent carnage also threw a pall of doubt over the very concepts of discipline, self-sacrifice and patriotism, over the need for a nation, if it is to remain free, to defend its freedom in the last resort by force. Many asked, to what end the Somme battles? It was but a step to ask, to what end any battle? Such sickly questionings have, with brief intervals, clouded our statecraft ever since that terrible sunlit morning.

Editorial, *Daily Telegraph*, 1 July 1976

Normandy's Horror

In vain twenty-five years later I searched with my son for the brickworks and the nearby wood in which, in June 1944, I was introduced to my new platoon. 'It must have been here . . . No, it doesn't quite fit. Perhaps there . . . ' Restored, smiling once again, Normandy has effaced nearly all traces of her agony. Memory has to work almost unaided. It brings back to me now the soldiers' faces looking up at me from their slit trenches, apprehensively wondering what fate had allotted to them for an officer in place of the one (or two?) they'd already lost, wondering perhaps what the cat had brought in.

Casualties had been very high, and continued so. Losses in Northwest Europe look trivial as a proportion of the whole force involved, including a vast preponderant tail which rarely heard a shot fired in anger. In this tail were many fit, experienced officers and soldiers who, among other duties, as the campaign wore on and losses mounted, callously passed on to be minced up in the front line mere children, younger even than I was, bewildered, hardly trained at all. In Holland we got a big draft from the King's Liverpool Regiment. They looked mostly like the original Beatles at the very start of their career. I put two of them on a charge for being, not for the first time, asleep on guard. Well I knew the colonel had at his disposal no punishment worse than these boys' daily lives. But I thought he might give them a lecture, fatherly or wrathful as he thought fit. He asked them their ages. 'Nineteen, sir,' 'Eighteen.' He dismissed them, and turned to me. 'Weren't you taught never, never to put two young soldiers on guard together?' I replied that we had almost no old soldiers left. 'How old are you?' he asked. 'Twenty, sir,' and I was dismissed too.

Also lurking in that huge tail, though fortunately in lesser numbers, were psychiatrists who frivolously sent back to the front as 'cured' or *malades imaginaires* poor shell-shocked boys who, so far from being cowards, endangered their own lives and everyone else's by their tragic antics in full view of the enemy. My opinion of psychiatry has never recovered. No blimpish colonel of either war would have behaved with such idiotic inhumanity.

In his exciting, thoughtful and informative *Overlord: D-Day and the Battle for Normandy*, Max Hastings reminds us that many infantry battalions suffered more than a hundred per cent casualties in that Normandy summer. My own battalion of the Lincolns, to which I was posted from the Royal Warwicks, lost, I think, a hundred and seventy per cent in the ten months from D-Day till my number came up in the Reichswald. These are typical First World War figures, unrecognised as such because we were relatively so few to begin with. In the first war the Warwicks had an admittedly exceptional forty-eight battalions on active service; in the second, not much more than a tenth of that.

Looking down on that first day, never have I seen faces more tired and ill, tired from sleepless nights, ill from bad food and fear, haggard and wan, puffed out and inflamed by ferocious mosquito bites. The men were unnaturally quiet, as if they were stunned or had seen ghosts. I don't suppose I looked too good either. Hours tossing about in a sickening dawn swell off Arromanches, followed by a day or two in a transit camp at Bayeux, must have left their mark .

Through this camp the authorities in their wisdom channelled not only reinforcements like us for the front line but bomb-happy officers on their way home. 'It's hell up there,' shrieked one, the wreck of a once impressive major, his hand shaking so much he couldn't water his whisky. 'HELL, I tell you. Run for it! Get out while you can! It's HELL!' We tittered nervously, shaken despite ourselves; and when the next day I looked down on those upturned faces it was not only with pity but with awe and humility. Here was I, woefully inexperienced, with my shreds of military lore, lectures half-forgotten and field training frivolously scamped, supposed to ' lead' men who had endured what had driven other men, supposedly their superiors, mad. They had shaved too; their weapons were clean; their spirit was subdued but not broken. I bowed my head to them, and was also unnaturally quiet. A part of my education was about to begin.

All schools have their particular smell, a whiff of which, carbolic, polish or sweat, will bring back days long past. The smell of Normandy was death. Holidaymakers will know Normandy as a province of fantastic fecundity, with tiny fields and lanes, all steeply banked and thick-hedged, rich orchards, old cottages and farm buildings of red brick and timber. You can hardly see ten yards in any direction, which led to many unpleasant surprises from Tigers and 88s invisible yet near enough almost to touch. Thick on the ground everywhere are fat animals, horses, cows, geese, ducks, chickens, pigeons and their blue-smocked peasant proprietors. It isn't military country: let loose a full-blast war in it, and the result is a gigantic abattoir, bodies everywhere, human, animal, theirs, ours, French, no chance to bury them, all stiff and hideously swollen, covered with white dust or mud, faces blown away or dreadfully distorted, crawling with flies, rotting, giving off that terrible sweet-sour stench which, once smelt, is not forgotten.

Add to it the reek of explosives and burning, of cider and calvados (which the soldiers drank too young, with results sometimes fatal) pouring from shattered vats and stills. Add, in the tormented cities, in Caen, Rouen, and others we saw later, the mephitic stink of sewers blown open to the sky. Memory unbidden still brings back these smells, and we shiver.

What did this school teach? Well, obviously different things to different people. I wrote twenty-five years ago in the *Daily Telegraph* about some of the things it had taught me. Few will remember that, but I wouldn't care to bore even them twice. Above all I think it imbued us with a deep, abiding and, to others, perhaps disproportionate hatred of disorder, violence and anarchy. The fragility and preciousness of civil society, as also the dire consequences of its collapse, were indelibly impressed on us.

In a way, we all became profoundly conservative, keenly

aware of what had been lost, desperately anxious to preserve what remained. Well do I know that most of the soldiers voted Labour in 1945, though there *may* be a distinction to be drawn between the front line, with its awe-inspiring experience of tragedy, and the progressive, argumentative, ABCA-lecture-infesting, barrackroom-lawyer types behind it. I don't know. But certainly Labour, with its passion for order, fairness and regulation, offered then no sort of anarchy – on the contrary. Someone described Hitler's Reich as 'systematised anarchy'. It was against that we fought, against a Caliban-like revolt of greed, lust, hatred, envy, cruelty and destructive rage.

It also imbued in us a great love of Europe. Not in all of us, of course – some could hardly wait to get out and stay out – but in many of us, by whom the spectacle of Europe prostrate, degraded, diminished, morally and materially ruined, could not be viewed coldly from outside. It hurt us personally and deeply, as if our own mother were lying there in pain and woe. Of course we didn't fight for the European Parliament as it is, still less for the CAP or Brussels' swarming bureaucrats. Rightly did Charles Moore in the *Daily Telegraph* ridicule politicians' claims that we did. But we did resolve that, so far as lay in our power, it must never happen again, that Europe must be given institutions which would prevent another civil war and guard her against enemies without. What exists now is a mere ghost or parody of what we sought: no one can look on it and think his task well accomplished. But never shall we be untrue to the idea of Europe, nor turn aside from any road, however muddy, twisting and arduous, which seems to lead towards its being made real.

The Spectator, 2 June 1984

The Spirit of Christmas 1944

Of Christmases in the army I myself treasure one memory. It is of Christmas 1944, when I found myself on leave in the little Dutch town of Helmond. First I went to my billet – a small house in a side street, rather bare, shabby but neat; and a bed, with sheets! My hosts were not well off at the best of times and the war had reduced them to real want: they and their children were half-starved, their clothes were wretched, they had no soap, they lacked all luxuries and most necessities. Then I went to the divisional club and, for various reasons, got shockingly drunk. When I returned in the small hours, I had lost my key. I wakened the whole household, fell over everything in the hall, and was sick all over the lavatory. The next day was Christmas Eve. Overwhelmed with shame, I slunk out early, wandered dismally about, wrote some letters in the club and crept back at eight or so to go to bed. On the bed I found an apple, a tiny bottle of *oude genever*, a little packet of gritty biscuits, some strange tobacco, and a card, painstakingly inscribed by one of the children in English and in many colours, wishing me a happy Christmas. As it turned out, it was for me a very happy Christmas. Of all the presents I have ever had, none has seemed to me to mean more than those pitiful objects, representing as they did not only a real sacrifice, but a gesture of understanding and love. And in my bedroom, bare as it was, hung the cross of Christ.

The Queen, 20 December 1958

The Odd Thing About the Colonel

Upon the gentlemanly, egg-like features of my first infantry colonel had settled a more or less permanent look of mild astonishment or bafflement. His waking life was full of little surprises, mostly disagreeable, which he greeted with composure or, at worst, restrained vexation. His temper, often tested, was normally equable. He had a rich, fruity, throaty, gargling voice, like Harold Macmillan's or Julian Amery's, emerging, as it were, hollow but crisp from the bottom of a deep well. This distinguished sound was often deployed to pronounce people or events, even of quite a humdrum kind, to be 'strange' or 'strange indeed', 'odd' or even 'very odd'. When he referred to our own regiment, which he often did with pride, he never abbreviated its full title, never omitted the sonorous opening 'Royal', and would have died rather than substitute, as the irreverent often did, the word 'scruffy'. The term 'line mob' shocked him. It was as if tradition itself had spoken in him: the unquestionable arbiter of what was strange or odd and what was not.

Certainly he was not scruffy himself, though his *chic* was rather of the First World War, in which he had won an MC, than the Second. One half expected him to carry his badges of rank on his cuffs, to refer to 'whizzbangs' and 'flamin' onions', to commend the comforting effects on cold nights at the front of Epps's Cocoa or Dunhill's V.O. Whisky. The silly fore-and-aft forage cap of 1939–45 did not suit him. He wisely preferred his glamorously battered and misshapen felt peaked cap, in the top of which was said to be concealed the full order for battalion parade, to be consulted if memory failed. His darkly gleaming old Sam Browne had a whistle attached to it, a memento of our role as mounted infantry in the Boer War.

I can see him now, advancing slowly in silent splendour across an enormous square towards the whole battalion drawn up, his jacket flared *à la* cavalry, his immaculate breeches a faded pinky beige, his boots gleaming and – yes – spurs clanking. Was a photograph to be taken? A soft mysterious sound was heard, as of ghosts faintly singing. It rose elusively, now from here, now from there. The RSM, a genial martinet who would call even his family to attention at the colonel's approach ('Wife and child . . . wife and child, HOIP! Wife and child present and correct, sir!'), strove in vain with a beady glare to locate and silence the music makers. Their chosen melody was 'I've got spurs that jingle, jangle, jingle', a ditty doubtless unfamiliar to the colonel. He must none the less have been vaguely aware of its unsuitability, just as a former Emperor of Japan, inspecting the guard of honour on a visit here, may have been uneasy to hear a selection from the *Mikado* booming, braying and crashing from the Guards' band. Odd, very odd, the colonel murmured.

Not all his surprises were unpleasant. On a rare pastoral inspection, slumming as it were, he visited the officers' club (or 'casino', as Thomas Mann's erratic lady translator has it) at Dover. Into a fruit machine there his feckless subalterns had inserted their all. 'A *fruit* machine?' enquired the bewildered colonel, 'Does it give out fruit?' We thought not, though how could we tell? It had never given anything out to us. Constipated beyond belief, what it engulfed it shamelessly retained. The colonel borrowed sixpence: did he, like the royal family, carry no money? Under instruction, he inserted it. Stupendous inner convulsions shook the machine. It settled and roared. A Danaë torrent of gold (or rather alloy) poured from it, overwhelming the cup meant for it, piling up and rolling about all over the lino, wealth beyond the dreams of avarice. 'Good gracious,' cried the Colonel, 'does this happen every time?' His astonishment, was on this occasion shared by us all. It was not unmixed with envy as we helped him to collect his loot, including, so rumour had it, the original stake not his – an oversight also rather royal in flavour, if stories of Queen Mary and others are to be credited.

A ray of sunshine, this, in a colonel's world otherwise clouded by cruel knocks, misfortunes and disappointments borne with fortitude: the young officers, for instance, allocated to him by a selection system which must have seemed to him perverse indeed – yes, me for a start. Yet, though no answer to any colonel's prayer, I caused him little distress that I am aware of. My smart creamy shirts caused him no pain; nor did the poetry which I then modishly read in bulk, a practice endorsed by no less an authority than Lord Wavell. Inefficiency and eccentricity were not profoundly distasteful to him, provided they didn't eat their peas with a knife or belch and say 'pardon, sir' or make mock of him or set fire to his *Times* while he read it.

On one such incendiary occasion, he cast the blazing organ aside with an oath straight into the waste-paper basket. The resultant conflagration was in fact swiftly extinguished by the mess waiter with a soda syphon, but dense clouds of smoke rose and billowed up the stairs, as did the colonel himself, spurred on by humorously exaggerated screams of, 'Fire, fire!' and, Run for your lives, gentlemen!' The colonel's reaction was if anything too swift. He hurled all his precious possessions out of his bedroom window, where many of them stuck in a bare silver birch outside. The next morning it looked like a very grand Christmas tree, decked out with the booty of Bond Street and Jermyn Street – things like exotic dressing gowns, ivory backed brushes, silk pyjamas, bespoke shirts and boots on trees, Floris hair water, silver hip flasks in leather cases and other splendours beyond our means or even our knowledge. The colonel was himself a bit shamefaced, but we rated him a proper toff.

More than acceptable initially to the Colonel was a very smart young officer, darkly handsome, called something exotic like Palaeologos or Thurn und Taxis, posted to us from Intelligence. Unfortunately this paragon had an overmastering sense of humour. One evening after dinner there were four of us in the mess, the paragon and I, the colonel and his guest, a brigadier. The colonel was telling a long, rambling anecdote about a hunt he had ridden to in Ulster, a very strange hunt, it seemed, with all the hounds of different sizes and breeds and many other marks of eccentricity, all lovingly recalled at length, together with confusing incidents illustrative of Hibernian oddity. The brigadier listened for the most part with polite attention, smiling or chuckling quietly at appropriate moments, waking with a start from little post-prandial dozes. The effect on the paragon was more disquieting. His face was completely hidden by the upheld *Times*, which shook alarmingly in his hands. From behind it came sounds of irrepressible mirth: chokings, gurglings, whinnies and violent explosions. Something was going wrong. The colonel's yarn was designed to please and amuse, but not to any such disproportionate extent. Finally the paragon lost control, abandoned all pretence, fled from the mess, shrieking and roaring, dabbing his streaming eyes with a vast silk handkerchief.

The colonel was astonished, 'What's the matter with the fellow? Has he gone mad or something?' And the paragon was forthwith transferred from acceptability to the remotest marches of strangeness.

Some of the other young officers caused the colonel almost unbearable pain from the start. Evelyn Waugh's Lieutenant Hooper was typical of them all, clerkish NCOs commissioned from unfashionable, banausic formations like the pay and ordnance corps, NQOCD, as debs' mothers were then supposed to put it – not *quite* our class, dear. He overheard with grief their flat precise suburban speech, viewed even their strong points without proper enthusiasm. They were mostly very good, for instance, at checking and re-checking their platoons' G 1098 – the complete inventory of equipment. An attribute not to be sneezed at, for what is the use of leading your men in a dashing upper-class way, of scorning convention and having nicknames like 'Boy' and 'Lucky', if face to face with the enemy you find – oh hell! – you've left half your weaponry behind. I lost my own pistol rather early on – not that I could have hit a gasometer with it, even from inside. My awkward antics with a pistol recalled Bob Hope rather than John Wayne. Far more effective in my hands was even the Sten, with its random bursts, misfires and unpredictable explosions, terrifying alike to user, friend and foe.

It was the colonel's settled conviction that these commissioned pen-pushers and orderlies, 'oiks' and 'grocers' (a snob word in use long before *Private Eye* attached it to Mr Heath), would all be happier and better suited in the searchlights. A kindly man, he devoted unwonted energies and even cunning to effecting these beneficent transfers. He would call the oiks' guards out at short intervals and unexpected times. One of them, with a bad attack of the trots, was caught giggling literally with his trousers down. I often wondered what the searchlights made of the gifts showered on them by the Colonel's social selection system. Perhaps they valued what he discarded. At least their lights would be present, polished and in working order. Nor could the German bomber caught in a hostile beam discern whether it was directed by someone with his trousers off or not.

Like other prejudices, the colonel's snobbery may have had some occult rationality in it, ill though it chimed with a People's War in the Century of the Common Man. It was often said that infantry soldiers didn't much like being commanded by upstart members of their own class, still less by promoted clever dicks from what they regarded as inferior mobs, administrative or supportive rather than brutal and licentious in character. They apparently preferred their officers a bit grand, odd, boozy, dashing, eccentric or even mad, humorous by nature or intent, to be celebrated in boastful anecdote or affectionately irreverent nickname. And of course officers produced by the inscrutable workings of a seemingly irrational class structure had at least the merit of having no damned merit nonsense about them. Respect for them was not enforced by some unchallengeable logic, though, if won, it was an enduring asset.

Towards the end of the war, anyway, there simply weren't enough more or less upper-class officers to go round. Some of the gentlemen called in to fill the gaps were very temporary indeed, far from *parfait*: the flashy heirs of rich pork butchers, endowed with sports cars and black-market petrol, public-relations types and salesmen, even, to the colonel's distress, *actors*. The obvious way out of these difficulties was to commission lots of those excellent infantry NCOs. The trouble was that all the 'Luckies' and Boys' were peculiarly dependent on good NCOs, who thus became precious, indispensable, to be hoarded

CW as lieutenant with the Royal Warwicks

like gold, and on no account to be recommended for a commission, which would normally mean their loss to some other regiment. The banausic corps, having an inexhaustible surplus of technically competent bods, were far more generous with their recommendations. This was sad, as I'm sure the colonel would have agreed.

One of the characteristics which the colonel shared with other great commanders was the ability to drop off for forty winks in all circumstances. Papa Joffre must have had that gift and at Tannenberg the battlefield guides used to point out various spots to visitors: 'Here Hindenburg slept before the battle; and here he slept after the battle; and here he slept during the battle.'

Our division had had a long, hot day at a Suffolk field-firing range, culminating in a night attack and a long drive home in the dark. The Colonel composed himself for sleep in the back of his Humber, delegating the task of map-reading to the battalion intelligence officer: he was not a man to keep a dog and bark himself. The IO sensibly attached himself to the last vehicle of the battalion in front. Under the tail board it bore, dimly lit, our divisional sign.

The great convoy set off. Confidently following his leader, the tired IO, too, relaxed. Round a corner and, lo, horrors! The road ahead was empty, nothing in sight. Frantically he ordered the driver to step on the gas. His torch wandered wildly over the map: where on earth were we? 'Left here, must be left again – no, right. Oh damn – make two lefts, Faster! We must catch them up.' Unheeded in the rush, unfamiliar soldiers leapt belatedly shouting from an open road block. The road widened dramatically, became concrete – were we on some by-pass? A huge and dramatically swelling mass of darker darkness materialised straight ahead, blotting out the stars. With a fearful roar it suddenly rose up, soared, missing the Humber by feet. We were on an airfield, from which a bomber had just taken off.

During the ensuing chaos and confabulations, the colonel stirred uneasily but did not finally surface. At length the convoy was re-formed, and set off headlong into the dawn. Along twisting lanes and through farmyards we thundered, scattering chickens, astonished and half-awake, reaching at last a road and then a better road, and at last – joy! – the distant divisional tail sign of a vehicle speeding lickety-split far ahead, presumably the last of our preceding battalion. The IO breathed an enormous sigh of relief: 'Follow that tail light,' he cried. No easy task, for it was receding at a fantastic pace, quite unlike the normal, stately Brucknerian *adagio langsam und feierlich*, of a military convoy.

It grew lighter. The colonel awoke, stretched and peered out of the window. Odd, he mused at last, how alike these Suffolk churches were. Doubtless a local style of medieval architecture, the IO, a cultivated man, suggested. Strange all the same, the colonel rumbled, as yet another church sped past, exactly like its predecessors.

Whatever misgivings may have assailed the IO, it was the colonel's keen insight which first realised that we were passing not similar churches but the same church over and over again, the same pub, too, with the same sign. The battalion transport had got itself into a huge circle. The tail the IO was chasing was his own. Moreover, the convoy was not quite long enough to fill the whole circle with ease. Hence the ever increasing speed as each vehicle strove in vain to keep up with the one in front. 'Very odd indeed' was the Colonel's first reaction. Reflection and wrath supplied him later with language stronger than he normally used.

The demands of garrison duty at Dover later forced us to do night battle exercises in the country during daylight. To one of these the colonel added a touch of realism by nodding off on his camp bed. Now battalion IO myself, I stayed awake. Over the sunny hill two figures approached slowly in an odd manner. One would walk forward a few paces and then stop. The other, who appeared to be reading a compass and giving instructions, would then join him. The process was again and again repeated. I woke the colonel, who was so astonished by these mysterious movements that he could hardly pull his trousers and boots on. His eyes stood out like gob-stoppers. 'God bless my soul: who are these strange people? Are they mad?'

I had recognised our new hyper-keen brigadier, who wore

enormous spectacles with heavy black rims like a Hollywood film director. I stepped forward to salute and delay him while the colonel completed his *toilette*. 'Good morning, sir,' I cried. 'Good morning?' the brigadier testily riposted. 'It's good evening if anything. And who am I? It's pitch dark. You can't see me.' The colonel joined us, his mouth hanging open in anxious disbelief. 'Where's your commanding officer?' rapped the brigadier, looking straight through the colonel as if he wasn't there. 'I'm here,' he faltered. 'I can't see you,' barked the brigadier: 'Identify yourself.'

The colonel later charitably acquitted the brigadier of mental derangement. 'It must be trouble with his eyesight, poor fellow. Desert blindness perhaps. Those specs, don't you know. Very odd all the same. You really can't command a brigade if you can't see an inch beyond your nose. They ought to invalid him out.'

Our paths later diverged, mine to the Lincolns in Normandy, his to command a battalion there. I bumped into one of his chaps out of the line, and asked him how the old boy was getting on. 'He had a bit of bad luck the other day. Very nasty.' I froze, fearing catastrophe. 'He'd managed to organise some breakfast for himself, you know, bacon, eggs, the lot – and he was sitting outside his command post, just about to tuck in, when a bloody carrier turned sharply in the dirt just in front of him. A huge clod flew and fell splat all over his fry-up.' 'He must have been livid.' 'Obviously, but all he said was "very strange", you know, in a mournful sort of voice, as if it were an act of God.' In every life, they say, some rain must fall. Blessed the life in which a ruined breakfast is memorably strange. Peace be with him.

The Spectator, 30 September 1989

Hitler the Arch-Romantic – and His Masterpiece

In 1939, on the eve of his invasion of Poland, the Führer declared to Sir Nevile Henderson, 'I am by nature an artist and not a politician.' This self-revelation is dismissed in William Shirer's new book* as 'a typical display of sentimental hogwash.' Yet is it not the sober truth?

The politician has always been a humble enough being, content to make arrangements calculated to secure at best the peace and prosperity of the world, more usually the prosperity of his own countrymen, at worst his own prosperity. Hitler was no politician.

Hitler cared for none of these things, not even the last. His private tastes were always simple: a bowl of rice and vegetables, a homely mistress, cream cakes, a few cronies and somewhere to doss down.

The artist's origins in our civilisation were yet more humble than the politician's. Treated by his patrons as a servant, he acquired nevertheless with the romantic movement a new arrogance and effrontery. He noisily asserted first his independence of his former masters, then his superiority to the common herd as to all men, to convention, duty and morality, to society as a whole. In the career of Hitler's favourite composer, Richard Wagner, the bold immodesty of the romantic artist reaches heights not surpassed till Hitler himself did so.

Hitler, of course, began his life as an artist in the most literal sense. But he was the unhappiest of artists: one in whom an irrepressible, almost volcanic urge to self-expression was united to the most meagre talents. In our day such men became action painters, and better far that they should do so.

* The Rise and Fall of the Third Reich

No such course was open to Hitler in a Vienna still dominated artistically by a frowsy academicism. The best that he could produce in this line were a few insipid views of the Ringstrasse and some showcards for shop windows. It is incongruous to think that such a genius could find for a time no more adequate outlet.

For genius he had, genius on the grandest scale, a genius which finally found expression in works beside which those of Wagner sink to the timid maunderings of a church organist. The Nazi party was his brush, the German nation his palette, Europe – the world – his canvas.

With these he created out of his sick imagination, out of all the anger, bitterness, frustration and contempt which boiled within him, one stupendous, horrible and tragic masterpiece. It was not in Ireland that Yeats's 'terrible beauty' was born: but in Germany.

In Hitler the romantic movement reaches a conclusion at once logical and grotesque. The artist, having established his independence of the world, now returns upon it as conqueror. The unacknowledged legislator is at last acknowledged, and lays down the law. The arch-romantic bends the world to his will, and expresses himself at the world's expense. He makes a picture out of our reality

A picture – yes: for the whole thing seems to have been to Hitler in a sense a show. Many have noted that in his last years his grasp of reality seemed uncertain and intermittent. Was it ever more?

It was not a firm grasp of reality that explains Hitler's triumphs. Indeed, they were achieved in defiance of the actual. Repeatedly he backed the impossible, and repeatedly the impossible cantered home.

Was it a sober realist who seized power in Germany, who denounced Versailles, who strolled audaciously into the Rhineland, who seized Austria and Czechoslovakia without a shot fired, who overran Poland, Holland, Belgium, France, half the Balkans and half Russia, all on wholly inadequate resources and often against overwhelming odds?

Was it not rather that reality itself seemed to shrink at the onrush of this armed Bohemian, to suspend itself, to dissolve, like the Reichstag or the French army, into mists and immaterial vapours? The forces arrayed against Hitler in Germany and later in the world: these were realities of the most imposing kind, but what until 1942 had *they* achieved?

It was only when at last in Russia reality took courage and struck back that Hitler first revealed what had always been true – that he had no respect for it whatever. When generals told him the truth, he dismissed them from his presence, and the facts they told him as brusquely from his mind.

Was anything outside this man real to him? Was he not a total solipsist? Did he feel any joy or pain except his own, or any sympathy for any human being?

Not clearly for any Jew or Slav: these were but tools to his hand, or blots to be erased. They were subhuman. He had no pity for their sufferings, perhaps no awareness of them. Their fate was for him nothing more than a part of the grand design.

More strangely, he appears to have had as little feeling for the Germans. He rejoiced publicly in their misery during the slump, as an artist rejoices to see the materials skilfully prepared for his use. He watched without compunction as, by his direct orders and through his own criminal negligence, vanity and folly, they were minced to death in Russia, never doubting for one moment his right to demand of them such appalling sacrifice.

And when at last they broke under the strain he was quick to disown them as unworthy. The Russians were subhuman, but they had defeated the Germans who must thus, by his own brutal logic, be sub-subhuman. Practically his last order was that Germany must be reduced to a wasteland, thus denying to its remaining inhabitants 'the basis of even the most primitive existence'.

With his own defeat and death, the Germans had lost their *raison d'être*. They must therefore cease to exist.

Goebbels once compared Mussolini unfavourably with Hitler and Stalin: 'He is so bound to his own Italian people that he lacks the broad qualities of a worldwide revolutionary.' Hitler was not thus bound to the German people. It was his strength, like that of Gulley Jimson, to be a lone wolf, bound to no one.

Fully to comprehend all the processes and activities of genius, genius of another sort is required. This Mr Shirer lacks, in common with his predecessors in the field. His style, too, is oddly uneven, ranging downwards from the workmanlike prose of good daily journalism (he was Berlin correspondent of the *Chicago Tribune*) to the purest Greyfrairs.

Just as Bunter is 'the fat owl of the Remove', so here is Goering 'the fat field-marshal' or 'the corpulent chief of the Luftwaffe'; Laval 'the traitorous Frenchman'; Rosenberg (not unjustly, I admit) 'the befuddled Balt' or 'this Nazi dolt'.

Such trivial lapses may obscure for the squeamish Mr Shirer's many qualities: his moderation and fairness, his absolute clarity, his comprehensive grasp of the whole story, his narrative vigour and, above all, his industry.

Mr Shirer witnessed at first hand as much of what he now writes about as did any man not a German. Yet he relies little on the impressions of the time. Even the redoubtable Mr Quelch would not deny that he has done his homework.

His judgement, too, is shrewd. For instance, he puts his finger firmly on the fact, often overlooked, that if Mr Chamberlain's German policy ever made sense it ceased to do so at the precise moment when he gave an unconditional guarantee, 'at the worst possible time in the worst possible circumstances', to come to Poland's aid.

Most disquieting too is his repeated reminder of what most of us have chosen to forget: that Hitler could be on occasion all sweetness and light, and could coo as peacefully and beguilingly as any dove or Khrushchev.

In sum Mr Shirer's is a major and most valuable work of public instruction, of history as Macaulay knew it. And if any purer historian, secure in his own specialisation, feels like quibbling at some *minutiae*, he might first consider how many of his learned confrères would dare embark upon or hope to complete such a vast enterprise (1143 pages, excluding source, notes and index).

For all Mr Shirer's thoroughness there are questions still to answer. Why on earth, for instance, did such a richly gifted people as the Germans prostitute themselves to become the tools of a maniac?

The imaginative insight of a Dostoevsky is required to show how Hitler, by achieving for the Germans legitimate aims by illegitimate means, dulled in them their sense of right and wrong: how, having drawn them subtly and inexorably into small crimes, he drew them on into great and unimaginable atrocities, until all were bound to him hand and foot, sink or swim, by chains of complicity and common guilt, of fear and despair, of dark knowledge, of acquiescence ruthlessly exploited, of exaltation; fatalism and actual insanity.

'This man Hitler,' said General von Fritsch ruefully in 1938, 'is Germany's destiny for good or evil. If he now goes over the abyss – as I believe he will – he will drag us all down with him. There is nothing we can do.'

Nothing, anyway, was done until 20 July 1944, and this heroic – but too little, and too late.

And there is another question, of course. Is it all fated to happen again? I will not rush in where Mr Shirer fears to tread. But I would like to make a few remarks about the German past, from which the German future – if we can know anything of it at all – must be extrapolated.

It is surely rash to assert – as Mr Shirer's dust-jacket implies more boldly than he does – that the whole of German history is nothing more than a sort of preparation for Hitler, an inexorable process of which he is to date the appointed culmination. If anyone asserted that German history was nothing more than a preparation for Dr Adenauer we should write him off as a fool.

Yet the latter view is hardly more fatuous than the former. Dr Adenauer has ancestors and precedents in the German past, just as Hitler had. A great tradition, rich though often submerged, nourishes and guides him.

What many wise men have noticed is the extraordinary *disconnection* of German history – the way in which now one strand is dominant, now another; the way in which different epochs succeed each other, like logs on a river, without any visible connection between them. In our own lifetime we have seen three such abrupt transformations: from Empire to Republic, from Republic to Reich from Hitler to Adenauer. We may not have seen the last.

Behind all this confusion may lie some pattern, but I don't know what it is and those who thought they knew were those who were most wrong about post-war Germany.

And until we *do* know, we can never be certain whether Hitler was truly Germany's destiny or whether he was rather a monstrous but isolated freak or perversion, a nightmare which vanishes with the rising sun.

Daily Telegraph, 8 November 1960

Constituency of the Dead

Do you remember when 11 November was truly Remembrance Day? How, at the muffled thunder of a gun, our whole nation would, even on a working day, halt and stand for two minutes in total silence, recalling with sorrow and gratitude the 'fallen'? If you experienced it you will never forget it nor what it said to you. Of course it was inconvenient and disruptive, to busy people in a hurry, vexatious. It was meant to be. It was an *aide-mémoire* addressed not only to those who wished to remember but to those who wished or were inclined to forget. It was designed to remind them that there are things more important than everyday life, things worth dying for as well as living for. This reminder it delivered by rudely interrupting everyday life, as wars do, though infinitely more so.

The idiots who moved it to the nearest Sunday were guilty of a crime like that of a brain surgeon who, in order to serve the convenience, comfort, happiness or 'mental health' of his patient, removes or deadens (as I fancy is now possible) that part of his brain in which memory resides. They must have done it deliberately. They must actually have thought everyday life more important than memory, and acted accordingly. They cannot themselves have regarded, as we should regard, all memory as sacred, all forgetfulness sinful.

Already dishonoured by being displaced, this year's Remembrance Day is further besmirched by the unseemly struggles of some politicians to get into the Cenotaph 'act' (as perhaps they see it) and of others to keep them out. Heartily do I agree with Bernard Levin that Mrs Thatcher should not have excluded Dr Owen, and that all concerned appear in a bad light. Yet much else with which he in *The Times* supported and embellished his characteristically sound judgement seemed to me sadly unworthy of one whose head and heart normally command warm affection and respect.

He declared, for instance, that 'the appearance at the Cenotaph of party leaders has nothing to do with the dead but plenty to do with the living, most particularly the political living'. Surely in fact it has plenty to do with both. Certainly politicians may derive political advantage from their presence there. But why so? Is it not because it is thought seemly for important politicians (who after all bear the responsibility for war and peace) to abjure for a moment all sectional strife and humbly to honour those who died that they might be there, and Mr Levin free to write about them? Is it possible, let alone desirable, to uncouple doing the right thing from whatever advantage may be derived from it? And since when has the right thing become the wrong thing just because advantage might flow therefrom? If the Cenotaph can still, so to speak, sway votes and exert influence, can honour some and shame others, how could it decently be otherwise when you think of that great constituency of the dead which it represents?

For Mr Levin it is perhaps 'time to wonder whether the official ceremony, with its bands and its guns and its royalty – and its politicians – should be put away forever and those who wish to remember their, and others', dead should do so in the peace and dignity of the country's local churches, or even the country's homes'. 'The whole business,' he writes, 'is as lifeless as an object in a museum . . . This is inevitable, for the living cannot indefinitely be looking over their shoulders at the dead; if the force has gone out of Remembrance Day, it is because people do not feel that force . . . and nothing will make them do so.'

In these sentences, don't certain words and phrases jar a bit? Those who 'wish' to remember the dead, for instance: as if it were just a personal whim. And again, 'even in the country's homes'. Can Mr Levin's home contain nothing to distract him, no little chores, no unpaid bills, no beckoning books, no telephone? Is his memory so perfect as to need no jog? Would he always remember unaided to set aside the due minute or two for meditation? Do we not all need external reminders, forms, dates and ceremonies, to keep us up to the mark? What if I were impiously to suggest that Bayreuth 'should be put away forever' and that those who love Wagner should listen at home? And again the phrase 'lifeless as an object in a museum'. Who has not contemplated some object in a museum and discerned in it, with a sudden pang of insight, a small, poignant but still surviving and quietly whispering part of the life of those who created it, used or thought it beautiful? I bet the sensitive Mr Levin has for one.

And 'the living cannot indefinitely be looking over their shoulders at the dead'. To be sure they can't *always* be doing this. As the dead knew well, the future has its claims as well as the past; and one of its most pressing claims is to have memories of the past lovingly preserved for it and handed on as fresh and clear and alive as lies in our power. In order to perform this noble task we do have to look back, not always but sometimes and – yes – indefinitely, at the dead.

And 'if the force has gone out of Remembrance Day, it is because people do not feel this force . . . and nothing will make them do so, not even,' Mr Levin continues, and again I agree with him, 'the sight of every member of the House of Commons, their ranks swelled by every defeated candidate, lined up around the Cenotaph listening, more probably not listening, to the Last Post'. Well, it must be a stony heart indeed which, hearing the Last Post, does not listen to it, is not moved by it, needs no furtive handkerchief. Perhaps there are such hearts, and I suppose there must be people for whom the 'force' has gone out of Remembrance Day. And if there are, why has the 'force' gone? Well, it must be partly because of the ignoble and shabby date switch, to which I have referred. But also there must have been an almost treasonable negligence or failure on the part of those writers, poets, orators, thinkers, historians, churchmen and – yes – politicians, on the part of those whom Coleridge (I think) called the clerisy and Benda *les clercs*, whose duty it is to guard and refresh the nation's memory and to preserve forever the full 'force' of whatever, like Remembrance Day, should rightfully have it.

To find Mr Levin even for a moment among these negligent *clercs* is a great sadness. Never to his honour does he forget the Russian dead, for instance, communism's victims, their sufferings before they died, the grief of those who mourned them. How then can he even for a moment wonder whether it be proper to forget (for this is in effect what he is wondering) our own? I know how much he venerates Nadezhda Mandelstam. Let her speak for me: 'What can we expect to happen in a country with a disordered memory? What is a man worth who has lost his memory?' Can a nation which has lost its memory hope long to preserve anything else?

> At the going down of the sun and in the morning
> We will remember them.

Binyon's lines were not just a prediction but a promise, a sacred compact which our forefathers made with the dead. To dishonour it would show us unworthy of all of them.

The Spectator, 12 November 1983

Eichmann in the Dock

JERUSALEM, A CITY OF GLOOM

(*Sunday Telegraph*, 9 April 1961)

Into this gloomy city is moved Adolf Eichmann to face, on Tuesday, the music long-delayed. No one knows exactly where he is: no one by design, for fear he should be assassinated.

No one knows exactly the number of Jews he is said to have murdered: six million is the conventional figure, four million the scholarly figure, slightly fewer perhaps the accurate figure.

Not that these figures matter over much. For if Eichmann were found guilty of the murder of any one Jew or of one or more millions of Jews it is the same thing: a vile and unforgivable crime.

Precisely, this man is accused, 'together, with others', of crimes against the Jewish people and against humanity:

> Being the person responsible for the physical extermination of the Jews and thus for the 'final solution of the Jewish problem';
>
> Killing millions of Jews in the concentration camps of Auschwitz, Chelmno, Belsec, Sobibor, Treblinka and Maindaned;
>
> Organising operational groups for the extermination of hundreds of thousands of Jews, especially on the Sabbath and other Jewish festivals, in Poland, Russia, Lithuania, Latvia and Estonia.

He is accused not merely of specific murders, as of a hundred children of Lidice, but of mass murder and of lesser crimes adding up to mass murder, of systematic persecution, starvation, of mass arrests, cruel beatings, of compulsory abortions and mass sterilizations.

Theft of 'vast amounts of parts of the bodies of murdered persons', such as hair, gold teeth, false teeth and artificial limbs.

Of these and other crimes Eichmann is accused by the Israeli State. It accuses him because he happens to have fallen within its jurisdiction; and because this State considers itself to be the legitimate heir of all the Jews who perished between 1933 and 1945.

He is accused with reluctance and with certain misgivings. These do not arise from any doubts as to Eichmann's guilt, which indeed are hardly permissible. They arise rather from doubts as to the strict legality of Eichmann's abduction.

For if found guilty how can Eichmann die four million or six million times? His life or death is by now an irrelevance. As well hang a fly for setting off an earthquake, one locust for causing a great famine.

The Israeli government says that the trial is also to set the historical record straight. But the record is already straight. In the English language alone there are at least three excellent, accurate and thorough books, by Messrs Reitlinger, Poliakov and Kogon, setting out all the facts about Eichmann for anyone who is sufficiently interested to bother to read them.

If anything important and new comes up at this trial it could well be false. There are glum premonitions circulating here that unless the Israeli judiciary is pretty smart the East Germans will start producing rubbish, like forged photographs of Eichmann shaking hands with such people as Dr Adenauer or General Speidel.

Another reason for holding the trial is to remind the Israelis of what their fathers suffered. It is far from clear what profit they will derive from being thus reminded of what they can never forget, much as they might like to do so.

If anybody needs reminding it is not the Jews but the Germans, which might be a good reason for forcing them to try Eichmann. Instead they are permitted only to defend him, which seems an odd and unsatisfactory arrangement.

Normally at this time of year Jerusalem is already hot and dry. Unprecedented weather greets this unprecedented event. Dark angry clouds roll overhead, the skies themselves weep cold, driving tears for the wickedness of which we are about to hear.

So this was Eichmann

(*Daily Telegraph*, 12 April 1961)

Without ceremony, accompanied by two Israeli policemen, a dull, birdlike man of middle age and middling height entered the bullet-proof glass house, placed to the left of the courtroom, looked round and sat down.

He was deathly pale and impassive, with short thinning hair and horn-rimmed spectacles. His lips were thin and withdrawn, suggesting shrunken gums and false teeth.

So this was Eichmann. Hard to see in him now the young and handsome SS officer in his glittering uniform, with his champagne and his Hungarian mistresses.

Somebody recently described him as a typical German official. As well describe Christie, Constantine FitzGibbon retorted, as a typical London policeman.

Yet it was Christie that Eichmann actually did recall – the same dim appearance, the same dreary, petit bourgeois respectability.

In the history of Nazi Germany two successive waves have often been noted, the first represented by the Nazi party proper, the second by the SS which, after 1934, gradually and unobtrusively replaced it in power.

The first were those 'armed Bohemians', described by Konrad Heiden: the second were not Bohemians but rather dry, cruel, ruthless nobodies – Mr Pooter, so to speak, possessed by devils.

The first, however disagreeable, were often driven to enormities by genuine eccentricities and fantasies, by real mental derangements or other aberrations.

The second were propelled rather by ambition and vanity, or by other motives basically rational, however monstrous the consequences.

It is to the second wave that Eichmann belonged. Anti-Semitism may be regarded as a sort of disease. Whether Eichmann really suffered from it or whether he had any real feelings whatever about his victims is open to some doubt.

If not, he was perhaps a sort of moral malingerer, a man who feathered his own nest by pretending to share, or by actually inducing in himself, a prevailing and professionally profitable form of madness.

The judges enter quietly. Mr Justice Landau, bald with lofty and glittering dome; on his right Judge Halevi, strikingly good-looking, with slightly grey jowl and cowlick; Judge Raveh, heavily bespectacled, heavily lined, his face infinitely grave and sad.

All three are of German birth, born in Danzig, Weissenfels and Aurich respectively. Had things not gone so tragically ill in Germany in the years between, Dr Servatius, German defence counsel, might have pleaded before these very men – but in Germany.

The indictment is read by Judge Landau in heavily accented Hebrew and repeated to Eichmann in German.

It took seventy-five minutes, throughout which time, Eichmann stood facing the judges, immobile, erect, his hands at his side, his head thrown back in calm defiance, or perhaps in resignation.

He was said by his colleague, Dieter Wisliceny, to be a coward. Is he in fact a very brave man? Or is he too dull, too stupid, to realise the enormity of what is read out?

He is accused of the most ghastly crimes – not all in vague and general terms, but some quite specifically, such as the murder of a hundred children of Lidice.

His face never alters, though he licks his lips from time to time.

Does he understand it all or take it in? He says he does and sits down.

Dr Servatius rises to perform his unenviable task. A bulky man, Teutonic, with thick, deeply creased neck and close-cropped whitish hair.

He does his best for his client, as he is bound to do. He suggests that the court might be prejudiced. But where could an unprejudiced court be found?

The judges, indeed, are Jews. But are we non-Jews not also only too aware of what went on in Nazi Germany and just as shocked as anyone else?

In what remote forest or other limbo bereft of communication with the outside world could judges be found to whom Hitler was but a name perhaps and Eichmann not even that?

He objects manfully, knowing full well the crucial importance to his client of these first rounds. The law the court now administers, he says, was passed after the acts were committed to which it is now being applied.

And so in part it was: the Israeli law against the Nazis and their crimes was passed in 1950.

But was it really a new law? Did it not merely express, perhaps for the first time, the settled moral views of civilised mankind?

The reason it was not passed before was presumably because no one had thought such crimes possible or such a law consequently necessary.

There may, in England, be no law specifically prohibiting the eating of one's own children. But where is the person who does not know that this is wrong?

This was more or less how Mr Hausner, chief prosecutor, argued when he rose in the afternoon.

The laws under which the Nuremberg and other war-crimes tribunals had been constituted were in no sense innovations. They merely gave expression to existing international law and to principles sanctified not merely by Grotius but even by the Book of Amos.

All those laws had done was to reiterate that, whatever the Führer, murder was still murder, theft still theft.

The linguistic babble in which the proceedings are conducted was further confounded as Mr Hausner read out in English many decisions of American courts, of the Supreme Court and of lower courts in Indiana, Idaho and Michigan.

All these were to the effect that it did not matter a hoot how Eichmann had been brought to the court, whether kidnapped by force or fraud or in any other way.

All that counted was that he is here: justice must now be done.

RELENTLESS ARGUMENT IN EICHMANN TRIAL

(*Daily Telegraph*, 13 April 1961)

Relentlessly, for hour after hour, the chief prosecutor, Mr Gideon Hausner, proclaimed the competence of this court to try Eichmann and the validity of the laws by which he is charged.

Mr Hausner is Israel's attorney-general. He cited a wealth of precedents from many courts in many lands, Germany itself not excluded.

His appearance is reassuring, but authoritative, like that of a bank manager. His pink bald patch, surrounded by a sort of tonsure, glistens in the neon-lights.

His manner is quiet and leisurely, with long pauses while he rustles for documents. He gestures rarely, but fluently and with effect.

But in moments of emotion his hands suddenly flutter out like butterflies, or a long finger shoots forth and wags emphatically at bench or defence.

He can be eloquent. His voice rises in fiery intensity as he denounces the unpardonable and inexpiable nature of the crimes of which Eichmann is accused.

They were crimes at the time they were committed, he cries, and have always been crimes. He hopes that the next generation of Eichmann's compatriots 'will be different'.

English lawyers nodded in recognition of *hostis humani generis*, the enemy of the human race: upon those who declare war on all humanity, all humanity must declare war.

A more sinister echo was aroused by the mention of the eminent jurist, Maurice Grynszpan, for it was the assassination of the German diplomat, von Rath, by a Jew named Grynszpan in 1938 which was the pretext for the first hideous pogrom in Germany, the night of the broken glass.

The proceedings are informal, simple, but dignified. Judge Landau has had to rebuke laughter, but permitted himself to smile once today – a smile of courtesy, not of amusement.

Even Eichmann appeared to smile once wintrily upon his

defence counsel, though it may have been only a momentary tightening of the lips.

On Mr Hausner's right sits at ease the most striking figure in the court, a religious Jew with skullcap and black beard adorning a magnificent Old Testament face. This is the deputy state attorney, Yaacov Baror.

He looks impassively at Eichmann, Eichmann impassively back at him, retribution personified.

Dr Servatius, for Eichmann, rises to object to something, but is mollified. He sits for the most part silent today, strikingly like the late John Foster Dulles.

Dulles-like, in another sense, perhaps, was his concession yesterday – possibly inadvertently – that the State of Israel might regard itself as the legitimate heir of European Jewry.

The defence was expected to contend that Israel was not the heir and thus had no right to speak or act on Jewry's behalf.

It can hardly do so now: at this point Dr Servatius appeared to tread on his client's toe.

An American voice suddenly shouts from the gallery, 'Hey, the red lights's gone out.'

A disturbance is expected, but does not materialise. The security arrangements are so tight that the chance of some fanatic getting in with a bomb or leaflets is pretty remote.

Feelings are high, at times almost uncontrollable. So many have lost relatives and friends.

There are those who have actually lost their reason as a result of what they went through. It is surprising that more have not done so, that many remain calm, humane and objective, often ready to correct politely some violent expression of anti-German prejudice.

As the argument proceeds, one almost forgets the grim figure in the bullet-proof glass case.

It is with a shock that one's eyes return to Eichmann's pale, drawn face, framed in its absurd earphones, the face of a spectator, silent, withdrawn.

It was noticeable that the ranks of correspondents thinned out during the continuation of the attorney-general's four-hour legal argument before the luncheon adjournment. Even Eichmann appeared indifferent as he occasionally adjusted his earphones or took them off when his counsel addressed the court in German.

From time to time Dr Servatius would interrupt the flow of legal language in guttural German tones. But for the most part he sat making notes on a pad.

The man on whose conscience?

(*Daily Telegraph*, 16 April 1961)

I can neither look at Eichmann nor stop looking at him, he fascinates and repels, like a snake.

Not that he looks in any way odd. It would be more bearable if he did. If he had horns, a tail and eyes blazing with diabolical malignancy, we could say, 'Ah, yes, these crimes were committed not by a fellow human being but by a monster. They are nothing to do with us.'

But, alas, he looks quite ordinary. He looks, in Nietzsche's phrase, human, all too human. He has, or had, a streaming cold. He coughs and sniffs, sneezes and blows his nose. He wears spectacles (with plastic lenses lest he cut his throat), a collar and tie (the latter only in court, for fear he strangle himself). He runs his tongue around his mouth, as though his false teeth fitted badly.

He is one of us, part of humanity. We are parts of each other; a little bit of each one of us sits in that dock with him.

Perhaps that is why we feel for him – yes – an overwhelming pity. I think that almost everyone in the court must feel this pity, though some of us might be ashamed to admit it.

It is not a sentimental pity. It is not because we forget or can ever forget, least of all here and now, those terrible washhouses in which showered down not hot and cold but Zyklon B, the reeking smoking chimneys, those ghastly trains stuffed with suffering, starving, suffocating, dying people, the exhausted columns of woman and children staggering through the night, the beatings, the cruel whippings, the kicks and blows, the systematic degradation, not only of guards and prisoners but also of all those who looked on without apparent protest.

All this was done to human beings, too, to six million of them or to many more. Heaven forbid that we forget that, or grow indifferent. Yet how can one not feel pity for any man who now faces death utterly alone and friendless, who may soon face a God whose existence he had denied (on the SS documents was entered 'Non-religious')?

That any one man should go to his death bearing such an intolerable burden of guilt is appalling. We must weep to see God's image so besmirched.

We long for him to repent. We long for him to show his humanity not just by sneezing but by sorrow and contrition. We long for one gesture from him which might help to bring peace and healing of wounds, to assuage the bitter but understandable hatred which some, though not all, Jews feel for his fellow countrymen.

We may long in vain. He may be too dull and stupid and unimaginative to realise the enormity of what he is charged with. What looks like courage or defiance may be no more than moral imbecility.

If so, he is still to be pitied. A man whose conscience is deformed or lacking is a man crippled. A man without settled moral principles is to that extent impoverished. Conscience is not a mere straitjacket, nor morality a prison. Both are privileges; while limiting freedom, both give security. And, as Burke said, liberty must be limited to be enjoyed.

If Eichmann is too dull to realise his guilt we must also suppose him too dull to have scaled unaided the peaks of depravity which we find described in the indictment. Such crimes as these are not the work of one man of indifferent intellect and scant imagination, however energetic and vicious he might be. Throughout the indictment appear the words, 'He, Eichmann, with others.' With others, how many others!

The indictment refers specifically only to Eichmann's accomplices, some dead, some still at large: to those who gave him his orders, whose guilt is indeed greater even than his but cannot diminish it (for the prosecution declares an immoral order is not an order that must be obeyed); and to those many more who obeyed Eichmann's orders. Already we see a mighty pyramid of guilt reared before us, with Eichmann somewhere near the summit.

But wait : the pyramid is nowhere near complete. What about the rest of us? What about all those of us who have long been working and are still working to undermine the whole foundation of Christian and liberal civilisation?

There have been men of immeasurably better education and greater intelligence than Eichmann who have proclaimed amidst the applause of millions that men are not responsible for their actions. 'Be hard! Be brutal!' some have cried: 'Man is a beast of prey!' And much vicious nonsense besides.

Very well, Eichmann behaved irresponsibly: he was or became hard and brutal as a beast of prey. Was this what they meant? If Eichmann can plead any one thing it might be that his betters set him a most shocking example.

Their guilt must be added to the pile, together with that of all those who helped to create a society which out of such a commonplace man, perhaps originally no more than slightly callous and over eager to get on in life, out of such a man fashioned a criminal. A society which did little or nothing to restrain him; a society which indeed exposed him to horrible temptation and placed at his disposal unprecedented material resources.

Here is a man fitted by nature to be, say, a postmaster or a railway traffic controller. He has made of himself, with our aid, the murderer of millions. May the Grace of God protect us from ourselves.

Epic address in trial of Eichmann

(*Daily Telegraph*, 19 April 1961)

In a voice, now rising passionately almost to a prolonged scream, now sinking to a sombre whisper, yet always with dignity, Gideon Hausner, Israeli attorney-general, today and yesterday told of the calamity, wide as the ocean that overtook the House of Israel.

It was an epic performance in the Eichmann trial. The best of it is destined to become a classic.

As we listen, we ourselves share the pain and humiliation of the Jews. We wince as we hear of their beards torn out by the roots. We, too, are ground down as they are forced to clean the streets with their prayer shawls.

Naked, bereft of clothing, pride and hope, we shuffle with them to the edge of a mass grave, kneel, are shot by a cigarette-smoking SS man and fall upon the piled corpses of those dead before us.

We hear of the children, 'separated by force from their mothers, murdered and thrown out of trucks, torn to pieces before their mothers' eyes, their little heads smashed on the ground'.

We go to the washroom, there to be gassed, our bodies to be burned if we are lucky.

For we, too, might die as did one who was found at Auschwitz, in the punishment-by-starvation block, clutching at the liver torn from another corpse.

Thus did the Jews of Europe perish at the hands of Germans and others. From Kant to cannibalism in a century and a half.

Echoes of an Indian summer

(*Daily Telegraph*, 20 April 1961)

Gruff, hesitant, as though a man were talking in his sleep at the bottom of a well. This was the voice of Adolf Eichmann, as recorded on tape under interrogation and played back to the court today.

Amplified, it boomed and murmered menacingly round the courtroom, raising the most fearful echoes, real and metaphorical.

Echoes of that Indian summer of 1941 – 'One could see the leaves falling.' How they fell, and not leaves only.

Echoes of the screams and shrieks of naked Jews murdered twenty years ago in the back of a gas van.

Eichmann saw their bodies tipped into a pit: he had to report to Mueller. He saw and then he turned and drove away: he was 'washed up'. It was quite enough for a 'white collar worker' – too much, perhaps.

By night he could not sleep; but by day he went to Auschwitz, as he was ordered to do.

Eichmann's manner in court has become slightly discomposed. He looks this way and that, fidgets, and rocks his head inanely to and fro.

He is under strain. Sooner or later, surely, he must break – into hysterical laughter or into tears.

Eichmann as an excursion manager

(*Daily Telegraph*, 22 April 1961)

Eichmann was just 'a transport officer and nothing more'. Such was the modest drift of his recorded testimony today.

From the administrative point of view, he simply had the duty of transportation. Just a little more perhaps: for 'the evacuating authority had to know with what categories of people to deal'.

It dealt with these, or course, 'in accordance with the instructions received from its superiors'.

And the Wannsee conference? Well, Eichmann had had to 'write the invitations'. He had also attended it, as it happened, but 'was not supposed to speak there – the small fry had no right to speak at such a conference'.

The Eichmann presented to us today was part station master, or perhaps, excursion manager, part social secretary, part petty bureaucrat.

He speaks in starchy, clerkish language, full of abstraction, pedantry and euphemism.

He speaks drily of documents, despatches, reports and negotiations; of 'emigration' and 'evacuation', of operations and actions and, of course, of solutions, of 'the legal basis' – of all things – of his activities.

A sensitive man, too squeamish, as we know, to contemplate

an open wound, he eschews such words as murder. Far too vulgar and precise.

Nor had he any particular responsibility, so it seems, for what happened to those he obediently pushed around.

'I received instructions to evacuate people, but not every person evacuated was put to death. This was out of the scope of my knowledge, who was put to death or not.'

Eichmann in the dock

(*Daily Telegraph*, 1 June 1961)

This sober and praiseworthy account of the Eichmann trial* is for those who feel that they can never know too much about this extraordinarily ordinary man.

Some may by now have wearied of the whole subject. Striving to comprehend, some find their imaginations will not stretch to the required point, and give up in despair. Others, conscientiously exposing themselves to the accumulation of horror, grow numb, as Eichmann himself must have grown numb.

Many must find themselves in some sympathy with the dignified closing speech of Eichmann's counsel, Dr Servatius. Referring to the ancient Jewish idea of 'superannuation', he contends that the passing of time must of itself bring peace and an end to suffering. Indeed, the Statute of Limitations surely has its place in nature: anger, hatred and the thirst for vengeance, like all worldly things, have their appointed term.

Yet it is still possible to argue that the cause of reconciliation and healing might be better served by Eichmann's death than by the mercy for which his counsel naturally pleaded. An eye for an eye: by no logic can the liquidation of one man avenge the liquidation of six million. Yet it may serve for a symbol: it could close a book and thus bring peace.

The trial, of course, lacked at least one element of drama: suspense. Eichmann's guilt was never in doubt; he had been tried and condemned a thousand times before he was brought to

* *The Trial of Adolf Eichmann* by Lord Russell of Liverpool

court. In this sense his trial was supererogatory. It had other purposes, indeed, as the court confirmed in its judgement.

> To put on record a precise historical description of the events which occurred during the catastrophe and, in so doing, to emphasise the heroic feats performed by the ghetto fighters and the resistance put up by the Jewish partisans in Poland and Russia.

Yet most of the events which occurred during the catastrophe were already on the record. Lord Russell of Liverpool among numberless others having already done his bit to put them there; the trial added little of importance. As for emphasising the heroic feats of resistance, alas, it could do little of the sort.

The battle-hardened young Jews of Israel listened with shame as they heard how their forefathers of the Diaspora were sent like sheep to the slaughter, meek accomplices for the most part in their own destruction, Eichmann himself agreed that there was in those dark times little civil courage to be found among Germans: could the Jews boast of more?

Yet, for all this, these proceedings still exert a fearful fascination. For example, let me commend to you the fantastic interchange between Eichmann and Judge Raveh on the subject of Kant's 'categorical imperative' – act always as though your action were to form the basis of a universal law. Upon this noble maxim Eichmann, so he says, had striven to found his life. In vain: the State had intervened, forcing him to bow to 'the reversal of values' which it dictated. 'I had no luck,' he complains.

It is possible at this point to see in Eichmann another Willems, the man who, in Conrad's *Outcast of the Islands*, when he left the path of his own peculiar virtue, intended to do so only temporarily, yet in fact never got back: the tragic logic of events was too strong for him.

Of the way chosen by Eichmann the Israeli attorney-general, Dr Gideon Hausner, had this to say:

> It is a terrible thing to realise that whoever sets his foot upon this path can no longer trace the way back to human

> values . . . His heart is destroyed; he is transformed into a chilly block of ice and marble, wrapped in documents, orders, instructions and proclamations.

At points along this dark road there seems to have been extinguished in Eichmann all pity, kindness, conscience and natural feeling. If so, how little now remains to die – a mere husk, all that remains of what was once a whole man.

MUSIC

❦

Message in the Magic

Never is *The Magic Flute* revived but it is again declared, whether by some of the critics, or perhaps by the producer or some of the singers, that Schikaneder's plot is a load of picturesque nonsense, a spectacular revue, a masonic farrago, either with no meaning at all or with many obscure and fractured meanings beyond the power of human will to comprehend.

David Hockney, the brilliant designer of the current Glyndebourne production, tells us that he 'read a lot of books – all the theories about the plot and meaning, etc., etc.' Yet, despite this, he concludes that, 'Well, even for a fairy story it is a bit silly.' He finds it rum, for instance that the hero, Tamino, starts on the road to enlightenment by running wetly away from 'a dragon' (actually Schikaneder specifies a *serpent* – more of that anon) which has to be killed for him by three ladies.

We are thus asked to believe that Mozart, a most intelligent man as well as a genius, lavished some of the most sublime music ever written on a twaddling text and kept for the result a special place in his heart. A bit thick this, surely, even if we did not know that Mozart *cared* about his libretti, took a keen and constructive interest in them. Doubtless he could have set, say, the telephone directory or the average sociology thesis to splendid music but he had more sense than to do so.

I have read none of the books. I should therefore be too modest to boast that the general meaning of *The Magic Flute* has always seemed perfectly – well almost perfectly – clear to me. Is it perhaps because I am too stupid to see all the difficulties? Anyway, I advance my case with great humility. If I sound too positive, it is only because phrases like 'may I respectfully suggest' become tedious with repetition. If what I say has been said before, I am sorry; but it is not plagiarism on my part, just pure ignorance. And please note that I am trying tentatively to describe the *Weltanschauung* of Schikaneder and Mozart, not my own.

Now the principal difficulty experienced by others, perhaps wiser, is the Queen of the Night's alleged change of character from goody to baddy (Brigid Brophy's elegant terms), a change variously supposed to spring from panic, incompetence, carelessness or a sort of dramatic amnesia on Schikaneder's part.

This 'change' is indeed vitally important. It is the clue to the Queen's identity. She is, I submit, the Roman Catholic Church, no less, as a Continental freemason of that time (Mozart and Schikaneder were both masons, which meant more then and there than it does here and now) would see her.

The timespan of the opera is the history of Western Christendom. During the Dark Ages (the Night) the Church which the Queen represents was a genuine force for good. Her agents deliver Tamino from the burden of inexpiable sin – the serpent. The gifts which she gives to Tamino, the seeker for wisdom and enlightenment, are genuine, precious and enduring – the magic flute itself, which carries him through all dangers, and the beautiful portrait of her daughter. They represent respectively music and the visual arts, the medieval Church being almost the sole faithful guardian, repository and patron of both. Enduring, too, is her gift to Papageno, the common man, the magic bells, which may stand for all the fun and festivals, the eye-catching ceremonial, spectacle and drama by which the Church endeared herself to humble souls.

Even the guides the Queen supplies for Tamino, the three wise boys, remain loyal to him throughout, to the end. They may represent scholarship and learning, also cherished by the medieval Church, against whom at the Renaissance they ungratefully turn.

Tamino is despatched by the Queen to rescue her daughter Pamina, who has fallen into the clutches of 'a powerful evil demon', Sarastro. Who is Pamina? She is all those who once called or still call the Church mother but have been attracted or seduced by reason and enlightenment – to a mason of that time irresistible and higher forces.

It is not really the character of the Queen which changes, but rather her role and circumstances. Once the last refuge of such remnants of culture as survived, she is debarred by her superstitious origins and nature from understanding or tolerating the new high culture of the enlightenment, represented by her enemy, Sarastro. In him, too, thought and the arts find a worthier and more liberating patron.

For Sarastro's character also undergoes a sort of change, or rather his true noble nature is gradually revealed He is no demon as the superstitious Queen thinks him, but the embodiment of reason and enlightenment, truth and goodness.

Truly bad by contrast is Sarastro's henchman, Monostatos, who suggests to me in his context the Ottoman Emperor but may be taken also to symbolise cruel earthly tyranny in general. Do not his attempts to rape and possess Pamina recall the presence of the Turks at the very gates of Vienna, only about a hundred years before *The Magic Flute* was written?

He is bound to Sarastro really by a sort of error, an illusion. As seen by the Church, both are equally evil, both infidels. Yet their characters and purposes are in fact wholly opposed. When he expects rewards from Sarastro, Monostatos gets rebukes and a beating instead (Sarastro is for once untrue to his creed of forswearing vengeance and forgiving his foes!). At last Monostatos rushes off to find more appropriate employment in the service of the Queen of the Night, who offers her erring daughter to him. Tyranny thus hurries to the aid of superstition, hoping – in vain as it turns out – itself to derive support therefrom.

Already in love with Pamina, Tamino joins her in Sarastro's realm. Far from 'rescuing' her, they together pass through the ordeals which dramatically symbolise the difficulties, the misunderstandings and loneliness (Tamino's enforced silence, for example) which the seeker for wisdom must courageously face. And on the other side we must presume them to find the heretical paradise predicted by the three wise boys – 'the Kingdom of Heaven on earth and mortals like the gods'.

And there is happiness, too, in the realm of reason for Papageno, in the thought of engendering numberless little Papagenos and Papagenas. But note that his 'dear little wife' appears first to him as a hideous crone – the fruits of reason are not at once attractive to the average sensual man (as Beatrice Webb should with contempt have called him).

By this time we have learnt who made the magic flute – Pamina's father, God the Father Himself, her mother the Church. Music is thus of divine origin.

More momentously still, we have learnt from the Queen of the Night that *that Father is dead*, that she has in consequence lost her power and that before He died 'He freely surrendered' to Sarastro 'His mighty shield of the sun' – i.e. His light, His power, His wisdom . . .

If Schikaneder and Mozart really meant all this, you may ask, why did they not make it clearer? At that time, in that place, they could surely be excused for being frightened to do so. Nobody who had ever been at the beck and call of the Archbishop of Salzburg could really be sure that the Queen of the Night had lost all her power. And then, too, there was the fear of damnation. For there was a priest present at Mozart's deathbed. You can't be too careful.

Daily Telegraph, 26 June 1978

Beatlemania

Mrs McCartney, wife of the distinguished composer and retired Beatle Paul, has sent a giant hamper from Fortnum's to the Greenham ladies. It contained champagne, *vol au vent*, stuffed vegetables, chocolate cake and delicacies (no dope is reported), also a message: 'You are doing a great job! Keep it up and don't give up. Love and kisses, Linda McCartney.' Whether the goodies were well chosen or not depends, I suppose, on whether the Greenham ladies actually like the weird messes on which they normally feed. That Mrs McCartney can afford to be munificent is beyond doubt. Her husband was hailed by Tony Palmer (though more distinguished critics made bigger fools of themselves at the time) as the greatest songwriter since Schubert. This judgement incidentally made him the superior of such lesser tune-smiths as Schumann, Brahms, Wolf, R. Strauss, Reger, Debussy, Fauré, Hahn, Duparc, Tchaikovsky, Rachmaninoff and others, not to mention innumerable composers of opera and operetta, all so far as I know actually able to write music, an accomplishment never attained by Lennon and only relatively recently by McCartney. Whatever his merits, he is certainly the richest songwriter in his own lifetime. The *Guinness Book of Records* places him, with a fortune of $500 million, as the most commercially successful musician in history.

Handsome in itself, Mrs McCartney's gesture has a certain peculiar resonance, as of a solemn bequest made by one generation of fools to another, a benediction, a torch or *ignis fatuus* handed on, an inextinguishable Olympic flame of simple wishful silliness. She can rest in peace, knowing that a little of the spirit of her own wild and wayward decade is alive and well and living at Greenham.

The Beatles were already much in my mind at that moment. I have just finished reading the excellent book about them by Peter Brown and Steven Gaines, *The Love You Make: An Insider's Story of the Beatles*. The authors boast, and I'm sure justly, that no other book on the subject has been so frank and outspoken. They describe how Hunter Davies's book was literally pulled to bits by the Beatles, whole pages torn out to excise 'curse words', to tone down drug abuse and delete references to such unsavoury topics as homosexuality, venereal disease and illegitimate children. The Beatles now appear before us warts and all, and emerge from the scrutiny looking not much better than the Metropolitan Police.

I can't in honesty say that the book came as a stupendous revelation to me. Rather was it confirmation of what I and other infidels had always suspected or sensed behind the glittering façade. It will be a revelation only to those who saw in the Beatles and still retain a seductive vision of youthful innocence and charm, powerfully attracting not only the young but some of their deluded elders. It is astonishing and to me shameful to recall how at their overcrowded concerts, at which the audience shrieked so loudly that not a note could normally be heard, applications for tickets poured in from VIPs, senior government officials and politicians, royal bigwigs and people eminent in 'the arts'.

It is tempting to imagine that the Beatles deluded almost everyone, young and old alike; tempting but not, I think, true. They deluded some of their elders, who probably wanted to be deluded, and who showered them with honours and invitations, often received with ill grace. Yes, it is true that they smoked a reefer in Buckingham Palace when they went to collect their OBEs, and had even brought one along for Prince Charles. Lennon thought his MBE better deserved than those returned in disgust by retired soldiers, which had been won for 'killing people'.

At a Washington embassy party they insulted and humiliated our ambassador, then David Ormsby-Gore, by giving him their names all wrong ('I'm not John,' said John. 'I'm Charlie. That's

John.'), by refusing to sign autographs and behaving with a graceless pomposity common in parvenus. The Beatles book is full of like warnings that those who lick the boots or worse of the unworthy are likely to gain nothing thereby but a dirty tongue.

An exception must be made here for Sir Joseph Lockwood, boss of EMI, who must have made a bomb out of the Beatles. This 'loyal friend', seemingly good for a million or two on request, is perhaps the most drably incongruous of the Beatles' entourage. He was a former flour miller (flour power?), director of an engineering works as of practically everything else under the sun, including various respectable quangoes, the Royal Ballet School, Arts Council and the like, author of a book stirringly titled *Provender Milling – The Manufacture of Feeding Stuffs for Animals*.

He appears to have stood in relation to the Beatles much as the elder Verkhovensky stood to Dostoevsky's *Devils*, or perhaps as Lafayette to the masses. Heine describes the latter as resembling, in his dealings with the mob, 'the tutor who accompanied the pupil in his charge to brothels lest he get drunk, to pubs that he should not gamble, to gaming houses lest he should duel and who, when it came to a duel good and proper, acted as his second'.

When Lennon was 'busted' for having marijuana (a tip-off had enabled him to rid his house of all heroin), Sir Joseph was urgently beseeched to 'use his political influence and connections to help John'. There is no evidence he did so. On another occasion Princess Margaret, favoured with a like request, prudently fled. Other VIPs were not too proud to serve the Beatles. Mr Callaghan, then chancellor, took an avuncular interest in the vast funds needed to buy a Greek island, and Lord Poole offered to sort out the finances of Apple, a Beatles' firm, free of charge.

Shortly after the 'busting', Lennon and Yoko proposed a record sleeve showing them both naked, 'her breast sagging', 'John heroin-stoned' exposing his 'shrivelled uncircumcised penis'. Sir Joseph's horror was almost pitiable. 'Why not show

Paul in the nude,' he feebly joked, 'he's so much prettier.' Though he 'deeply regretted turning John down', EMI could not possibly distribute such a cover, though it was quite ready to manufacture the record (which consisted mostly of 'Yoko's peculiar screaming and John's earsplitting feedback') for them 'at its usual fee'. Here indeed we see a man sticking fearlessly to his principles! Or perhaps another example of those capitalists who, in Lenin's shrewd assessment, would be quite willing to sell to their executioner the rope with which he will hang them.

Yet I don't think the Beatles deluded the young, not all of them anyway, only the most genuinely innocent. The rummer of the young clearly discerned something rum about the Beatles, a sly and hidden decadence which was what they liked about them, the basis of an elective affinity. And if most of their elders saw it not, so much the better: they did not undeceive them. It was as if the Beatles and the young had in common a secret language, incomprehensible to others, yet full of dark meaning to them. They got the point all right, but kept it to themselves.

The perceptive music critic Fritz Spiegl charged the Beatles with doing more damage to music than any four other people in history. This they did by offering instant bliss without effort. In other words, their music lacks that reserve which characterises all really good music. Of course good music can be very attractive on a first hearing; but it always has something extra held back for later. The Beatles offered others what drugs and the Maharishi Mahesh Yogi offered them: 'instant relief and salvation', as Brown and Gaines put it, 'a mystical trance that sent you into a psychic dreamland . . . the key, the answer . . . the Next Big Thing'.

* * *

Brian Epstein, the Beatles' homosexual manager, died of an overdose of drugs. At his funeral, the officiating rabbi described him as 'a symbol of the malaise of our generation'. Brown and Gaines, hail him as one 'who had influenced the course of history'. All three are surely right. For, as the authors point out, the Beatles whom he launched and guided into space became not just entertainers but 'avatars and prophets', heroes and philosophers of a whole generation, exemplary in their meretricious triumphs, political posturings, shallow 'thinking' and sentimental feeling. 'To a whole generation' is a bit stiff, when many remained indifferent or resistant to their spell, or contemptuous of it. Yet of that generation most were touched, diverted or made restless by it, many scarred or crippled for life, some tragically destroyed, lost. To blame the Beatles alone is also far-fetched. Their numberless imitators and heirs, many worse than they, all played their part, not least Sir Michael Jagger, as *Private Eye* mordantly predicts he will be at eighty, honoured for such fancied lyrics as 'I Wanna Jerk off the Whole Bloody World' and the metaphysical 'Hullo, Mr Freakout Devil Man'. But the Beatles remain as the progenitors and type of them all.

To me they seem Pied Pipers, leaders of a second Children's Crusade, doomed, like the first, to land its followers in slavery. What they did to our children (not all, not mine, I hasten to add) was analogous in effect, if not in intent or method, to what the Greek communists in the civil war of the late forties did to Greek children. As Nicholas Gage reminds us in his harrowing *Eleni*, they abducted them.

In this forlorn fairyland what manners and *mores* prevail? First, all natural links between parents and children are severed. While parents weep or shrug, their children dance away, arrayed perhaps like John and Cynthia (Lennon's first wife), George and Pattie at London Airport, 'like wizards and fairy princesses in . . . purple and yellow satin . . . garlanded with flowers, bells round their necks which tinkled', all high on LSD. (Poor Cynthia was later that day near to stepping out of a second-floor window to 'float' down to join the stoned throng below.) Not all, to be sure, can afford Lennon's psychedelically decorated Rolls-Royce. But drugs may produce in the mind some equivalent, transforming dirty torn jeans into satins and velvets, conjuring up flying saucers, for instance, or the 'air car', powered by 'psychic fuel', in which Lennon and Yoko were supposed to arrive at a 'peace concert'.

This brave new world rather resembles the Club 18–30, in which, according to a macabre poster I saw the other day, there are 'no oldies, no babies, no has-beens, no no-nos . . . only party-party on the beach. Bop till we drop . . . if you don't belong, just f–f–fade away.' The grim message is driven home by 'oldies' caricatured as if participants in, say, *Carry On up the Costa Brava* – a fat ratbag simpering and ogling in a short flowered little-girl dress, her husband a grinning moustached runt with a green wig, FIT T-shirt and leopard-print jeans. A sort of mules' paradise is adumbrated, without parents or progeny.

In the brave new world past and future have been abolished, the present too so far as hallucination can obliterate it. Reality may be not merely suppressed but actually enhanced by drugs. Paul McCartney piously announced that LSD 'opened my eyes. It made me a better, more honest, more tolerant member of society.' Whatever disagreeable facts remain may be sung, wished, loved or dreamed away. Lennon sang of his secular paradise: 'Imagine there's no heaven . . . No hell below us . . . Nothing to kill or die for, And no religion too. Imagine all the people living life in peace . . . And the world will be as one.' When Lennon proclaimed the Beatles 'more popular than Jesus now', and His disciples 'thick and ordinary', he appears to have intended no more than a statement of facts, without pejorative undertones. Yet, if facts, they were clearly to his taste.

Lennon of course was the most explicitly political of the Beatles, though McCartney adjured us in song to 'Give Ireland Back to the Irish' without pausing to ask which Irish, or whether it was ours to give. Other Beatle political views can be readily inferred. But Lennon had, or affected to have, a complete range of progressive sentiments. His MBE disgusted him, as did the 'royals' and class structure which it symbolised; he 'came out' against war in Vietnam and Biafra, returned his MBE partly for these reasons, partly (and characteristically) because his song 'Cold Turkey', about kicking drug addiction without help, was 'slipping in the charts'. In between 'walloping' Yoko, as Cynthia before her, he waged his 'peace' campaign, conferred with the egregious Trudeau ('a beautiful meeting'), hooked up with Michael X, later with Jerry Rubin and Abbie Hoffman, wrote 'Power to the People', 'a proletarian anthem which begins with a chorus [*sic*] of marching feet', as a way of 'struggling with being rich', always so embarrassing for left-wingers. All this was according to Brown and Gaines 'also a phony pose'. Nor can the cause of world peace have been much advanced by a Coryphaeus apparently too drugged for months even to record a simple promised message on the subject, and finally delivering only a tape of a baby dying.

In the brave new world, there is neither God nor copybook headings. Reason sleeps, monsters are brought forth. Cause and effect are sundered; so are sowing and reaping, self-indulgence and tears, toiling and eating. The old world of work and business, of 'men in suits', is derided by those still totally parasitic on it. We find ourselves in a Bohemia without talent or skill, in which the crazed life of a Utrillo might be held forth as a norm for emulation: no need for the magical pictures. If art be required, films of naked bottoms, or 'concerts' at which microphones are 'hidden in the toilets so the patrons could be heard urinating and flushing on stage', will do well enough.

From this world certain boring virtues are completely missing. All the military and marital virtues, all fidelity, restraint, thrift, sobriety, taste and discipline, all the virtues associated with work, with the painful acquisition of knowledge, skill and qualifications. All these give place to a decadent self-expression, in which nothing is expressed because nothing has been cultivated to be expressed. One must do one's 'thing'; yet no 'thing' can be done without the drudgery of learning, practice and thought, without other *ardua* unknown to Cythera.

We are all too well aware of objective economic factors which cause and gratuitously increase unemployment among the young, with attendant demoralisation and hopelessness. Yet it would be fatuous to ignore what some of the young, abetted by the negligence, weakness, silliness or despair of their parents, have done to render themselves unemployable. The *Daily Express* recently devoted a horrendous page to pictures and interviews with unemployed punks. One had his head part shaved, part bristling with long spikes, hardened with superglue and deemed by a former employer a safety hazard. 'Freedom' was for him 'more vital than a job'. 'I don't want a job, no matter the money, unless I can be employed as I am, for what I am.' Others were equally intransigent. The Beatles did not teach these children to look as they do. What they did teach, however, is that what you look like is more important than what you do. To be conceited about anything is bad; to be conceited about nothing compounds vanity with idiocy. How far are the Beatles' teachings and example responsible for the ruin of their native city?

Meanwhile, may I wish to all babies, and to all my fellow has-beens, oldies and no-nos, a very happy Christmas! And to all young people in internal exile a safe return from their 'bad trip'! And to all parents thus bereaved, a swift reunion!

The Spectator, 17 December 1983

Money Matters and False Notes

I watched *The Money Programme* on television the other night. Appearing on it were Lord Armstrong, Sir Arnold Weinstock, and some articulate *dirigiste* planner whose name escapes me.

They were discussing, in the sombre, quasi-technical language appropriate to their theme and with a proper gravity of manner, our present economic plight and future prospects.

None of them was wearing skin-tight *ciré* jeans or cat-suit, still less 'drag'. Alice Cooper might never have existed for all the make-up they wore. None of them displayed any of the mannerisms of the pop-fan – the nervously snapping fingers, the twitching features, that unending yeah-yeah-yeah noise. None of them at any point showed the slightest sign of suddenly seizing the mike or compulsively croaking into it, with those obligatory pelvic gyrations, the latest top of the pops – Abba's recording, so they tell me, of 'Mama Mia'. Their decorum was unruffled and irreproachable as finally, under the direction of the chairman, they summed up with mournful courtesy their views.

They concluded, and suddenly all hell broke loose – mindless blasts of uproar, some sort of pop group playing like fury what is apparently the signature tune of *The Money Programme*. Thanks to my colleague, Sean Day-Lewis, I can tell you what that is too – a rearrangement, commissioned by the BBC from Barry Forgie, of the Jimmy Smith version of the Elmer Bernstein theme for the film *The Carpet Baggers*, of which the Jimmy Smith version is available on a commercial record, VLP7079. Perhaps there are people who might prefer such a record to one of Lord Armstrong and his associates ruminating about the economy. *De gustibus* . . .

What bothers me is why music of this demotic sort is thought suitable to begin and end *The Money Programme* (as most other television programmes, the gravest as well as the gayest).

Is it presumed, perhaps, that this is the sort of music which the venerable participants would, were they asked, choose to hear? I cannot see Lord Armstrong, at the end of a strenuous day of decision-making at the Midland Bank, or formerly at the Treasury, repairing to the nearest jazzed-up pub, ordering a lager-and-lime and putting 5p in the juke box to hear, content at last, 'Love Machine' or 'Love to Love You, Baby'. If such are in fact his recreations, they are a sad decline from what his parents would have thought suitable: for one or both, unless memory errs, played in a Salvation Army band.

About Sir Arnold's tastes we do not have to speculate. He was heard recently in *Man of Action* (indeed, heard not once, but twice) and revealed himself on both occasions a staunch and cultured Mozart man – no Moog for him.

The third participant was the sort of quiet bespectacled chap with a tie and jacket, perfectly OK in a bank, who would stick out like a sore thumb at Watchfield or in Windsor Park.

The fact that such inane music accompanies perfectly serious programmes (even dear St Malcolm Muggeridge is thus mocked on most of his earthly manifestations) may be simply due to a long standing but perfectly innocent British inability to find the proper music for any occasion whatever.

Sir Frederick Ponsonby long ago lamented that, at King Edward VII's court, great ladies were presented to the strains of 'His Nose Was Redder Than It Was' and that the bands, under Captain Rogan, played comic songs while distinguished men were knighted and a ridiculous two-step while the inspiring deed which had won some hero the Albert Medal was being solemnly recounted. More recently I myself witnessed the Palace Guard, on the morning of devaluation or some other Wilsonian débâcle, marching away not wholly inappropriately to the absurd and lugubrious dirge, 'You'd Be Far Better Off in a Home'.

On the box I suspect a less innocent explanation. Might not the music chosen express the television producers' semi-conscious desire to reduce everything to the same vulgar level, to a 'turn', an act, a show – 'Lord Armstrong's Half-Hour'? In an equal world, there can be no unpunished distinction, no unassailable eminence: the uneminent, the undistinguished must always have the last word, have their revenge. Every reputation, deserved or no, must be punctured or diminished.

When the famous American banker J. P. Morgan testified to a Senate Committee in the thirties on the causes of the great depression, a smiling female midget was suddenly to his consternation placed on his lap, resulting in a photograph still remembered. The motive of the press agent who put her there was none the less one which Mr Morgan must have found perfectly intelligible; it was frankly and innocently commercial, to publicise Ringling's Circus.

Different and darker may be the motives of those who subtly make Lord Armstrong look a bit of an ass, who might in other days have sandwiched Churchill's wartime speeches, or Montagu Norman's evidence to the Macmillian Committee on the economy, between records of 'Run Rabbit Run' or 'All By Yourself in the Moonlight'. And what on earth would they have found for the Gettysburg Address?

What next? Will pontificating bankers and bureaucrats be forced to wear those novelty sets of combined nose, spectacles and moustache? Will jets of water suddenly stream from the tops of their heads, or ribald motor horns honk as they solemnly discuss the money supply? Can the laws affecting pornography be debated in future by reverend bishops and moralists without the lewd intervention and caresses of streakers and strippers and Miss Whipps, with appropriate displays of breasts, copulation and pudenda?

So far I have been shockingly unconstructive. What is the right music for *The Money Programme*? Well, there is always the *Ring* which is largely about money, a commodity of which Wagner appeared to think less highly than the rest of us do (though the *Ring* incidentally was originally intended to have a happy ending, in which case its moral would presumably have been the opposite – that the quest for gold ennobles, that Adam Smith was perfectly right, that Marx and George Bernard Shaw could jump in a lake and that the music would consequently be just right for *The Money Programme*). And there is Schoenberg's *Moses and Aaron* which depicts the worship of a golden calf. Ho hum.

Less controversially what about Richard Strauss's *Die Liebe de Danae* which ends with a gigantic shower, a veritable deluge of gold? What could possibly be more refreshing in these hard times?

Daily Telegraph, 9 February 1976

An Undignified Incident

Two pet hates of mine are people who keep their names out of the telephone directory and people who have black glass in their car windows, so that they can see but not be seen. I mean, of course, only people who do these things without good reason, out of vanity or affectation; not because they really are persecuted but because they think themselves (or would like others to think them) important enough to be persecuted; not because they are pop stars, but because they have sunk so low as to wish to be thought pop stars.

Outside some horrible new flats near our house a huge glossy car was drawn up the other morning, its windows impenetrably black. A certain inscrutable and expressionless menace emanated from it, as though it were some object identified by Dr Who as coming from another age or planet. On my way to the station, and thinking myself unobserved, I executed a discreetly ridiculous dance of hatred. As I drew nearer the mysterious vehicle, I heard issuing from the interior the sound of broadcast pop music, subtly polluting the ambient air. Somebody must have left the radio on. My dance grew wilder my features ludicrously distorted, tongue protruding grotesquely.

Suddenly I became hideously aware that I was not unobserved at all: dimly through the smoked glass I could discern a female human form in the passenger seat, her face not a foot from my own, gazing out presumably in terror and astonishment on the incomprehensible spectacle presented to it.

How difficult to walk away from such a scene with any semblance of dignity!

Daily Telegraph, 31 May 1976

Men and Music amid Barbarism

When Dmitri Shostakovich stared with grim impassivity from the television set I often wondered, as did our music critic Robert Henderson, what on earth was going on behind those thick spectacles. Whenever I heard his music, so bitter, tortured and sad, I wondered always whether this could really be the work of a man who, according to his official biography, was 'a faithful son of the Communist party', constantly reaffirming 'the ideals of socialist humanism', and who, according to *The Times* obituary, was 'a committed believer in Communism and Soviet power' and other such heresies.

Well, if his memoirs are authentic, as they seem to me, we can now see the soul behind the spectacles. And it is, to be sure, not the stone soul of the public appearances and idiotic tributes, but the soul which the music had portrayed for all with ears to hear. No faithful son of the Communist party this, no committed believer in Soviet power, but a man absolutely consumed with anger and sorrow at the ghastly destiny of his country, by the corruption and prostitution of her music to the vilest ends, by the cruel expulsion or murder not only of friends but of millions unknown but never forgotten by him.

With the *Yurodivy* (untranslatable: prophetic idiot?) in *Boris*, he cries: 'Sorrow, sorrow for Russia, weep, oh weep, Russian people.' And where is comfort to be found? Not in socialist humanism or any such rubbish, alas, nor yet for him in God. To live in Soviet Russia *without* religion, that must have been hell.

The 7th symphony is not, as was asserted, inspired by the heroic siege of Leningrad. No, it is a requiem for Shostakovich's pre-war Leningrad, the city of his birth that Stalin destroyed and Hitler only finished off, for its butchered citizens and for those who mourned. The 8th quartet has nothing to do with 'exposing Fascism', as was stated. No, it is as it sounds, a desperately mournful personal document, quoting not only from earlier works but also from the tragic Russian song 'Worn out by the hardships of prison'.

'All my symphonies,' says Shostakovich, 'are about the terrible pre-war years . . . the majority . . . are tombstones.'

Yes, we were right. As they seemed, so they were and were meant to be not triumphal arches but tombstones; they did not lie, though lies were told about them. It is astonishing, and in this case appallingly sad, how directly music *can* (it need not) tell us about its creator. As Robert Henderson told us in his memorable review, the memoirs only confirm what the music has already said.

The result is a grim and not wholly edifying self-portrait. Yet even in these terrible pages the sun also shines, and this especially when Shostakovich recalls at great length his old, loved and respected teacher A. K. Glazunov.

I remember once reading with wrath a sleeve note on one of Glazunov's recorded symphonies. It recalled an asinine Chicago critic in the late twenties who, after hearing a concert of Glazunov's music conducted by the aged composer, impudently asked in effect (I quote from memory) what use Chicago had for this fat, reactionary, out-of-date old penguin waving his flippers about, conducting worthless music with no message for today and which even Mendelssohn would have found old hat.

My hat, I thought – if only I were a poet and could write in suitably memorable terms Glazunov's 'reply to unjustified criticism'!

Whenever I hear his sumptuous ballet music *Raymonda* (admired by Shostakovich), I see, among many visions, this: old St Petersburg at Christmas time; cosy in her velvet stall at the Maryinsky, a little girl in the fashions of 1900, as if painted by Renoir, at her first ballet; her hands in her muff, her cheeks flushed, her lips parted in wonder, her eyes sparkling with awed delight as the resplendent score unfolds; as the breathtaking procession of melodies, themes and effortless variations passes by, now noble and gracious, now ardent and impassioned, now charged with romantic splendour or mystery, now magically radiant, now fizzing and tingling and sparkling with irrepressible life and joy; all brightly clothed in that orchestral raiment at once gorgeous and delicate which was born and died with St Petersburg, all displaying that true virtuosity which expresses feeling rather than masks its absence.

I think of that little girl and I wonder what composer with a message for Chicago could have conferred upon her such happiness, such memories. So might my poem have gone.

But now, better, at last the dear old boy, so often pooh-poohed and faint-praised ('a salon composer,' 'drily academic') gets his due – and from Shostakovich of all people! Why, he even likes some of his music, though not so much as I do.

The absurd and unsaintly aspects of Glazunov are not ignored. His piano playing (very good) but with cigar clamped between third and fourth fingers (try it!); his hippo-like appearance (alas, after the Revolution, haggard and drawn, his old clothes sagging as from a coat hanger); his venereal disease picked up from a ballet dancer, his consequent bachelordom and dependence (most unseemly in the director of a great institution) on a fussy mama; his sad alcoholism, his unsteady sinking behind the desk, while teaching quartet classes, to suck vodka up a tube, his incomprehensible muttered comments – yes, but despite all he emerges as a heroic figure, kind and wise, generous, honourable.

Never can the St Petersburg Conservatoire, of which he was director from 1906 till the twenties, or music itself have known a more loyal servant or champion!

His salary he gave to poor students. He attended every exam, listened to every student's works and read scores by the thousand. His own taste and principles were of the highest, but never so as to prevent him tirelessly helping duds and unfortunates. He quietly finished other composers' works for them (notably Borodin's). He listened to every sad tale, took trouble, wrote endless recommendations, pestered officials, dried tears, saved lives. Asked before the Revolution how many Jewish students were at the Conservatoire, he replied with dignity, 'We don't keep count.'

After the Revolution, comfort for himself, though starving, he rejected; for his beloved Conservatoire he boldly demanded instead, and got, firewood. His musical memory, his ear and erudition were all prodigious. He knew thoroughly and loved Josquin, Orlando, Palestrina and Gabrieli before they were fashionable. He found merits in 'cacophonous' composers he didn't care for, listened again and again to new works till he understood them. He could play nearly every instrument.

And when at last, old and worn out, hurt and ill, he left Russia 'for a rest', never to come back, it was only after his courageous defence of Rimsky-Korsakov's memory had exposed him to the venomous insults and menaces ('shark of imperialism', 'last imperialist toady') of the ideological hacks who had already attacked his dead friend.

On second thoughts, I think that both the music and life of this man do have messages for Chicago, as for all of us, at Christmas and at all times, but especially in harsh times, such as we here too may know.

They are perhaps: hold fast to what is good and true; guard what is beautiful; help the unfortunate; stoop not to malice, back-biting and denunciation; defend precious standards and traditions and institutions; honour the masters; master your craft; respect the past; be loyal to your art and to fellow artists; guide and cherish the young; pass on the sacred torch; this above all, remember.

Remember – in his loving portrait of Glazunov, Shostakovich recalls with piercing anguish a vanished Russia in which these noble values could and sometimes did prevail, a world which, alas, poor man, he hardly knew save as embodied in his old teacher. Another requiem, not the least beautiful, another tombstone . . . May God rest them both, and bring you a very happy Christmas.

Daily Telegraph, 17 December 1979

WAY OF THE WORLD

❦

Soporific

Various theories have been advanced as to why people in Moscow sleep soundly. According to Mr Khrushchev it is because there are no American bombers overhead. According to Western ambassadors, it is because everyone knows that the Soviet Union will never be attacked.

For what it is worth, my own theory is that everyone in Moscow as in any other parts of Mother Russia, is more or less permanently plastered and thus in no condition to know what is overhead or who is being attacked.

In support of this theory I can advance the facts that the Russians, according to their great novelists, always were more or less plastered; that they certainly have no less reason to be plastered now than under the Tsars; and that Mr Khrushchev, himself no militant teetotaller, has just denounced 'the cult of heavy drinking'.

In the illicit manufacture of alcohol, the Russian peasant has usually displayed an unexpected energy and resource. A former Tsarist officer once told me how in the First World War, vodka being unobtainable, each peasant became his own still or brewery.

First he would swallow quarts of sweetened fruit juice, issued by the State to prevent scurvy; this was followed by a few pounds of yeast. The reveller would then lie flat on the hot stove and, in unconvivial silence, punctuated only by the rumbles of fermentation, pass slowly into oblivion.

Sir Maurice Pangloss

'All is for the best in the best of possible Oxfords.' This is more or less the theme of an urbane article by Sir Maurice Bowra about modern undergraduates.

The Oxford scene of today, Sir Maurice concedes, may be 'unfamiliar or even distasteful' to those who knew it before 1939, still more to those who knew it before 1914. These fogies, however, are briskly brushed aside. Each successive generation, according to Sir Maurice, regards its own as the Golden Age; the present generation is no exception, 'and who shall say that it is wrong?'

Tap this argument, and what a hollow ring emerges!

Of course memory may play us false, painting the past in rosier colours than it deserves. Is this any reason to ignore it? If we wish to compare past and present, what else but memory can support us?

In days to come, we may imagine Sir Maurice, seated amidst a desert of radioactive ruins, blandly informing his fellow survivors that they deceive themselves in imagining that times were ever better.

Personally, I doubt if all those now at Oxford believe that theirs is the Golden Age. And if they do, I for one will say they are wrong.

Sir Maurice does not deplore the expulsion of 'the incorrigible idler no matter how agreeable or picturesque'. I do. He does not lament the heedless conviviality of years gone by. I do.

These things gave Oxford and Cambridge an irreplaceable charm and style. They were a continual and necessary reminder that learning and application are not everything in life. Without them, the universities are a stew without salt: nourishing but tasteless.

I regret them, and not for themselves alone. For, if idleness is at a discount, so is independence of mind. I do not deny there is more learnt at Oxford and Cambridge now. But I am sure there is less learnt for its own sake.

For an undergraduate without resources of his own, learning must be geared to results: his tutor's approval, a good degree, a fellowship or a good job to follow. He cannot pursue his own bent: he must produce what happens to be academically acceptable at the moment or get out.

And if this is not deeply regrettable, I hardly know what could be.

Diddling the Meter

By by-passing his electricity meter a Chatham voter managed for ten years to obtain electricity for a cooker, two fires, a radiator, two tubular heaters, eight lights, a drill and a television set. This is a splendid performance but not superior to that of a Dublin sculptor once known to me.

This improverished genius used to lodge free in the bare attic of a friend's house. His clothes, composed largely of bits of matting and old newspapers tied together with string, were informal but striking.

On buses he would always ask the conductor for a ticket to wherever the bus had just come from. Told that he was going the wrong way, he would sadly dismount, catch the next one on and repeat the performance.

By making passes at the electricity meter with a complex arrangement of magnets, he learnt how to reduce the reading to an economical level.

This accomplishment led to his downfall. One day he absent-mindedly reduced it too far for plausibility, and found himself unable to increase it by magnetic means.

He immediately telephoned all his friends (this he was able to do free by pressing buttons A and B simultaneously), urging them to bring round all the electrical equipment they could lay their hands upon. Soon the attic was like a fantastic showroom.

Two-way and three-way plugs sprouted from every socket and from each other. Wirelesses and gramophones blared day and night, hair-dryers and Hoovers howled, refrigerators froze, cookers cooked and stoves glowed: a myriad brilliant lights blazed all around. All the fuses blew and were replaced by hairpins and wires of elephantine thickness. The meter ticked on madly but in vain.

Prison, he told me later, was a rest-cure.

Trollopevsky

One of Trollope's most joyous inspirations was the introduction to Barchester of the indolent Canon Stanhope and his exotic family. The presence of the impressively robed and bearded Metropolitan Pitirim of Minsk at the Lambeth Conference is a comparable stroke of genius.

This happy mingling of the worlds of Trollope and Dostoevsky makes one regret the more that the former never completed a sequel to *Barchester Towers*, the rough draft for which is in my possession.

In this lost masterpiece, the saintly Alexei Karamazov is appointed to succeed Mr Slope as Bishop Proudie's chaplain. His arrival, accompanied by his remarkable family, causes a stir in the quiet cathedral city.

One of his brothers, the violent and reckless Dmitri, becomes engaged to Miss Dunstable and borrows £5,000 from her to throw a wild Saturday night bacchanale for the Signora Vesey-Neroni in the Bishop's stables. Mrs Proudie, entering to complain about the noise, is immediately the subject of an indecent assault by Karamazov *père*.

A tremendous scene follows in which Mrs Proudie accuses old Karamazov of being intoxicated on the Sabbath. In the ensuing *mélée*, Mrs Proudie is stabbed to death by Ivan, a crime for which, by a twist of savage irony, Mr Harding is later tried and executed.

Trollope was finally persuaded that this theme, however powerful and dramatic, was one unsuited to his talents. As Bagehot pointed out in a letter, 'this sort of thing is really best left to people like Mrs Gaskell'.

HOME AND ABROAD

❦

Chaos and Laughter in Nkrumah's Gold Coast

On what would have been Klemperer's one hundreth birthday, BBC2 re-broadcast a film of him, already seventy-eight, conducting Beethoven's choral symphony. For the most part Klemperer sat impassively beating time, bringing in new sections of the orchestra as unemphatically as one might pick a jar of jam off a shelf. The results throughout were stupendous. At times his gaze would rise far above the orchestra, as if he were seeing visions, exploring for the first time a virgin land of unimaginable splendours and beauty.

I found it all terribly moving, though well aware of the perils of building fantasies on facial expressions. Pater and others have concocted pages of purple prose out of what the Mona Lisa was thinking about. Veal for supper, D. B. Wyndham Lewis irreverently suggested, or fish?

I was once badly misled by the face of Geoffrey Bing – you remember, 'left-wing' MP from Hornchurch, later Nkrumah's 'attorney-general', a sort of dilute Vishinsky, half Ulster by origin, half, I think, Vietnamese, in which case his name were perhaps better spelt Binh than Bing, with its sturdy English associations – Douglas ('put a rose in your hair, Mavis – there's a cabload of sailors at the door') and the Admiral shot *pour encourager les autres* (though he was Byng). 'You mean,' said Kingsley Amis, 'that he might just as well have been called, say, Bong?' Just so.

I was in the Gold Coast, as I still prefer to call it, for the *Daily Telegraph*, one of a series of correspondents each greeted with fiery denunciations of his predecessor, each to be denounced in his turn. My predecessor, Ian Colvin, had characterised the Asantahene's 'palace' at Kumasi as built of mud and corrugated iron, an observation which, true or not, gave no pleasure. I was denounced for having confirmed that a senior expatriate police officer had gone to Switzerland to investigate ministers' bank accounts.

I stayed at the rambling ramshackle one-storey Seaview Hotel in Accra. Ghana's hotels were not then of the faceless inter-continental variety, but of rich individuality. At the Kingsway in Kumasi I had a room with shower. This last consisted of a cold tap on the fungus-stained wall, from which a rusty pipe ran up to and across the ceiling. I turned the tap. Distant gurgling, knocking and coughing sounds ensued, then silence. A large weird insect emerged from the pipe and peered irritably around, plainly annoyed at being disturbed. Of water no sign, and the insect huffily withdrew.

A welcome fellow-guest at the Seaview was Kingsley Martin, editor of the *New Statesman*, as ever friendly, bright, bird-like, 'progressive' and optimistic. Our rooms all opened, through half-doors like those of stables or school lavatories, on to a rough courtyard filled with rusting tricycles, debris of a failed ice-cream venture. Kingsley's bed was positioned diagonally in the middle of the room, like a battleship in the paper game Jutland. Against my advice, he moved it tidily into a corner. That night there was a terrific storm, with rain bouncing six feet and fireballs hurtling like flaming onions in all directions. Kingsley was drenched; before it was moved, his bed had been in the one dry area. Moral for radicals: respect what seems irrational; it may serve some deep but hidden purpose.

The next night Kingsley had Geoffrey Bing to dinner, and kindly invited me. The meal itself was memorable. The menu announced 'Fish No. 1' and 'Fish No. 3'. These were monsters with eyes on stalks and vestigial legs, dredged up by the Colonial Development Corporation from depths hitherto unplumbed, for which no name had been found. They ate like lumps of coarse kapok, full of needles, on which a fish had expired and decayed, leaving behind a ghostly taste and noisome fragrance. Kingsley asked for the wine list. 'We have two waines, sah,' the waiter beamed: 'whaite and black.'

Even more unexpected were the affability and humour of Mr Bing. He talked mostly absolute nonsense about the African consciousness, Western exploitation and oppression, negritude, Ghana bled white by the British (actually it had been bled by the Cocoa Marketing Board, which Nkrumah, also partial to a drop of blood, gratefully retained) and the 'hopeful experiment in democracy' which was taking place there. Mr Bing had a guttural German 'r', so that 'democracy' turned out something like 'demochrrracy'. Each tirade concluded with a broad grin, as if in self-mockery.

Not a bad chap after all, I thought: at least he can laugh at himself. I grinned too. Ever wilder grew Mr Bing's self-parodies, ever broader the grins. I laughed out loud. Kingsley laid a warning hand on my knee. Bing exploded. It dawned on me that they weren't grins at all, but a fearful involuntary rictus, containing no trace of mirth. A fragile solemnity was with difficulty restored.

My first call in Accra had been on our Liberian stringer, proprietor and editor of the local paper, so lavishly inked that, after reading it, one's fingers and bedclothes were black. As in Peter Simple's *Nerdley Clarion*, the same block could readily have served to depict a smart wedding, a road smash or a massacre. The office, in a maze of open-drained side streets, was held aloft on seven-foot pillars, approachable only by a ladder which could be withdrawn against creditors, government narks and those who fancied themselves wronged. Against one of the pillars reposed a blind man – the ace parliamentary reporter, I was told, who, with that total recall which God sometimes confers on the blind and illiterate, could reproduce *verbatim* hours of rhetoric: 'And Mr Gbedemah, he say . . . ' The editor was at first reserved, thinking I had come to sack him. As it became clear I had no such intent or power he cheered up and produced beer. He confided that he had had a real scoop for the *Telegraph* the other day, but, alas the damn goat had abstracted the copy from the out-tray below and eaten it. Primitive and eccentric as his printing plant was, it must have been powered by electricity. Rumour had it that he had once run the whole lot off a lead plugged into the nearest street-lamp.

Kingsley Martin had to fly to Lagos. I went to see him off. West African airways pilots were then mostly 'Wasps'. Towards the cockpit of Kingsley's aircraft, however, strode a gigantic Paul Robeson-like figure, covered in gold braid. Kingsley blenched and fell silent. A test of egalitarian nerve was at hand. 'Hang it,' he cried, 'I've left my tickets at the Seaview. I'll have to take a later flight.' As he turned, his jacket swung open, revealing a BOAC wallet. 'They're in your pocket.' 'Thank God,' he sighed, without conviction. Remembering the three or four horrendous pile-ups we'd passed on our way to the airport, I could have bitten my tongue off.

The Spectator, 29 June 1985

Australia's Charm, Refinement and HP Sauce

'I have greatly enjoyed my first visit to Australia,' the earnest man from *The Times* declared. 'I hope it will not be my last. Meanwhile, I would like to take back some souvenir or memento, something wholly characteristic of, ahem, "down under", which will recall to me and suggest to my wife, unable alas to be with us here, Australia's unique and gracious charm. Now what, Mr Watson, would you suggest?'

More than thirty years ago, it was my first intercontinental freebie. BP had very kindly invited a party of hacks from London to witness the opening of its new refinery at Kwinana, Westralia. At Sydney we were reinforced by antipodean hacks, including Mr Kingston ('King' to his friends, of course) Watson, then editor of the Sydney *Daily Telegraph*. King's humorous face was as wrinkled as a walnut, a bit like a sun-baked Sid James. Long and carefully he pondered *The Times* man's request. At last he spoke: 'What about a bottle of HP sauce?'

His wise counsel came back to me when I read a recent headline, 'Reagan lifts US ban on HP sauce'. A kindly president had noted that the ban had brought 'unanticipated consequences' and 'severe hardships' to 'users' of the sauce, not only Britons but presumably Australians too, whose national symbol King had pronounced it to be. Good on yer, Ron! King's pronouncement was indeed a symbol perhaps of Australia's coming of age, marked by an ability to laugh at herself, as also by a heartening eagerness to absorb and learn from hitherto shunned swarthy Mediterranean immoes: already then pavement cafés proliferated at King's Cross.

Our party was in the charge of a delightfully avuncular BP boffin, his converse liberally spiked with self-parody, lemon juice and Tabasco. Even at Heathrow he had introduced me to a

THE STORY SO FAR:
BARRY HAS BEEN SEASICK SEVERAL TIMES OVER SEVERAL PEOPLE. HIS LAST TECHNICOLOUR YAWN HAS OBLIGED HIM HURRIEDLY TO QUIT THE FERRY AT CALAIS WITH HIS FRENCH SPEAKING COMPATRIOT COLIN LUCAS
NOW READ ON...
VITE VITE MON BAZZIE, THOSE PAUVRE OLD POMMIES WILL JUST HAVE TO STEW IN YOUR OWN JUICE. WE'LL BE IN PAREE IN NON TEMPS, AFTER WE'VE BEEN THROUGH THE FRENCH CUSTOMS!
FRENCH CUSTOMS? CRIPES, I DUNNO WHETHER I COULD FACE A FANCY ROOT RIGHT NOW. SOME SHEILAHS DON'T LIKE KISSING BLOKES WITH CHUCK ON THEIR BREATH!
SOON OUR FRIENDS ARE ON THE TRAIN TO PAREE
COUGH! COUGH! STONE THE CROWS COL! WHAT'S THAT FROG SMOKIN' DRIED UP SHEEP'S DAGS OR SOMETHIN'? I RECKONED LONDON STANK OF B.O. AND SNEAKY ONES, BUT THIS DUMP'S ON THE NOSE AS WELL!!!
LE RIRE
AUSTRALIA DOESN'T SMELL OF ANYTHING.
DON'T COME THE RAW CREVETTE MON LE SPORT. ICI IS EUROPE. NOW IT'S AN ILL VENT THAT DOESN'T BLOW ANY BUGGER ANY BON!
JEEZ YOU'RE AMAZING FROGGERS! I DONE A BIT OF FRENCH BACK IN THE OLD MOONEE PONDS STATE SCHOOL DAYS AND I DIDN'T THINK IT FLAMIN' WELL SUNK IN, BUT I CAN JUST ABOUT UNDERSTAND EVERY WORD YOUSE BLOODY WELL SAYS... AS FOR THE FROGS THEMSELVES, THEY MIGHT AS WELL BE YAPPING IN DOUBLE FLAMIN' DUTCH. I RECKON THEY'D BE SMART TO IMPART A FEW DINKI-DI AUSTRALIAN FRENCH TEACHERS!
C'EST LA VIE. COMME CI COMME ÇA. TOO RIGHT.
REGARDEZ PAREE MON BAZZIE! ISN'T IT FLAMBE BELLE. LET'S SKIDADDLE OFF TO THE NEAREST BISTRO AND GET STUCK INTO A BIT OF CHAUD TUCKER. I'M THAT FAIM I COULD EAT OUT OF A CHINESE GENDARME'S JOCKSTRAP!
CRIPES, NOW YOUSE MENTION IT COL, I'M PRETTY PECKISH MESELF. ALL THEM LIQUID LAUGHS I HAD ON THE BOAT HAVE LEFT ME FEELIN' WEAK AS PISS!
THE PALS ADJOURN TO A FRIENDLY BISTRO...
GIMMEE A NICE JUICY STEAK PLEACE GARÇON
VARIOUS CRUDITIES???
ME TOO!
AND 'OW WOULD YOUR FRAIND LIKE HEEZ STEAK MONSIEUR?
JUST KNOCK OFF ITS HORNS, WIPE ITS ARSE, AND BUNG IT ON THE PLATE SPORT!
BARRY HAS ORDERED A VERY NICE MEAL. WILL THE CHEF FOLLOW HIS INSTRUCTIONS? SEE NEXT LAUTREC-LIKE EPISODE.

fantastic refinement of U and non-U behaviour. A gorgeous Qantas hostess came with a box of cigarettes. She innocently enquired, 'Do you smaoke?' 'Damn cheek, these interrogations,' he burbled as she wiggled off up the aisle. 'What's it matter to her whether we smoke or not? Why doesn't she just offer us a cigarette and have done with it?' True courtesy would have left us free to smoke it, chew it or install it over the ear.

The boffin had been in Abadan during the crisis. Of Dr Mossadeq he took a more jaundiced view than that propounded by Brian Lapping in the *End of Empire* television series. So far from thinking him 'well-connected, incorruptible and dedicated to the principles of liberal democracy', he compared the doctor unfavourably with hatters, fruitcakes, coots and other symbols of insanity. 'Trouble is, we never bribed them properly. They expect it, you know. The Yanks told us to butter them up, but we were too grand and stuffy. Don't ask them if they drink or smoke – causes offence. Just slip 'em Havanas and the Widow – that's the drill.'

Mr Dick Stokes had flown to Teheran to impress upon Dr Mossadeq the dire consequences of seizing the Abadan refinery. Frustrated, Mr Stokes reported back to the Cabinet: Dr Mossadeq's only response to every threat had been, '*N'importe, n'importe!*' 'Namport, namport,' Mr Attlee broke in: 'a Persian term, I take it?' 'I ask you!' the boffin wailed. 'Rotten school, Haileybury. Hope you weren't there?'

Memories crowd back. At a Perth barbecue I was introduced to a tall, voluptuous girl: 'Shirl, meet Collen, Collen, meet Shirl, and this is Kevven.' Shirl's opening gambit was unexpected, though highly topical in view of her attire. 'When I sit on a wickerwork chair in short shorts, Collen, I get a criss-cross pattern on my bum. Look!' I left her with Kevven and sought advice. Provocative her remark certainly was. Was it meant to be? Was it a 'come-on'? Or was it the fruit of innocent naïvety? 'Certainly the last,' my host judged, 'make no mistake. Just take the conversation straight on from there.' 'Another sort of damn cheek,' the boffin mused. I returned, disappointed.

We were driven in a Holden limousine to a nature park. The

driver stopped abruptly and pointed: 'A kookaburra!' There it sat in solemn silence on a nearby branch about six feet off the ground. *The Times* and *The Economist* conscientiously tiptoed across and stopped beneath it, ears cocked attentively, as if expecting delicate flute-like tweets, trills and melodies and eager not to miss a limpid note. King, familiar with the bird's utterances, stayed in the car, surveying the music lovers with a saurian eye. 'Look at those two drongoes. If that bastard issues a statement, it's like an engine whistle. You can hear it five miles off.' Taciturn as Coolidge, the bird had no message for the nation.

Two wild New Zealanders left Perth early. We took a bottle of Corio dry gin to the airport to soothe the pain of parting. Farewells were effusive and boisterous, with much back-slapping and embracing, culminating in the wilder of the two snatching the gin with a triumphant guffaw and charging off zigzag across the tarmac like an All Black wing three-quarter. We only gave up the chase when, appalled, we saw the thief's head pass unscathed between the revolving blades of the propeller.

Fate brought us all together in Sydney – the New Zealanders, a luxuriant Australian who'd served in the Brigade, or so he said ('No, not the fire brigade, Collen, the f—ing Grenadiers'), a couple of nurses. Drinking hours in Sydney were then restricted, so we adjourned to my bedroom for room service. At about three in the morning Peter Kirk, not yet an MP, insisted on ringing up his (I think) godfather, E. W. Swanton, in Brisbane. 'He'll never forgive me if I don't.' 'He'll never forgive you if you do' – but the genial old boy did. He took it well.

Waking hesitantly and with forebodings the next morning, I found myself lying stark naked on the bed-cover. A 'don't disturb' card had been thoughtfully hung on a – well – convenient projection. I looked around with mounting horror. Debris of last night's knees-up: only to be expected. Less reassuring a cup of cold tea, white-filmed, beside the bed, and a huge breakfast congealing on a tray; a suit back from the cleaners hung on the door hook; on the stool a parcel of clean shirts; on the floor, the day's *Sydney Morning Herald*. My shame must have been witnessed by half the staff (and who knew who else besides? The *nurses*? Well, at least they must have seen it all before) of a hotel so respectable that it couldn't tolerate shirt-sleeves at 100 in the shade!

Yes, yes, but what about the refinery? Ah, the refinery . . . Did I ever get to it? I dutifully wrote an article for the *Daily Telegraph*, but lavish press kits may have sufficed for that. Memory is a perverse sieve, retaining curious trifles, allowing to escape what is 'important' and 'serious'. Enthusiastic Israeli government press officers showed me on a later trip a potash works. What do I recall of that save that it was at Sodom?

The Spectator, 15 June 1985

The Weirdo Wizard of Oz

In August 1971 a judge and jury found a special school kids' issue of the hippie magazine *Oz* obscene – a finding later found unsafe. (Is 2 + 2 = 4 safe now in any court?) The trial had been turned by the accused into a 'media event' with 'stoned' defendants in gymslips in the dock and street theatre raving outside, 'a wailing wall of weirdies'.

Reaching the old *Daily Telegraph*, the tidings set me off in the leader column on a long, predictable and ineffectual blast against *Oz* and its transvaluation of all values. If memory serves, I lambasted particularly its rabid sentimentality, its infantile clamour for quite incompatible things, for cause without effects, for sex without sorrow or consequences, for crime without cost or punishment, for strawberries in winter, for revolution without tears, and so on.

The results were for me bizarre. Much obscene and colourful abuse. More than a hundred letters of support, balanced by a passionate public wigging from our proprietor's spirited and loveable wife Pamela, Lady Hartwell. She furiously denounced the leader as, 'DREADFUL, QUITE DREADFUL.' She dismissed the supporting mail as emanating from people 'like retired Cheltenham colonels' – which it perhaps did, and none the worse surely for that.

In his splendid book about the *Telegraph* and the Berrys, Duff Hart-Davis understandably if mistakenly assumed that the leader must have been *favourable* to *Oz*, and critical of that Establishment which Lady Hartwell in her position as a dazzling Tory hostess might be expected to defend.

Not she; not the 'smart' world; not the intelligentsia; not then, anyway, not at the end of the 1960s; not now either, for all I know.

THE STORY SO FAR:
BARRY IS IN PARIS WITH CHARMING, BI-LINGUAL COLIN LUCAS, AUSTRALIAN EXPATRIATE EXTRAORDINAIRE. BARRY HAS NOT EATEN ANYTHING FOR MANY EPISODES, AND RECURRENT BILIOUS ATTACKS HAVE LEFT OUR HERO DEBILITATED AND HUNGRY. HE HAS JUST ORDERED A NICE STEAK.
NOW READ ON...
YOUR STEAK MONSIEUR–BON APPETIT!
CRIPES SPORT— I LIKE IT RARE BUT THIS ONE'S STILL ON THE HOOF!
SHHH! MON PETIT. SHUT YOUR BOUCHE AND MANGE IT. IF THE GARCONS SEE YOUSE DON'T LIKE THEIR TUCKER THEY'RE NOT ADVERSE TO HAVING A DIP-AROUND!
WHAT!!! A DIP AROUND?
MAIS OUI! A DIP-AROUND. IF THEY DON'T LIKE THE LOOK OF YOU THE BASTARDS GET TOGETHER BACK THERE IN THE CUISINE AND POINT PIERRE AT THE PATISSERIE!!
JEEZ, THE DIRTY ROTTEN MUGS! NEXT TIME I BETTER ORDER A GOOD HOT CURRY JUST TO BE ON THE SAFE SIDE. LET THEM TRY DIPPING THEIR DONGERS IN THAT LOT!
APRES LE REPAS...
I RECKON I'VE HAD AN ELEGANT SUFFICIENCY COL. TO TELL YOUSE THE HONEST TRUTH I'M PRETTY STONKERED. WHERE CAN WE GET A SNOOZE ROUND HERE?
COME CHEZ MOI MON BAZZIE. I'VE GOT A CRASH HOT MAISON JUST ROUND THE COIN...
...ONLY ONE MORE FLOOR. THERE'S A SPARE LIT AND EVERY SANGE THING THAT OPENS AND FERMES!
WHO'S THAT SORT UP THERE? I COULD... ER... I MEAN SHE'S QUITE AN ATTRACTIVE LASS!
THAT'S GERMAINE SHE LIVES NEXT DOOR CHEZ MOI SHE PUTS IT AROUND A BIT BUT SHE'S TREZ BONZER!
WELCOME TO PAREE MON PETIT. IF YOU STAY WITH M. LUCAS REMEMBER LEETLE GERMAINE EEZ AT VOTRE SERVICE!!! (SLURP!)
CRIPES, A BIG JUICY ONE RIGHT ON THE CHOPS. I HOPE I DON'T GET A RASH OR ANYTHING. I HEAR THESE FROG SHEILAHS ARE RIDDLED WITH WHATEVER IT IS!!!
BARRY IS SUSPICIOUS—WHAT SORT OF RASH DOES HE FEAR FROM THE NICE AND HOSPITABLE GERMAINE? SEE NEXT RASH EPISODE

No, the *Oz* world and philosophy had variously touched, interested, fascinated, beguiled, tempted, enchanted, hallucinated, lobotomised, confused, corrupted and/or affected, perhaps permanently, many or all those whose overthrow it sought. As the French say, the fish perishes from the head down . . .

Well, the reader may demur, you were around at that time: were *you* then touched, tempted, etc.? Well, I couldn't in all honesty without qualification deny it. Nor perhaps could such now respectably repentant persons as Mary Kenny, Paul Johnson, John Birt and David Dimbleby. These and others are all quoted by Richard Neville, perhaps to their embarrassment, as onetime friends of *Oz*, with something now to laugh off . . .

Neville's account of *Oz*'s 1960s heyday* is itself fascinating, vivid, proof of a fantastic memory, very frank and foul-mouthed (I wouldn't commend it to my wife, servants or gamekeeper). It is also very amusing, and might have been funnier still had the opposing Establishment not been so wet and equivocal. As it is, one hand claps riotously, a stormy dialectic unfolds with one of the participants silent or enfeebled.

Nor is the book at all times absolutely clear. The plot line is often obscured and entangled by hippie jargon and slang, leaving much scope for clarificatory judicial interrogation: 'What is a "spliff"?' 'What is "psychedelia"?' 'What does the defendant mean by "get folked"?'

What Neville does make absolutely clear is *Oz*'s mysterious and incongruous power to command the tolerance, or even enthusiastic support, of the sort of important top people – academics, philosophers, media moguls and so on – who are still expected by judges, often vainly, to 'know better' or to 'set an example'.

It was so already in Australia, where *Oz* and Neville were born. His fond and loyal parents remind me forcibly of Dostoevsky's Verkhovensky Senior, the bewildered begetter of the Devil in Chief. Charged in Australia also with obscenity, *Oz* was able to wheel out no fewer than seventeen 'experts' (the

* *The Dreams, the Trips, the Trials, the Love-ins, the Screw-ups . . . the Sixties*, Bloomsbury, 1995.

most formidable gathering of intellectuals ever in an Australian court), to testify to its literary and other merits. Are there now, I wonder, university departments of merit-finding, with professors skilled unerringly to find merit on every public-lavatory wall?

Here are a few treasures of Nevillish wisdom, picked at random from his dark, macabre and exotic store.

His artistic collaborator Sharpe gets 'a timely inheritance from an aunt'. Will there then be in the alternative society aunts and legacies, as in Dickens and at the Drones? Parasites are indeed wise not to destroy their hosts but to cherish them.

Neville incongruously laments that London phones are broken and public transport is rotten. Better perhaps if the staffs, crews and users were all 'stoned'?

Clive James is reported to have said: 'I believe in civilisation: as long as you guys keep preaching revolution, you're setting yourselves up to be knocked off – politics isn't a nursery – you'd be the first to go.' Good on yer. Clive.

And Ken Tynan too (of all people) prompted by a hippie clap epidemic, wonders, 'In the alternative future, who's going to build the hospitals?'

'So this is how low we've sunk,' wails an unknown man storming out of a Germaine Greer show in Amsterdam, in which an Austrian humourist (said by Neville at present to be serving a seven-year sentence for indecent acts with underage girls) extracts a woman's tampon with his teeth and gives it to a bearded colleague to eat. Answer: Yes, this low, and lower . . .

John Mortimer QC, defending *Oz*: 'When you're laughing, you are unlikely to be corrupted.' What of those who mocked Christ on the Cross, who told Jewish jokes at Auschwitz?

Bob Dylan to parents: 'Don't criticise what you don't understand.' Good advice to German parents, say, in 1933 and after? Their children too 'wanted to solve old problems in a new way' (Mortimer again). When they learnt what their daughter was up to, I understand that Irma Grese's rude peasant parents chucked her out. Unwise, perhaps unkind: but would Mr Mortimer utterly condemn their 'lack of confidence and compassion' for her 'tender ideas'?

'In *Oz* there is no one word of tenderness. That's because *Oz* does not deal with love. It deals with sex – sex with a capital S' (Brian Leary QC, prosecuting). Neville was oddly impressed by Leary's address: 'It was true. And strangely so, given that we once claimed that love is all you need.'

As the book unfolds, a strange reflective and elegiac tone occasionally dilutes Neville's ravings; doubts thicken and abound.

Timothy Leary (not Leary the QC!) said that 'to kill a policeman is a sacred act'. Neville muses: 'Really?' Neville tells us he'd 'cheated and lied, and dressed it up as brave new politics. I guess I am emotionally retarded . . . love remained a mystery.'

Jimi Hendrix choked to death on his own vomit, releasing in Neville a sense of *memento mori*, of his own disappearance. 'Yeah, some revolution! But it was too late to stop now . . . We blithely declared World War Three on our parents while forgetting to look after our friends.'

More mundane horrors were also salutory: excrement is smeared all over Neville's walls by the visiting hippie son of an aristocrat. 'Party's over,' rules Neville's nice girlfriend Louise. 'A perverse incarnation of freakdom,' ponderously reflects Neville. A freezing Isle of Wight festival, blankets all sold out, no food and stinking latrines, also favours by implication an ordered life.

Let off again on appeal, Neville at thirty wonders whether it is time to settle down. He returns, now in Australia, to a quiet house in which his children are sleeping. Has he repented? Well, he remains, according to the blurb, 'a controversial social commentator'. Watch it, Richard.

As a cure for Nevillish possession I would recommend a visit to the enchanting film of *Little Women*, a certain exorcism.

Otherwise, read and ponder the mournful letter to *Oz* from a hippie (failed), reported on page 164 of Neville's book. The Northern author, alas, can't take his clothes off ('nasty embarrassing spots'). So no Living Theatre, 'the sex scene' in the North is non-existent: 'we have to do it painfully with our hands.' A smoke? The drug squad is too efficient . . . 'I can't play the guitar, write poetry, act or sing, don't understand politics or economics, so what happens to me in the great cultural revolution? In my nineteen years I've had three women, a nervous breakdown and some bad education . . . '

As Lenin put it: 'What is to be done?' What indeed.

The Times, 18 May 1995

Mr Patel's Post Office

If it wasn't for the ATS,
Where would England be?
—ed if I know.

Thus lugubriously chanted private soldiers of the Royal Warwickshire and other distinguished regiments as they prepared, if not to hit old Hitler for six, at least to survive precariously till the tea interval.

The stirring old dirge came back repeatedly to me over the prolonged British Christmas hiatus. At this time, so it seems, a whole nation, moved doubtless by a profound and annually increasing religious emotion, abandons all worldly pursuits, forswears all base, mercantile, usurious and industrial preoccupations and falls to its knees for ten days or more of fervent and uninterrupted orisons. Or so, in my innocence, I presume.

Yet others of us, baser mortals to be sure, cannot free ourselves wholly from the toils of this earth. We want to eat, indeed drink, even – horror upon horror – smoke! Worse, some – a benighted and dwindling few – even have at times to work.

A self-confessed member of this ignoble band of sinners, I could not help repeatedly wondering

If it wasn't for the dear old Paks,
Where would England be?
—ed if I know!

I use the term 'Pak' loosely, only because it fits the traditional metre. No disrespect intended: I fully realise that many of those on whom England now depends for sheer survival are in fact Indians, or British subjects, often of Gujerati origin or springing from one of the other great Indian trading peoples. Others are or were Pakistani, but from the bit now called Bangladesh. Others again are Chinese. To simplify, and to conceal my ignorance, may I call them all Asians?

When the great dark influx began, it was widely predicted that the West Indians, having if any culture then something approximating to our own, would settle down well and become 'assimilated'. Not so the Asians, it was said, who would keep themselves rigidly to themselves in numberless impenetrable tightly knit and unassimilable lumps, like a sort of incurable ethnic fibrositis.

Well, assimilated indeed they have *not* been. They remain unmistakably themselves – hard-working, enterprising, independent though clannish, strangers to restrictive practices, strikes, go-slows and the rest, immune to the British disease, obliging, infinitely adaptable.

They have not normally been here very long. Yet the little shops they run, open all hours, all days, have everything the English need, including substances which must seem to the proprietors and to their brightly clad and glittering womenfolk wholly alien, incomprehensible, disgusting or even polluting. Hindus sell beef, Moslems ham – anything to oblige, and on Christmas as on any other day.

Again, the Welfare State has been regarded as in some way the creation of the whole British people rendered articulate, the miraculous embodiment of its social thoughts, debates and aspirations. It must be said that of the British people who I see stumbling bemused in and out of Mr Patel's sub-post-office, few (including myself) seem to have the foggiest notion of how our brain-child works, of how to extract its bounty, of which lever to pull for the jackpot (or donation, as Lord Home called it). We confront it as an elderly ewe might confront a computer.

Not so Mr Patel himself. Within six months of landing here from East Africa, he has acquired a mastery of the Welfare State far superior to that of the late Lord Beveridge – inevitably superior, in that he is master of numberless new forms of the 'social wage' introduced since that wild nobleman's death.

'No, no, no, darling,' he cries, with much illustrative

gesticulation, to some mumbling and trembling old lady (he has acquired all the local endearments): 'you have got utterly the wrong form. What you are entitled to is the Dependent Widow's Seasonal Discretionary Displacement Rebate, and for this you will require this buff form GX/wid/856/214632852(9a). There now, darling, let me fill it in for you. Date of birth?' And soon the Biro is scratching rapidly over the forms with all their bright promise of scheduled benefits, supplements, grants, free cheese, pensions and whatever else cheers the British journey from the cradle to the grave.

Hardy less adaptable is his neighbour Mr Rashid at the Bangladesh Curry Mahal (fully lic). A dim English and continental menu is appended to the list of his own fiery specialities. Even this last is supplemented at Christmas by seasonal yuletide delicacies such as Turkey Madras, Turkey Khorma, Turkey Dopiaza, Turkey Bangalore (very hot) and Turkey Biriani.

Throughout the festive season, the Mahal remains, like the Windmill, always open. The swarthy 'boys' wait eagerly amid yards of spotless vacant linen for some solitary, sad, drunk, belated and improbable customer, or perhaps for some luckless family whose turkey has vanished, gone up in flames or exploded. At the door beams Mr Rashid himself, the embodiment of courteous welcome. With the same earnestness as the Statue of Liberty, though in a low buzzing Bengali accent, he seems to beseech

> Give me your tired, your poor.
> Send these, the homeless, tempest-tossed, to me.
> I lift my lamp beside the golden door.

It is for some reason assumed that the English absolutely detest all these admirable people and utterly resent their presence here. If we do not say so, or even resort to violence against them, it is assumed that this is only because we are restrained by a straitjacket of ridiculous laws and Lanes boards, Bonham-Carters and what not.

Well, I for one like Mr Patel and Mr Rashid and Co. No board forces me to do so, and I am sure I am not alone in doing so.

Amid a lavish display of tinsel and paper chains, a holly-begirt notice in complex Indo-Gothic script proclaims Mr Rashid's ecumenical Christmas message – 'The season's greetings, and a happy new year to all our customers.' A bit late, but with great warmth, I reciprocate: 'A happy new year to you, Mr Rashid, and many more to come.'

Daily Telegraph, 9 January 1978

The Indian Mutiny – May 1857

To the Europeans of Meerut, cut off from the seething life around them, May 10th, 1857, seemed quite an ordinary Sunday: odd only was the inexplicable absence of many servants. In the evening Mr Rotton, the chaplain, was about to start with his wife and children for church. The Indian nurse implored her mistress to remain at home: there was danger, she said – a fight with the sepoys. Mr Rotton scoffed at her fears, but on the drive to church he saw and heard enough to make him leave his family at a safe place *en route*. He heard the rattle of musketry, the shrill blare of bugles calling the assembly; he saw armed men hurrying to and fro, the panic-stricken looks of the unarmed, pillars of smoke rising against a fast-darkening sky: the sepoys had revolted. The Indian Mutiny had begun.

Within a few hours, the mutineers had thrown open the jail and released eighty-five of their comrades imprisoned for disobedience the day before. They had slaughtered every white man, woman and child they could lay hands on, fired the European bungalows and stolen or destroyed the contents. In the middle of the night they made off for Delhi, the ancient Mogul capital, where, with the tottering king as its nominal, bewildered and unwilling leader, their revolt assumed a national and political character.

This sudden eruption set a pattern which was to be reproduced in the next few months over most of northern India. Revolting regiments, sacked treasuries, arson and massacre, then the flight for Delhi: had all happened simultaneously we must have been lost. As it was, British confidence and sense of security in India was gone for ever. We never quite recovered our nerve. Remembering warnings and precautions neglected before 1857, we felt we could neglect nothing again. Gone was the old careless confidence that what Indians thought and did was of no importance. Among those who did not love India and her people, indifference or contempt were replaced by a great fear. The massacre – or what you will – of Amritsar, and the nervous tension, reasonable or otherwise, which led to that disaster, were consequences of the Indian Mutiny. So, too, in its way, is Indian independence. From the Mutiny sprang alike the belief that we could not rule India without extraordinary vigilance and – when necessary – violence, and the suspicion that we could not forever rule India at all.

What led to this disaster? 'It is quite evident,' wrote Sir Henry Maine, 'that the greatest fact in Anglo-Indian history, the mutiny of the Sepoy army, is as much a mystery to the average man of the West as are certain colours to the colour-blind; and even historians are compelled to supply wholly or partially fictitious explanations of the events of 1857 to a public which cannot be brought to believe that such a vast popular uprising was caused by a prejudice about a greased cartridge.' Maine was no fool, and he knew India. There is much sense in what he says. Certainly it is no use pretending that the East, to us, is not mysterious: it is. And apart from the cartridge there are many things about the Mutiny which are strange and unaccountable: how it spread, for instance, the lightning movement of rumour, the ominous *chapatis* which passed from village to village, which obviously meant something – but what? Even those who passed them seem to have had no clear idea. Nevertheless, to point to the cartridges as the spark which caused the explosion is not to explain all that had assembled the combustible matter which it lit. That we were powerless to check the spread of a rumour – quite false in its essentials – argues that the Indian sepoy had *already* lost contact with his superiors and confidence in their good faith. That the resulting conflagration spread far beyond the Bengal army and assumed – as it most certainly did – the character of a general revolt is something that no fuss about cartridges can explain.

The truth is that we had ceased to fit naturally into India. We had ceased to participate in India: we only worked there. Nor did we any longer work with Indians at their level: we worked above their heads, imposing our decisions upon them.

The Englishman of the eighteenth and early nineteenth centuries had one signal advantage over his successors: he was not *shocked* by India. He was not shocked by dirt and corruption. He had little reason to be: there was plenty of both at home He did not despise the Indians for their technical backwardness: little more advanced himself, how could he? Confronted, indeed, by the wealth, majesty, and antiquity of Indian civilisation he sometimes had the grace to confess himself a parvenu.

The nineteenth century brought with it an Englishman of a new type, a Steam Intellect Society Englishman – arrogant, radical, contemptuous and self-righteous, a leveller and a prig, convinced of his mission to direct and improve, untroubled by doubts, indifferent to – or even ignorant of – what Indians thought, felt or said. To him Indian religious beliefs were mere superstition, Indian social organisation a laughable charade. All that stood in his path was to be swept, like so much lumber, ruthlessly aside. The thought that what he swept away might one day have protected or been of service to him in troubled times never crossed his mind: he thought himself invulnerable. Nor did he doubt for a moment that things were better done well by himself than done ill, or at least differently, by Indians. It was an axiom of his that the Indian was good for nothing: unfit to command troops, unfit to share in the government of his own country, unfit even to own land and to exercise the responsibilities that go with it.

As early as 1817 Sir Thomas Munro had written: 'They [the advantages of British rule] are purchased by the sacrifice of independence, of national character, and of whatever renders a people respectable . . . The consequence, therefore, of the conquest of India by British arms would be . . . to debase a whole people. There is perhaps no example of any conquest in which the natives have been so completely excluded from all share of the government of the country as in British India.' And a year later: 'Foreign conquerors have treated the natives with violence, and often with great cruelty, but none with so much scorn as we;

none has stigmatised the whole people as unworthy of trust, as incapable of honesty, and as fit to be employed only where we cannot do without them. It seems to be not only ungenerous but impolitic to debase the character of a people fallen under our dominion.'

Sir Thomas's protests were barren. During the succeeding four decades the tendencies he deplored were vastly accelerated, pushed on by such evangelists of efficiency as Lord Dalhousie and John Lawrence – great men, both, who did much *for* India and nothing *with* India, and whose achievements were thus the more transitory. Sir John Kaye's character of Dalhousie is the character of a whole type. 'He had but one idea of them [the Indians] – an idea of a people habituated to the despotism of a dominant race. He could not understand the tenacity of affection with which they clung to their old traditions. He could not sympathise with the veneration which they felt for their ancient dynasties . . . He had not the faculty to conceive that men might like their own old ways of government, with all their imperfections and corruptions about them, better than our more refined systems . . . He could not form a true dramatic conception of the feelings with which the representative of a long line of kings may be supposed to regard the sudden extinction of his royal house by the decree of a stranger and an infidel, or the bitterness of spirit with which a greybeard chief, whose family from generation to generation had enjoyed ancestral powers and privileges, might contemplate his lot when suddenly reduced to poverty and humiliation by an incursion of aliens of another colour and another creed.'

The estimate formed by the Steam Intellect Englishman of the Indian character was based not, perhaps, on racial prejudice but on observation. But observation unchecked by sympathy or understanding is a most faulty guide, and the resulting judgement soon degenerated into racial prejudice or something indistinguishable from it. By 1857 we were half-strangers in India, arrogant and aloof: and our aloofness deprived us of any foreknowledge of the revolt our arrogance had provoked.

Indians were different from us: therefore they were inferior – and not merely technically but *morally* inferior, wholly inferior, and that to such an extent as to put their very humanity in doubt. We had ceased to see Indians as our fellow-beings. I am sure that this is the explanation for the fantastic brutality with which the Mutiny was suppressed. Certainly our forces were enraged by accounts – sometimes grossly exaggerated – of the atrocities committed by the sepoys: 'If I had them in my power today,' wrote Nicholson after reading of the massacre of the English at Delhi, 'I would inflict the most excruciating tortures I could think of on them with a perfectly easy conscience,' and much else besides. Certainly we were terribly outnumbered – 36,000 British troops faced 257,000 sepoys and heaven knows how many non-military rebels. Certainly this was no time for half-measures: Kaye, a humane man, did not doubt that 'the severity of the hour would be the humanity of all time'. But neither the logic of retribution, nor fear wholly, nor any grounds of public policy can explain – let alone justify – the wild vengeance which we let loose, its indiscriminate nature, or the self-righteous hysteria or cruel levity with which it was often accompanied.

Before May was out, on the march down from Ambala, villagers believed to be guilty of inflicting injuries upon fugitives from Delhi were seized and condemned after the most rudimentary trial; before execution they were pulled by the hair, pricked with bayonets, and forced by soldiers to eat cows' flesh while officers stood by smiling. Before the middle of June a sort of judicial mincing machine had been set up in Benares, hanging old and young with indiscriminate ferocity, 'as though they had been pariah dogs or jackals'. Even children who mischievously flaunted the rebel colours were hanged. Volunteer hanging parties, with amateur executioners, swept the surrounding countryside. One gentleman boasted of the numbers he had hung 'in an artistic manner' from mango-trees, with elephants for drops; his victims were whimsically strung up 'in the form of a figure of eight'. In Allahabad in June, Indians were slain, regardless of age or sex, after scant trial or no trial at all. When

Renaud set out for Cawnpore, he hung forty-two by the roadside in two days, twelve of them, according to Sir William Russell, 'because their faces were turned the wrong way. All the villages in his front were burnt'. In his wake he left a desert of burnt, deserted villages, untilled fields, and dangling corpses rotting in the heat.

These examples are chosen almost at random. They are what we would call – if committed by foreigners – atrocities. They are in no way untypical of what was going on in all parts of India affected by the Mutiny. All were committed before either of the two massacres at Cawnpore, which are generally regarded as the highwater mark of Indian treachery and infamy. They cannot thus be justified by them, and may in part have provoked them. All were highly damaging to that universal respect for the law on which all government rests, and thus calculated in the long run to postpone rather than hasten the restoration of order. Some – those of Renaud, for instance – were directly and immediately prejudicial to the success of our military operations. We depended on Indians for supplies, transport, information, service – everything: and how could these be got if every Indian fled in terror before us?

I could list further acts of cruel injustice – the wholesale sack and slaughter after the capture of Delhi, for instance, in which guilty and innocent, ill-wishers and well- alike were robbed or put to the sword – all illustrating one fact, that we had ceased to regard Indians as individuals; that we had ceased to discriminate between them; that we regarded them only as a mass, known by its colour, judged hostile by its actions, to be crushed indiscriminately. And from this failure to discriminate sprang a racial bitterness which naturally clouded all the rest of our time in India.

In no place, unfortunately, was the divorce between English and Indian more absolute than in the pre-Mutiny Bengal army – precisely, indeed, where it was most necessary that the union should have been close.

I remember seeing old prints of the Bengal army at the turn of the nineteenth century, which really do seem to portray a sort of easy, informal family life. The regiment in those days, as Kaye says, was the officer's home, his sepoys his children (*babalog*, or babies). He had no distractions outside; intercourse with Europe was rare, English women almost non-existent. Outside the mess, his only interest was in his sepoys, to whom he chatted off duty, whose comfort he ensured, whose wrongs he redressed. In the evenings he and the Indian officer would smoke and gossip in his bungalow; at night, as often as not, he slept with an Indian mistress. He did not merely command Indians: he was half an Indian himself.

The next fifty years twisted this idyll almost beyond recognition. An excessive centralisation robbed the officer of his power. His rights to reward or punish, promote or demote, became ever more circumscribed. From a patriarch or despot, he shrank to the mere mouthpiece of the adjutant-general's office. His decisions were frequently set aside; he was forced to eat dirt before his men; he looked a fool himself, and was powerless to protect them from the folly or pedantic bad faith of headquarters.

It was fortunate indeed for us that the Mutiny itself immediately shattered the centralisation which had done so much to cause it. The telegraph wires were constantly cut, communications were slow and uncertain. John Lawrence at Rawalpindi wrote to Canning, the governor-general, on June 10th. 1857, and had received no reply by the end of July. Delhi fell to us in September; yet rumours of its fall in June were believed, for want of other information, by the governor-general himself. This breakdown of communications is often represented as a great disaster to us. Hodson of Hodson's Horse for one thought otherwise, and I am sure he was right. 'Well, here we are,' he said in May, 'the wires cut north, south, east and west; not a soul can interfere with us; we have the cracking of the nut in our own way.'

It was the rupture of the normal chain of command which gave men like Hodson and Nicholson their chance: they grabbed the reins which the senile and unfit were compelled to drop and restored order in their own utterly disorderly way. 'Had there been no struggle for life and death,' wrote Edwardes, 'when would Neville Chamberlain and John Nicholson have attained the rank of brigadier-general? . . . Amidst the ruins of the regular army these two irregular pillars stand boldly up against the sky, and I hope the tomnoddies admire their architecture.' British rule in India, comments Kaye, was saved by men 'who did what they had no right to do'; and it was the severed telegraph wires which enabled them to do it.

The fabric of pre-Mutiny army life was further shaken by the greed of the central government, which actually robbed regiments of half their officers – and those the best. Ceaselessly active, its appetite for administrators was insatiable. New territories to be governed, surveys and public works to be directed, new irregular regiments to be raised: these were now the plum jobs, and regimental soldiering became a bore. Not only were regiments denuded of officers, but those that remained had no heart for the job: nearly all were in restless expectancy or sullen despair.

As important as any of these factors – if not more so – was the increasingly English tone of society. English books, magazines and newspapers, English morals and habits, English stiffness and etiquette, above all, English women: all these raised an insurmountable barrier between the Indian and ourselves, and utterly destroyed the old friendly intimacy and informality which had helped to make our predominance both effective and endurable. And thus it came about that by 1857 the officer riding at the head of his company might – almost certainly did – know far less of what was passing in his men's minds than the *guru* squatting half-naked under the peepul tree at the wayside.

The extent of this ignorance was revealed when in 1857 officer after officer swore to the absolute staunchness of regiment after regiment, each one in fact poised on the very brink of mutiny. On May 22nd, angered by aspersions cast at his regiment, Colonel Simpson wrote to the *Englishman*, furiously protesting its 'utmost loyalty'. A day or two later his officers were butchered and he was lucky to escape with a ball through his arm. The commanders of regiments about to be disarmed at Peshawar 'unanimously and violently declared their confidence in their men. One advised conciliation, and another threatened us that *his men would resist and take the guns*' (my italics: an odd proof of loyalty, surely!). When Nicholson handed them packets of intercepted letters, proving the men were up to the hilt in sedition, the colonels were more angry than interested. Colonel Spottiswoode of the 55th blew his brains out at the disarming of his regiment. When Nicholson disarmed the 33rd, its colonel burst into tears, protesting that he would answer with his life for the loyalty of every man. Such scenes as these were reproduced all over India. The blind confidence they illustrate has its touching side; completely misplaced as it was, however, it argues that, for all they knew of their men, the officers might as well have been in another continent.

And thus the mutiny spread from regiment to regiment, spurred on by mysterious murmurs and fears, directed – if at all – by unseen hands, moving rapidly in the vacuum left by over-centralisation, over-confidence, and the remoteness of our officers from those they were supposed to command.

Perhaps if the Mutiny had been confined to the army, it might have been stamped out as quickly as it arose, leaving only superficial scars behind. But it was not. Indians have constantly stressed the *national* character of the Mutiny. They often speak of the Mutiny as 'the war of Indian independence': Savarkar wrote a famous history of it, banned in British India and published therefore in Paris. Reacting against this view, British writers have tended to over-emphasise the *military* character of the revolt, its local and particular causes, its lack of general significance, its opposition not to British rule as a whole but to mistaken aspects of that rule.

I am not sure the facts support either side. To speak of 'nationalism' in connection with the semi-feudal India of 1857 is certainly an absurd anachronism It is equally absurd to deny, however, that behind the obvious, spectacular and carefully recorded military aspects of the Mutiny can be discerned the outline, vague yet unmistakable, of a vast civil convulsion. In many parts of India our administration entirely collapsed and all that we had achieved was swept away. No mutiny, perhaps, no civil convulsion: the two are certainly connected yet absolutely distinct.

In the so-called North-Western Provinces – the 'model' provinces, our most vaunted administrative triumph – the civil population rose quite independently of the sepoys: without their presence or aid, before they had risen, or after they had left the district. In some places sepoys, still loyal, actually helped us in our attempts to restore order. In the parts of India, moreover, where the revolt was confined to soldiery, its effects were temporary and superficial. A day or two of massacre, loot and arson, then the sepoys would make off for home or Delhi and our authority was swiftly restored. It was not the violence of the sepoys that caused the governor-general to write officially of the North-Western Provinces as 'lost to us' or Henry Lawrence to say of Oudh, 'throughout the province, *all is anarchy*'. Indeed, the truth was – as Kaye points out – that in these provinces and in some others 'all classes with any power of rising had risen against us'; our government consequently 'collapsed like a house of cards – it had no more substance or stability.' We found ourselves powerless and friendless. How had this come about?

The explanation, I am sure, lies somewhere in the paradoxical nature of modern British imperialism. To the traditional imperialist pure and simple, order is self-justifying, its establishment and maintenance the supreme, overriding obligation. In controlling a country therefore, his thoughts and actions are directed to this one end. All that can strengthen his position is fostered, all that can weaken restrained. Forces, energies and institutions in the subject people are not seen as good or bad in themselves, but good or bad in so far as they can be harnessed to his single purpose. Reform he views with the same cold eye. I do not write disparagingly. Order is in itself a great blessing: nothing can flourish without it. A pure imperialist of this type, moreover, is commonly tolerant of native ways of life, respectful of native rights, and friendly to native participation in the government: where others see only brakes or inefficiency and obstacles in the path of progress, he wisely finds sources of strength.

The beginning of the nineteenth century saw the rise of a quite new school of imperialism: *a radical imperialism.* Out of the conflict inherent in this idea the Mutiny sprang. It was the central tenet of the new school that we were in India not merely to rule it but to reform it – to change it out of all recognition. Progress must not merely be maintained. It must be ruthlessly hastened, even at the expense of stability, by the central authority. There was no time to consult Indians, to pander to their tastes, to associate them with what was being done: there was too much to do.

On assuming the government of the annexed Punjab, Henry Lawrence, an imperialist of the older type, dealt more lightly than was generally approved with the native aristocracy and respected their traditional rights. This meant that much revenue which could have been well used elsewhere was alienated in grants and pensions, often to quite worthless recipients. Lawrence was quite prepared to tolerate such abuses, as not the most expensive means of reconciling the influential classes to our rule. Such an outlook was quite incomprehensible to the *new* imperialism: if one can only rule by tolerating abuses, why rule at all? Again, I do not write disparagingly. The intemperate reforms of this school were based on lofty motives: on a deep sympathy for the poor, backward and oppressed, on a passion for what we would now call social justice. Yet the results of trying to do so much were to shake the state to its foundations and thus jeopardise our power to do anything at all.

The two great pre-Mutiny issues on which the new imperialism met and routed the old were, one, policy towards the native states and, two, policy towards the native aristocracy. To men such as Colonel Sleeman, reared in the old school, the native states were valuable breakwaters: 'When they are all swept away,' he predicted, 'we shall be left to the mercy of our native army, which may not always be sufficiently under our control.' Like Sleeman, Colonel Low of the Supreme Council in Calcutta had seen everything the native states had to offer in the way of vicious misgovernment, waste, cruelty, sloth and inefficiency: and it was not little. Yet he too was convinced of the impolicy of annexing native states whenever the occasion presented itself, for the most trivial reasons and often in defiance of the letter or spirit of long-standing agreements.

The cautions of Low and Sleeman were powerless to check Dalhousie's expansive zeal. The native states were to him at best tiresome anachronisms, at worst sinks of every known political iniquity. Lying as they often did between one British territory and another, they were inimical to the efficiency and uniformity even of our own administration. The idea that people might prefer a tyranny to which they were accustomed, and which was exercised by men of their own race, to a novel tyranny imposed by aliens seems not to have crossed his mind.

'As it lies in the midst of other British districts,' wrote Dalhousie of Jhansi, 'the possession of it as our own will tend to the improvement of the general internal administration of our possessions in Bundelkhand. That its incorporation with the British territories will be greatly for the benefit of the people of Jhansi a reference to the results of experience will suffice to show.' 'The results of experience,' comments Kaye drily, 'have since shown to what extent the people of Jhansi appreciated the benefits of that incorporation.' The consequence of Dalhousie's annexations was to spread insecurity far and wide; no native ruler felt sure that his house would not perish with him. With the annexation of Oudh, the loss of confidence was complete: who could be safe, it was asked, if we treated thus a state which – whatever its faults – had always been our most faithful ally?

Thus, in our passion for expansion and standardisation, we knocked down several of the pillars which might have supported us in our need and shook them all. In our dealings with the native aristocracy we showed an equally astonishing disregard for interests potentially harmonious with our own and thus, indirectly, for our own interests. If the primary duty of a state is to maintain and strengthen itself, it is a duty which the British in India seem at this time entirely to have neglected. Instead of acting as a tranquillising and stabilising force, they appear to have regarded themselves as the agents of a veritable agrarian revolution.

The idea of a native aristocracy was clearly an abomination to us. We wished to see nothing between us and the masses; we wished to see nothing strong and self-reliant except ourselves. It was an axiom with us that whoever we found in enjoyment of wealth or social position must have acquired it by force and fraud and maintained it by cruelty and oppression. And thus with a perfectly clear conscience, in province after province, we went to work with the inhuman precision of a gigantic planing machine, reducing Indian society to a dead level. Where rights existed without documentary proof we swept them away; where documents were produced we ignored them, pleading defects in the character or conduct of the owner; forced sales and heavy taxation sped on the process; we acted on numberless pretexts and in numberless ways.

Warnings of what would happen were not wanting. Mr William Edwards, magistrate at Budaon, pointed out ceaselessly that, 'although the old families were being displaced fast, we could not destroy the memory of the past, or dissolve the ancient connection between them and their people'. In the event of an insurrection, he continued, 'we should find this great and influential body, through whom we can alone hope to keep under and control the rural masses, ranged against us on the side of the enemy, with their hereditary followers and retainers rallying around them, in spite of our attempts to separate their interests'. Many pointed to the folly of such arbitrary behaviour in the provinces out of which the Bengal army was recruited: 'If we persist,' warned a Calcutta paper in 1838, 'we shall very soon have to trust for our security to British troops alone.'

All these and other warnings were neglected. And thus when the Mutiny broke out we found ourselves confronted by revolution. It was led by men whom British rule had deprived not only of their land and privileges, but of all hope of profitable or honourable employment; by ruined men forbidden by us to be either drone or bee; by men who had nothing left to lose; by men who were our natural allies but who had been alienated by our doctrinaire egalitarianism, ruthlessly and recklessly applied. Edwards's experiences are perfectly typical: 'In Budaon the mass of the population rose in a body, and the entire district became a scene of anarchy and confusion. The ancient proprietary body took the opportunity of murdering or expelling their successors, and resumed possession of their hereditary estates . . . To the large number of these sales [forced sales by decree of our civil courts] and the operation of our revenue system, which has had the result of destroying the gentry of the country and breaking up the village communities, I attribute solely the disorganisation of this and the neighbouring districts . . . The rural classes would never have joined the sepoys, whom they hated, had not these causes of discontent already existed . . . Those who could really control the vast masses of the rural population were interested in bringing about a state of disturbance and general anarchy . . . '

Sir George Trevelyan writes of the forces which converged on Cawnpore: 'Intelligence of the revolt attracted to the spot the entire available blackguardism of the neighbourhood. The disloyal and insolvent landlords for thirty miles about called out their tenantry and retainers. Some chieftains brought two hundred armed followers; others four hundred. One rajah came with a tail of forty score: while Bhowany Sing, whom Nanukchund designates as "that old and notorious scoundrel", marched into the rebel camp at the head of 1,200 matchlock men. No one seems to have entertained any doubt as to the final extinction of our sway. The old order of things had disappeared for ever, and it behoved any feudal leader who had ambition or necessities to be present and ready to assert himself ere the new order was definitely established . . . '

Blackguards, disloyal and insolvent, old and notorious scoundrels – in these Falstaffian figures with their scarecrow armies we see the last protest of the old India against the dead level which crushed it. They failed: and across the dead level, across a plain strewn with broken powers and thwarted energies the British marched to a bleak and glorious victory.

But not, indeed, to a final victory. The unity, uniformity, and equality which we successfully reimposed on India shaped the agitation of the future; gave to the movement for Indian independence its national, mass and democratic character. In this one sense, and in defeat rather than in the possibility of victory, the Indian Mutiny was truly the war of Indian Independence.

Encounter, May 1957

*To Our Visitors**

A word to the countless foreign visitors who throng London and other parts of the British Isles at this joyful Jubilee time. We bid you most warmly welcome. We hope you will not be outrageously fleeced, always a risk when there are huge crowds about, and that you will return home not only with all the handbags, cameras and so forth which you brought with you but also with a great store of happy memories.

We would also like, if we may without disrespect, to say something about what you are about to see. You may suspect that this great show, magnificent as we hope you will find it, is put on for your benefit, or more harshly, that it is base lure to get you here so that we prodigal bankrupts may the more easily empty your wallets. Indeed, in the *New Statesman*, in an 'anti-Jubilee issue' of Caliban-like malignity, you will find it baldly stated – 'It's all for the tourists, really.'

Such a cynical point of view makes quite inexplicable the stupendous public rejoicings which marked Queen Victoria's two great Jubilees, well before the age of mass tourism. It is also an insult to both you and us. It suggests that we are the sort of people who have no use for history or patriotism, or for our time-honoured political and religious institutions, of which the Queen is the peak and embodiment, except to make money by prostituting them. On the other hand, it suggests that you are the sort of vulgar mindless dupes who might easily and fitly be deceived by such a fake. What absolute nonsense it all is, anyway, as ridiculous as saying it is all put on for brewers, or for the makers of flags or pork pies.

* Editorial on the Queen's Jubilee.

If you doubt us for a moment, take a look not at the national press, but at any local paper. What will you find? Here is a typical list of forthcoming events in an ordinary South London borough: dancing displays; hot-air-balloon shows; ecumenical services of thanksgiving, many in the open air; parades of steam engines and veteran cars; a gymkhana; forty-odd street parties (pray, please for fine weather!); a wellington-boot-throwing competition; concerts by children and local performers, some of them distinguished; fairs; processions, many in fancy dress; a pageant; barn dancing; bars and barbecues; a bonny baby show; art exhibitions; a fête; an 1890 cricket match – for pity's sake, you cry, stop! Very well, but could anybody in his right mind suppose, that this innocent saturnalia was for the tourists, really? When it was all planned did anyone for a moment hope for a single tourist's presence? Not, of course, that you would not be most welcome everywhere – for the best family parties (which is what this really is, on the huge scale) are by no means exclusive.

A further point: you will probably have been told by your *media* that we are a bitter and class-ridden society, shackled by outworn conventions and tradition, groaning and suffocating under the vast pyramid of snobbery and privilege of which the Queen is the very apex. You may even feel a momentary twinge of guilt if you are lucky enough to see her: how can you happily admire the passing plumage without remembering and lamenting the dying bird it adorns?

Reject all this, we beg you, and enjoy yourselves with a perfectly good conscience. To encourage you, see how others do it. If you have time, go to the poorer districts, far off the processional routes, at the very bottom of the pyramid, where the streets are normally drab and dirty. You won't find all of them utterly transformed and, indeed, it is hard to make tower blocks look festive. But look at some of the streets, especially the ones where the parties are going to be, now ablaze with red, white and blue, with royal emblems and pictures of the Queen. The people of these parts do not seem to see in her an outmoded and alien class-symbol (or, if they do, they disguise it pretty well). Rather do they seem to regard her as a symbol of their own country, as a trusted friend who shares and expresses their own profound and passionate patriotism. They seem far more aware of what they have in common with her than of what divides. Her Jubilee is therefore something not only for her to celebrate but for them as well, and for you too – the more the merrier.

Remember too that this is a very old and settled monarchy, and ponder then what this implies. If it were new, then indeed some might reasonably argue that it *was* the enemy of social change, the guardian of an ossified and hierarchic society based on privilege rather than merit. But it is old. It has presided over a society notably mobile by most standards (oh, yes, this is true, however unfashionable) and over the most profound and striking social changes, to which it has adapted itself with grace, ease and success. It offers thus not only a reminder of past achievement but also the best hope of future achievement, and a thread of continuity running like memory through all.

Above all do have the courage and good sense to believe that what is obvious may also be true. The Queen does not drive about at a tremendous speed, like the cruel head of the Russian state, in an opaque and sinister bullet-proof limousine, one of twenty for safety's sake, through streets cleared, fearsomely guarded and overawed. No, you will see her drawn, quite defenceless in her ancient coach, at a snail's pace through cheering millions to give her thanks to God. You will see her afterwards mixing freely with her people. You will see the smiles of welcome, joy and pride on every face.

You might suppose that she trusts us, and that we love her. And you would be absolutely right.

Daily Telegraph, 7 June 1977

BOOKS

❦

*The End of the Tether**

Greatly and a shade guiltily privileged, we read the private letters of distinguished men, eavesdropping on conversations not normally meant for our ears. What we hear can be disconcerting.

'Criticism,' writes Conrad to his publisher and benefactor William Blackwood, 'is poor work and to expose the weaknesses of humanity as exposed in literary work is a thankless and futile task.' Hmm. Conrad concedes that that criticism is worthy which attempts

> to point out to the crowd beauties not manifest to the common eye, to flash the light of one's sympathetic perception upon great, if not obvious, qualities and even upon generous failings that hold the promise of better things to come . . . But the blind distribution of praise and blame, done with a light heart and an empty mind, which is the very essence of 'periodical' criticism, seems to me to be a work less useful than skirt-dancing and not quite as honourable as pocket-picking.

Eh, what? Who? Me? Conrad must have had someone else in mind, but ruefully I pick up the proffered cap. Does it fit?

Conrad had actually been asked for his opinion of an early John Buchan story in *Blackwood's*. He preferred for the above

* Review of *The Collected Letters of Joseph Conrad, Vol. II, 1898–1902*, Frederick R. Karl and Laurence Davies (eds), Cambridge University Press

reasons to say 'nothing critical' of 'that – production', as he fastidiously called it. Heaven help poor Buchan had he decided otherwise. For what he *did* say was that

> its idea, its feeling, its suggestion and even the *most subtly significant incidents* have been wrenched alive out of Kipling's tale *The Finest Story in the World* . . . One does not expect style, construction or even common intelligence in the fabrication of story; but one has the right to demand some sort of sincerity and to expect common honesty. When that fails – what remains?

To Edward Garnett, Conrad denounced Buchan as a fraud and an 'unspeakable impostor'.

Well, Buchan's subsequent literary career demonstrates the cruel injustice of Conrad's judgement. And to single it out for quotation, as I have light-heartedly and empty-mindedly done, does Conrad an equally cruel injustice. Why then did I do it? Sheer *diablerie*, I suppose, at finding a great man doing with relish what he despises, getting it wrong and denying he has done it; and, more seriously, to emphasise the value set by Conrad on the sincerity and honesty which he mistakenly found absent in Buchan.

Conrad's appreciation of all honest and sincere efforts produced by his fellow toilers in the literary vineyard is normally percipient and generous to a fault. Apart from Buchan, only Grant Allen ('*un imbécile*'), Marie Corelli and Hall Caine ('male Marie Corelli', 'megalomaniac' and 'simply mad with vanity'), feel his lash. Conrad was exceptionally kind to Galsworthy, for instance, as that good man was kind to him (and to so many others, many ungrateful). Galsworthy was unobtrusively lavish with banknotes (he may himself have characteristically suppressed all references to his munificence in earlier selective editions of Conrad's letters), Conrad lavish with advice, encouragement and praise. In a Galsworthy story he finds things 'that I would give a pound of my flesh to have written'. He urged Galsworthy, however, to remove himself from his work, to keep his distance from his characters, to treat them with greater scepticism and indifference.

Such advice Conrad himself surely took more to heart than did his disciple, creating Marlow, for instance, to stand between him and his characters, and thus bogging down *Chance* in impenetrable forests of inverted commas within inverted commas, indicating that Marlow is telling us what B told him about what C had told D about what E or F had told G – or is it A?

Conrad, incidentally, noted not unkindly in Galsworthy 'a certain caution of touch which will militate against popularity', which should lead him never to expect more than 'limited appreciation'. Well, who then could have predicted Galsworthy's prodigious sales, international success and Nobel Prize?

In Conrad's letters, we might expect to find not only advice to the young but estimates of his peers, intimate wit and wisdom, private comments on public affairs, innermost thoughts, some tricks of the trade, what inspired or lay behind published masterworks, how these were achieved and why thus rather than in some other way, a host of insights peculiarly valuable when vouchsafed by a writer some of whose major works are mysteriously veiled, enigmatic and withdrawn. In this engrossing volume we do indeed find – though some inner mysteries remain – such insights by the sackful, conscientiously and helpfully edited, even with humour: mention of Grant Allen's *Woman Who Did* reminds the editors of the answering *Woman Who Didn't*, by the aptly named Victoria Cross.

Conrad's general views on mankind's natural viciousness, fatuity, cowardice and selfishness (which last he provocatively valued as the preserver of 'absolutely everything') are durably illusion-free. His comments on the Boer War, for instance, have lost none of their point. His Polish sympathy for oppressed peoples led him to deplore the 'stupid' war, but did not blind him to the fact that Boers are by nature oppressors too. He hoped for a quick British victory, on the dispassionate ground that, if you can't prevent murder being done in the next room, it were best done quickly; but he shrewdly doubted the will of the British to keep the Boers for ever in their place.

It would be shockingly misleading, however, to suggest that we find here a great soul at ease in dressing gown and slippers, mellowly dispensing what life has taught him with a cynical worldly-wise smile. Oh dear, no: on the contrary, we find a great soul in torment, often or normally in utter despair, borne down by worries and poverty, and by debts which inflation has reduced to an appearance of triviality (but think what five pounds meant then!), as also by the severe and agonising illnesses of his wife, his little son and himself, his own including gout, piles, backpain, toothache, the lot. He dwelt in the heart of darkness, at the end of his tether. His letters groan *de profundis*.

'He is poor and a gentleman and proud': Stephen Crane put his finger on the point at which Conrad's character and circumstances joined to produce misery. Sometimes it took the poor gentleman all his resolution and self-control 'to refrain from butting my head against the wall. I want to howl and foam at the mouth.' After sleepless nights and fruitless days, he 'would be thankful to be able to write anything, anything, any trash, any rotten thing – something to earn dishonestly and by false pretences the payment promised by a fool'. These terrifying revelations to Edward Garnett, and others worse, are the norm rather than the exception when he writes to real friends.

At first I thought the editors mistaken to have fattened an already fat volume (470 pages for the letters of only four years: the whole will fill eight volumes!) by including every one of Conrad's pounds-shillings-and-pence letters, begging for loans and advances, for a few bob more per thousand words. But no: to have suppressed these would have been gravely to distort and bowdlerise the pitiful truth. It was this truth which caused Conrad with bitter cynicism to write about *Lord Jim*, 'The artistic pleasure is neither here nor there. Bread is the thing' – remarks which could only have cheapened him did we not know the agony from which they sprang.

'Of course there is a material basis for every state of mind,' Conrad asserts, 'and so for mine.' If he strays here, as material adversity causes most of us to stray at times, near to a sort of kitchen Marxism, he had – strange for a Pole – no religion to prevent him from straying further, only a profound and stoic pessimism, which found evil in all 'causes' and 'isms, except perhaps one, a mysterious and 'absolutely lost cause' to which he remained forever faithful. Whatever this was, it certainly was not Christianity, in which 'nobody – not a single bishop' (he can say that again) ' – believes. The business in the stable isn't convincing; whereas my atmosphere (*vide* reviews) can be positively breathed.'

If Conrad seems here for one blasphemous moment to compare *Youth* and *Heart of Darkness* favourably with the gospels, this good opinion of himself as a writer is absolutely exceptional. He was certainly not buoyed up through all his vicissitudes by any inner conviction of his worth. Indeed, he faced not only a staring monster without, which 'will devour me', but terrible doubts, enemies and menaces within. *The Rescue*, which hangs over all these four years like a black cloud, was 'unredeemable trash', 'unutterable bosh'. *Heart of Darkness* itself had earlier been 'rotten': 'all I write is rotten now'. Fame was for him in 1900 a fraud, beyond his reach; 'profit I do not get'; he no longer believed in 'the illusion of being a writer'; 'it is not my depth but my shallowness which makes me 'inscrutable'. *Typhoon* was 'too silly for words', *The End of the Tether* 'heart-breaking bosh'. To crown all, the whole manuscript of the second part of this bosh was incinerated by an exploding lamp. To write it all for a second time, belief in it doubly destroyed: 'Imagine trying to clothe in flesh a naked skeleton, without the faith to help you in the impossible task.'

Of the despised *Romance* (a magnificent tale, surely?) he seems to have thought better, or perhaps affected to for the sake of his dear collaborator, Ford Madox Ford. And he did once write defiantly to Blackwood, rejecting the idea of his own worthlessness, declaring that he knew exactly what he was doing, denying the possibility of utter failure, invoking the names Wagner and Rodin, 'who both had to starve a little in their day'. Yet only ten days later he wrote to Garnett confessing that 'all my art has become artfulness in exploiting agents and publishers', that he had lost utterly all faith in himself, 'all sense of style, all power to tell the simplest fact in a simple way'. To whom was he telling the truth as he saw it, to publisher or to intimate friends?

In fact, these letters would be unbearably painful if it were not for two consoling possibilities. One is that much happier times were in store for Conrad, though they may not have been all that happier for a man of his dark temperament: we shall see. The other possibility is that, throughout his sojourn in the valley of the shadow, the author never lost two things of supreme importance to him, his courage and his honour. There are two letters referring to a mysterious and distressing act of 'scoundrelism' done to R. B. Cunninghame Graham, involving £20. The matter was seemingly put right, and the word 'scoundrelism' is probably justified only as reflecting Conrad's own knightly standards of personal conduct.

Nor did Conrad ever lose his warm zeal to help others in distress, notably Mrs Cora Crane, whose plump and pleasing likeness (with hip-flask) is here reproduced. She had been the first ever woman war correspondent, a brothel-keeper before as well as after being married (or rather not married) to Stephen Crane, and one-time proprietress of the Hotel de Dream (*sic*), Jacksonville, Fla. 'What the world calls scandal,' Conrad wrote to her, 'does not affect me in the least.' Nor did it: bully for him. *De profundis confortavit, creavit et vicit.*

The Spectator, 16 August 1986

Dear Little Noddy: A Parent's Lament

It you have small children and they don't like Noddy, you are very lucky. I have; they do; I am not. This insipid wooden doll, with its nodding head crowned with cap and bell, with its taxi and its friend Big Ears, has opened a rift between parents and children which time alone may heal. They love it; we don't. And we can't agree to differ, live and let live, because we parents have to sit and read the stuff to them.

The Noddy business has by now taken its place among Britain's major non-warlike industries, along with sauce-bottling, the pools, cheesecake photography and the manufacture of ice-lollies, righteous indignation and plastic pixies. The business is founded on the mass-production of Noddy books, of which twelve million had been sold two years ago: twelve titles, that is to say, and about a million sold of each. The export branch produces Noddy books in countless foreign languages, including Tamil, Hebrew and Swahili. By-products, controlled by five separate companies, include Noddy soap and Noddy chocolates, Noddy pyjamas and nighties, Noddy painting books, jigsaws, Christmas annuals, cut-outs on cereal packets and models ('smashing fun modelling Noddy and his friends: all easily made from Sculptorcraft Rubber Moulds'). Noddy has also appeared on television and the West End stage, though not yet at the Royal Court.

Noddy's onlie begetter is a former schoolmistress called Enid Blyton. She has been described by William Hickey as 'a sweet-looking woman in her middle years. The outstanding thing about her is her eyes. They are deep and kind.' The really outstanding thing about her is her industry. In the five years 1948–52 inclusive, she managed to fill nearly four close-printed columns of Whitaker's Cumulative Book List – 261 titles by my count. In 1955 she clocked up 59 titles, more than a book a week (not all of them about Noddy, of course). Last year, flagging slightly, she only managed 28. She also produces a fortnightly magazine ('the only magazine I write'), runs four children's clubs (the Famous Five Club, the Busy Bees, the Sunbeam Society and the Magazine Club), and personally answers a thousand or more fan-letters a week.

The scale of her activities has naturally aroused suspicion that she must be a corporate entity like Dumas et Cie, or even some sort of electronic brain. These allegations she indignantly denies: it is all her own work, all done by hand. 'Once I get started,' she has said, 'I've just got to go on and on. Oh, I love it . . . Stories flow from my imagination like cotton from a reel.' According to her husband, 'It has been a constant battle to restrain her from working. The sheer effort of turning out 10,000 words daily – sometimes 14,000 – has resulted in heart-strain. She never lets up . . . She is a remarkable woman, but now she must rest.' 14,000 words daily – if we assume a seven-hour writing day – means 2,000 words an hour, about 33 words a minute, a word every two seconds. Miss Blyton's style may be flat, her material banal, her method unreflective; written at such a lick it is astonishing that her works make as much sense as they do. Measured beside this literary Stakhanovite, such prodigies of productivity as Trollope, Zola and Balzac shrink to mere idle dilettantes.

Miss Blyton is, by Johnson's definition, no blockhead. Even two years ago, the royalties on Noddy alone totalled £400,000. With an income estimated at £50,000 a year, she must be about the highest paid woman in the British Isles. It would be quite wrong, however, to assume that she writes only for money. She writes not merely to amuse, but to edify. Her art is not for art's sake. She is committed: she has A Message.

'Into my books,' she says, 'I pack ethical and moral teaching . . . I do not write merely to entertain. My public, bless them, find in my books a sense of security, an anchor, a sure sense that right is always right and that such things as courage and kindliness

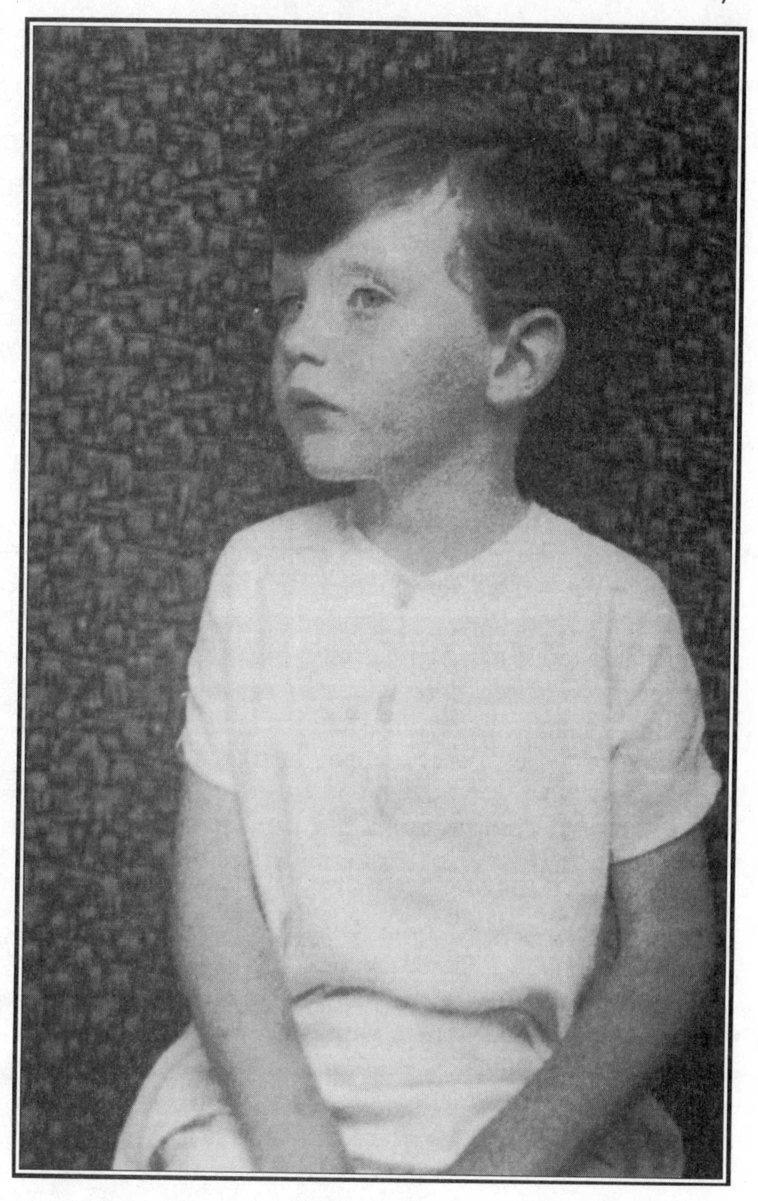

CW aged four

deserve to be emulated.' Thus does she range herself firmly with Dr F. R. Leavis against Lord David Cecil's hedonistic aestheticism.

If not 'merely' entertaining, however, the Noddy books undoubtedly do entertain the people they are meant to entertain. The sales are unanswerable – the more so, since the books could not possibly entertain anyone else. Noddy books are not enjoyed by grown-ups and forced upon children: they are enjoyed by children and forced upon grown-ups. The story behind practically every copy sold is of a delighted child and an adult's dead body.

The essence of a children's classic – perhaps of any classic – is that it can be enjoyed at a number of different levels. The *Adventures of Alice in Wonderland* and *Through the Looking-Glass*; the tales of Grimm and Andersen; the wistful nonsense of Edward Lear; Beatrix Potter's strange stories, in which the matter-of-fact surface half conceals a sort of mysterious poetry; *The Wind in the Willows*, *Doctor Dolittle* and *Winnie the Pooh* – all these books have delighted generations of children. They have also delighted generations of grown-ups. And when parents read them to their children, it is to experience a complex harmony of pleasures: they find delight in the book itself; they recapture the delight it once brought them as children; and they see awakened that same delight in a new generation. These books thus form a most precious link between the generations, binding them together, part of the family, forever part of the life of each member of it.

To compare say, Winnie the Pooh with Noddy is not really unfair. Both appeal primarily to the same age group, both with complete success. In other respects, the difference is startling. The Pooh stories are written with wit, taste and economy of means, and with an almost magical felicity of form. For sheer craftsmanship take the story 'in which Pooh and Piglet go hunting and nearly catch a woozle'. The mounting suspense as these two enchanting fools plod round and round the tree in the snow, tracking first one woozle, then two, three and four, and the effortless way in which the illusion is finally pricked, make this in miniature a perfect short story. Compared with such happy mastery, Noddy is mere drooling, shapeless meandering – 'cotton from a reel'.

If children enjoy Noddy, is that all that matters? Miss Blyton, of course, wouldn't think so; neither would I. By writing ruthlessly *down* to children, she does not merely bore and antagonise grown-ups. Her Noddy books also fail to stretch the imagination of children, to enlarge their experience, to kindle wonder in them or awaken their delight in words. They contain nothing incomprehensible even to the dimmest child, nothing mysterious or stimulating. They have no 'contact with nescience'; they never suggest new and exciting fields to conquer. By putting everything within reach of the child mind, they enervate and cripple it. 'Those children,' says Miss Blyton, 'who find exams easier to pass and scholarships easier to win, are nearly always those who have been much read to in their earlier years.' It is hard to see how a diet of Miss Blyton could help with the 11-plus or even with the Cambridge English Tripos. It certainly did not help poor Christopher Craig, of whom, at his trial for murder, it was stated that 'the only books he knows anything about are the books of Enid Blyton, which he gets other people to read for him'.

The idea that children should have special books is a fairly modern one. Until Victorian days, children by and large read grown-up books or none. In Noddy, 'the book for children' is carried logically *ad absurdum.* Victorian children's books often involve long words and quite complex intellectual and moral problems. Since then children's books (not excluding *Winnie the Pooh* of course, in which 'writing down' is used half-ironically) have been more and more closely geared to the supposed intellectual powers of their public. Enid Blyton is perhaps the first successful writer of children's books to write actually *below* her audience. 'Only not-so-bright children like Enid Blyton,' was the acid comment of a town librarian. 'My books,' replied Miss Blyton, somewhat irrelevantly, 'are read in palaces as well as in working-class homes. They are suitable for every child's mentality.' In fact, her appeal is not only to the not-so-bright.

Her books seem to possess a mysterious fascination for all children, bright and not-so-bright alike.

To what ends, then, does Miss Blyton use her influence over children? It is not easy to say. For all her protestations of lofty purpose, there is little explicit moralising in the Noddy books. One can only go by the characters Miss Blyton appears to find sympathetic. Of these the chief is Noddy himself.

Noddy is not perhaps intended to be admirable. According to his creator, he 'is like the children themselves, but more naïve and stupid. Children like that – it makes them feel superior. He is the helpless little man who gets into trouble and invites sympathy – a children's version of the early Charlie Chaplin.' But he is undoubtedly intended to be attractive and influential. He is always 'dear little Noddy'; he is 'always so friendly and polite that everyone likes him'; 'he is quite the nicest person in Toy Village'; he cleans his teeth, brushes his hair, polishes his shoes, drinks his milk, eats his bread; he can make children respect policemen, tidy their rooms, eat up their porridge; echoing his creator, he thinks it 'good to work hard and earn lots of money'; he is also an artist who composes (or rather 'feels coming', like Elgar) songs which, sung by the composer, are invariably received with rapturous enthusiasm. Mr and Mrs Tubby Bear like to hear one every morning; 'Isn't he clever?' says Miss Rabbit; 'How *does* Noddy think of his songs?' asks Miss Blyton: 'no wonder everyone is clapping him and calling for more.' Several critics have thought Wagner rash actually to incorporate in *Die Meistersinger* a melody, the Prize Song, which he himself declared to be of transcendent beauty, a masterpiece: wiser, perhaps, to have funked the challenge and left it to the imagination. Miss Blyton is equally intrepid. Her pages are lavishly enriched with the fruits of Noddy's genius, of which the following – greeted as usual with universal applause and cheers – is a fair sample:

> 'I'm only little Noddy
> Who's got a song to sing,
> and a little car to ride in,

And a bell to jingle-jing.
I've a little house to live in
And a little garage too.
But I've something BIG inside me,
And that's my love for YOU –
My love for ALL of you!'

The 'little-man' sentimentality and crooner's clichés of this declaration are in fact redolent less of 'the early Charlie Chaplin' than of the mature Norman Wisdom – to whom in other respects Noddy bears a certain resemblance.

His poetic gifts apart, to call Noddy 'more naïve and stupid' than any normal child is a gross understatement. His imbecility is almost indecent. It is somehow symbolised by the ceaseless nodding of his head, a movement – presumably involuntary – upon which great emphasis is placed. The clinical explanation of this palsy or St Vitus's dance is that the victim's head is supported by a spring. Yet, in the light of Noddy's manifest feeble-mindedness, it is bound to acquire a deeper and more sinister significance. One recalls Zinsser's description of St John's Evil, a medieval scourge in which whole villages, driven mad by want and misery, went about shaking and nodding. As characters in Dickens and Wagner have their own catch-phrases or themes, so Noddy nods – or 'nidnods' .'There goes the little nodding man,' cries everyone in Toyland. 'Look at his head nid-nodding as he drives.' Noddy himself seems to regard his affliction with pride; it also appears to give pleasure to others. Noddy's milkman is paid in nods: 'He tapped Noddy's head again as soon as it began to stop nodding and made it nod again, up and down, up and down. 'Payment for *two* bottles,' he said.

More striking even than Noddy's imbecility is his timidity, which again borders on the pathological. Courage may be 'a thing to be emulated'; it is not emulated by Noddy. He is terrified of everything. His friend, Big Ears, a hundred-year-old Brownie who acts as a sort of father or male-nurse symbol, knocks at the door: ' "Rat-a-tat-a-tat." Little Noddy woke up in a hurry and almost fell out of bed in fright. His little wooden head began to nod madly.' Bouncing balls scare him so much that he wants to get down a rabbit-hole. He is terrified by the sea ('It's too big. Let's go and find a dear little sea. This one's too big and it keeps moving') and by holidays: ' "They sound sort of prickly," said Noddy. Big Ears laughed and laughed. "Not *holly*-days made of prickly *holly*!" he said.' (Big Ears' laughter is timely: this is about as near a joke as Miss Blyton gets.) When four golliwogs steal his taxi and all his clothes (including 'his dear little trousers and shoes'), 'Noddy couldn't move an inch. He was so full of alarm that he couldn't say a word . . . He wriggled and shouted and wailed, "You bad, wicked golliwogs" . . . Noddy was all alone in the dark wood. "Help!"' he called. "Oh, help, help, HELP! I'm little Noddy and I'm all alone and LOST." ' He is overwhelmed by self-pity. 'He stumbled along through the trees, tears running down his cheeks.

"I've lost my hat,
I've lost my car;
I simply don't know
Where they are!
I'm all alone;
Won't ANYBODY
Come to help
Poor little Noddy" '

Help, of course, is soon forthcoming, in the shape of Big Ears and Mr Plod the policeman, who arrest the golliwogs and restore Noddy's possessions to him. Though utterly resourceless himself, Noddy is never in trouble for long. There is always somebody to run to, someone to whine and wail at. The machinery of benevolent authority (Big Ears) or of the state (Mr Plod) can always be invoked to redress the balance between cowardice, weakness and inanity on the one hand, and vigour, strength and resource on the other. In some respects, the Noddy books give the impression of being an unintentional yet not wholly inaccurate satire on – or parody of – the welfare state and its attendant attitudes of mind.

If Noddy is 'like the children themselves', it is the most unpleasant child that he most resembles. He is querulous, irritable and humourless. ' "Whoo-ooo-ooo!" said the wind at the top of its voice, and blew some flowers out of a jug on Noddy's table. "Don't," said Noddy. "Now look at the mess you've made! It's my busy morning, too!" ' A clockwork clown turns somersaults in Noddy's garden. 'Do stop, clown,' Noddy frets, 'you always make me feel so dizzy . . . Oh, don't start going head-over-heels again. Look, you've squashed one of my plants.' He is unnaturally priggish. 'I would rather like to see you knock a lamp-post down,' says the clown: 'BANG! What a noise it would make.' 'Now you're being silly,' is Noddy's sanctimonious reply. He is also a sneak. An elephant from Mr Noah's Ark wants Noddy to drive it to the wood, so that it can knock down trees: 'That's what real elephants do,' it explains. Noddy, of course, is 'alarmed'. 'That's silly and dangerous . . . you're a very bad elephant. I shall tell Mr Noah of you.' The elephant struggles into the taxi. ' "Please get out," begged little Noddy' – all to no avail. Off they go, Noddy's head nodding sadly ('Whatever was he to do?') and the elephant thoroughly enjoying itself, blowing the horn and making everyone jump 'dreadfully'. Soon the elephant goes to sleep. Noddy's head nods 'madly'; he smiles to himself: 'he knows what to do'. 'What to do' is, of course, to drive the elephant to Mr Noah's Ark, report it, and request that it be smacked: 'Certainly, certainly, certainly,' says Mr Noah.

In this witless, spiritless, snivelling, sneaking doll the children of England are expected to find themselves reflected. From it they are to derive 'ethical and moral' edification. But Noddy is not merely an example: he is a symbol. Noddy, according to Miss Blyton, 'is completely English, and stands for the English way of life. He's very popular in Germany. It's interesting to think that a generation of young Germans is absorbing English standards and English morals.' The Russians, it seems, have pirated some of Miss Blyton's books, but not yet Noddy. 'I wish they would,' says Miss Blyton. 'I don't care about the royalties – I should like the Russian children to read English stories. It might help them to understand our way of life.' It is disquieting to reflect that they might indeed.

It remains only to add that Miss Blyton was a strong supporter of Suez. So, I bet, was Noddy: indeed, circumstantial evidence might suggest that he was the moving spirit behind the whole enterprise.

Encounter, January 1958

*A Black Blimp**

It was with a leaden heart, I must confess, that I embarked on 690 pages of Baldwin – you know, the black New York novelist and publicist, buddy of Eldridge Cleaver, Bobby Seale and the Revd Martin Luther King. (Of this last friendship, to be sure, *honi soit qui mal y pense*. As Baldwin reminds us, King was no inner city Runcible; informing his black flock that negroes, ten per cent of the population of St Louis, were responsible for fifty-eight per cent of its crime, he stoutly adjured them to hoist their moral standards, to save money and to stop blaming the white man.) Apart from my own strong if insecurely founded prejudices against Baldwin, how unreassuring the dust-jacket! On the back peers forth from modish gloom, like a ravaged dark moon in its second quarter, half of the author's face, epicene, 'sensitive', wounded, anguished, deeply trenched (perhaps in part by beatings from cops and other whites?) It recalled for me the odious ET or the features, burnt-corked, of Robert Helpmann or even Dirk Bogarde – another death in another Venice, Black Death perhaps in Venice West? Not less daunting is a blurb from the *Times Literary Supplement*: 'His art is nourished and sustained by an unquenchable rage.' Presumably intended as a compliment in an age in which anger is no longer regarded as a deadly sin, is it really more flattering than to pronounce his art to be nourished and sustained by prodigious doses of brandy or heroin or even by clinical insanity, all equally destructive of every faculty a writer needs? Is the company of a man unquenchably angry more to be sought than that of a dog with *la rage*?

* Review of *The Price of a Ticket: Collected Non-Fiction 1948–1985* by James Baldwin, Michael Joseph, 1986

Well, the great tome first fell open for me at page 101, and I was confronted with an extraordinarily sad, penetrating and sympathetic study of Gide and homosexuality. Nothing odd about that, surely, you say: isn't Baldwin himself a homosexual? Indeed he is, though no stranger to women nor any sort of misogynist. He ruefully recalls his own quick discovery downtown that 'his existence was the punchline of a dirty joke', that he was not 'gay' in those distant days, but a queer, faggot or pussy. Yet he records that what initially made him dislike Gide was the latter's 'Protestantism and homosexuality'. Two surprises here for the price of one, since Baldwin is not widely famed as first wicket down for the Counter-Reformation either, but what he is really deploring in Gide is his *puritanism*, which invests all his work 'with the air of an endless winter'. More genuinely surprising, Baldwin goes on to a melancholy disquisition on the modern homosexual's lot: the possibility of having his pleasures without paying for them; the consequent search, ever more desperate and grotesque, for pleasures; the discovery that sex is only sex, conquests therefore futile and demeaning; the danger of falling into an underworld in which 'he meets neither men nor women, where the possibility of genuine human involvement has ceased'. In the fact that there are two sexes Baldwin finds 'the hope and glory of the world'; 'no matter what demons drive them, men cannot live without women and women cannot live without men': 'when men can no longer love women, they also cease to love or respect or trust each other'. Baldwin expresses great sympathy for Gide's 'agony' in his 'male prison', not less for the long anguish of Mme Gide. Unless my *précis* is sadly misleading, we are in the presence not of 'unquenchable rage' or anything so fatuous, sterile and degrading, but of warm understanding and pity, of woeful yearnings and aspirations, of a profound sense of the tears which are in things, of an envious respect for nature and normality which must appear, in the present social and sexual anarchy, well, *conservative*.

I was amazed and moved by this fine essay, I must confess, and rebuked too: judge not . . . Nor does it stand alone. I could fill the rest of my space with Baldwin's opinions which are highly traditional, or highly critical of aspects of radical *chic*. Baldwin denounces, for instance, the failure of (black) protest novels as caused by their rejection of life and of the human being, by their insistence that categorisation (by colour) alone is real, not to be transcended. Contrasting in *Encounter* in 1951 the black American with his African counterpart, he notes that the American was born in a free society: he wished not to overthrow it but just to make it work for his benefit (a view Baldwin has often since contradicted). He deplores the enormous bitterness left by the American Civil War, suggesting that indignation and goodwill are not enough to make the world better; clarity and charity too are needed, and social indignation may kill personal humility. He hates the 'housing projects' in Harlem, new ghettos far worse than the old, because friends, neighbours, amiable tradesmen and familiar churches are gone. The one great difference between the southern white and the northerner is for him that the southerner remembers with a pang a sort of Eden in which he loved black people and they loved him; is it thus from the south that healing will come?

In the Place de la Concorde Baldwin saw, and sees, the guillotine: 'Anyone who has ever been at the mercy of the people . . . knows something awful about us (the people), will forever mistrust popular patriotism, and avoids even the most convivial mobs.' Yet he finds the 'total indifference' of the French not only better than the 'welfare and chicken-shit goodwill of American liberals', but even in its way a mark of respect: 'If I could make it, I could make it.' He scorns alike 'anti-poverty programmes' in American ghettos and 'foreign aid to the underdeveloped nations', profiting only local adventurers and fat cats, deeply frustrating to the most dedicated, increasing the misery of the voiceless millions. He laments the passing of the old Harlem, still essentially southern, in which any dutiful grown-up would whip the young Baldwin for wrong-doing blocks away from home, and then carry him back for another whipping from mamma or daddy. He learnt there respect for his elders, not fear: 'the child knows whether the hand that strikes is raised in love or not, to help or harm'. He mourns the flower children as doomed orphans. Young whites Baldwin meets in the Village astonish him with their cruel alienation, lacking seemingly all antecedents and connections. 'Do you really *like* your mother?', one asked him, disbelieving in the very possibility. Such questions deepen Baldwin's mistrust of psychiatry, 'a desperate moral abdication', striving to make empty lives tolerable, rendering parents incapable of giving their children any sense of right and wrong, creating that 'howling inner space' which engenders first flower children, then monsters, Weathermen, Symbionese and Mansons.

All these quasi-Blimpish sentiments, so congenial to me, are also authentic Baldwin. Are they typical? Of course not. They bloom shyly and survive with difficulty amidst – indeed, are often contradicted by – great swirling torrents of the religiose radical rhetoric ('white man, hear me!') and resentment, the bitter cant and apocalyptic prophecies for which Baldwin is usually noted. His distaste for the Weathermen and the like would be decidedly more impressive if it were not mocked by bizarre assertions that the Black Panthers are 'a great force for peace and stability in the ghetto'. His fear of 'convivial mobs' in Paris leads to little understanding of white fears of black convivial mobs. His ceaseless denunciations of white brutality to blacks in America would also profit by being balanced against blacks' brutality to blacks in Africa. He notes that an African mistreated in the States can, unlike the American black, appeal to his embassy. Very well: to whom could the millions murdered in Africa have appealed? Baldwin wonders what the Christian world, 'so uneasily silent now' (!), will say when the blacks in South Africa start to massacre the masters who have 'massacred' them for so long? He plainly expects it to express effective disapproval; I expect it won't. Nor will it express effective disapproval of any massacres of blacks by blacks which follow; nor will Baldwin. According to the double standards upheld by Baldwin and most of the Christian world, it's not what you do that matters, but who you are. Anything goes provided it's blacks doing it, whether to someone else or to each other. If two wrongs don't make a right, Baldwin asserts about South Africa, neither does one. Nor do three, may I add?

He accuses the American whites of nursing in their hearts the possibility of genocide, a 'Final Solution'. Indeed, with great reluctance he advised his flock to vote for Carter rather than Reagan to 'outwit the Final Solution' – not to prevent it, but to 'buy time'. Americans are for Baldwin the sickest and 'certainly the most dangerous people of any colour' extant today. He accuses the West of creating famine in Africa, of deliberately starving Africa 'out of existence'. The world's present economic arrangements doom most of it to misery. A form of socialism is therefore needed, to provide 'an ox to be ridden on by the people'. Has not Baldwin noticed that, under most forms of socialism, it is the ox which rides on the people? He laboriously and stridently explains and justifies black anti-Semitism and racism. Yet, as so often, he supplies his own antidote: 'One cannot deny the humanity of another without diminishing one's own.' Poor man, who admires in himself what he pities in others.

Again and again his own old-fashioned humanity reappears, helping to explain his bitterness and to lend it a certain injured dignity. His rage against American society seems to spring not so much from any consistent belief that it is valueless as from a conviction that it has cheated the black man, robbing him of his own history and identity without offering him full access to its own. He does not so much deny the rights of inheritance as roar that he has been swindled out of his own. He quotes with mournful approval Aimé Cesaire of Martinique, about how Europe, to make money, destroyed in Africa with utter ruthlessness languages, tribes, customs and lives, to keep her subject in 'cultural anarchy, in a barbaric state'. With the consequent sense of loss I can sympathise, as with a man who has lost his shadow. Yet I can also envisage another might-have-been world, without slavery or colonialism, in which the black man was left in undisturbed enjoyment of his own 'history'. In such a world Baldwin would not 'divide his time between New York, Massachusetts and the South of France', but would live or die in some remote Borrioboola-Gha, beyond the reach even of Mrs Jellyby's munificence, communicating perhaps with clicks and drums. Would he have lost *nothing* thereby? Would we?

The Spectator, 11 January 1986

Cosmetics for a Nazi

Do you remember those long Scottish expresses which puffed, snaked and struggled through the Highland passes, pulled not by one huge steam locomotive but two? The prudence of the LMS engineers is shared by those now dragging the great Norwegian novelist and Nobel Prize winner, Knut Hamsun, out of the sinister shadows in which he has for forty-odd years languished into the sunshine of critical and popular approval.

For the new paperback edition of *Hunger* is headed by no less than two introductions – the first by Isaac Bashevis Singer, the second by the excellent translator, Robert Bly. Whether or not as a result of their efforts, the book sells like hot cakes, is universally praised and discussed. It deserves to be, for it is a masterpiece of sour, half-mad humour and despair.

Mr Singer's tribute is distinguished not only for its generous enthusiasm but also for the following thought-provoking passage, in which I have italicised the most odd and ambiguous words and phrases:

> During World War II, the 80-year-old Hamsun was guilty of the most *tragic mistake*. Nazi critics *read into* Hamsun . . . support for their ideologies and Hamsun *deceived himself* into thinking that Nazism would spell the end of the left-wing radicalism which repelled him . . . [he] allowed himself to be *taken in* by Nazi demagogues. It was a sad day for many of Hamsun's followers when a picture of him greeting Hitler appeared in the newspapers. In it, Hamsun's face reflects *shame*, while Hitler looks at him *mockingly*.

Now, 'a tragic mistake' – in supporting the Nazis, was Hamsun no more culpable than any eighty-year-old dotard who incautiously steps off the pavement and is run over by a bus?

The word 'guilty' suggests something a bit worse but not much: something akin to the negligence of a dotard who at the wheel unintentionally knocks over a child. Such 'mistakes' are usually regretted by the perpetrators. Not by Hamsun – after the war and in full possession of his brilliant faculties (when charged with collaboration his defence pleaded, to his furious indignation, that he was gaga), he displayed himself totally unrepentant.

Again, the Nazi critics 'read into' his works what they desired to find. Did they? Was there nothing of the sort already there?

And why should Hamsun have 'deceived himself' into thinking that Nazism meant curtains for the left-wing radicalism he loathed? Surely that, among other things, was what Nazism *did* mean? Some of us indeed might argue that Nazism was itself in part an aberrant form of left-wing radicalism: but Hamsun cannot join us here without self-contradiction.

'Shame' on one face, mockery on the other: why should this be so at a meeting which both men had eagerly looked forward to? Centuries of guff about the Mona Lisa's enigmatic smile have shown what can be read into the expression on a pictured face: Timothy Shy thought she was probably wondering whether to have fish for lunch or not.

Yet one must have deep sympathy for Mr Singer's predicament – all the more agonising in that he was born in Poland in 1904 to a family of Hassidic rabbis, and still writes in Yiddish. For him 'the whole modern school of fiction . . . stems from Hamsun . . . they were all his disciples' – Mann, Schnitzler, Stefan Zweig, Wassermann, Bunin, D'Annunzio, Scott Fitzgerald, Hemingway, others, Singer himself.

Yet Hamsun was a Nazi – impossible! So he must be turned into a pseudo-Nazi, a Nazi by mistake or ill-luck, by self-deception, by being hoodwinked, an ashamed Nazi, a Nazi *malgré lui*.

Hamsun might have found this plea, with its suggestion that he was not responsible for his own thoughts and deeds, repugnant and humiliating. Or on the other hand, he might not: for everywhere else in the two introductions is emphasised his 'curious, almost superstitious faith in the unconscious', his joyous obedience to impulse which thus (idiotically) defines 'the essence of right life – "when you are hungry, eat; when you are tired, sleep".' A man governed by such occult or sub-human forces could easily become a Nazi, or murder his mother or what you will, without being fully responsible.

Elsewhere in the introductions in the book itself and in other works of Hamsun, we meet his heroes (variants of himself?) 'frivolous in word and deed', anti-social, 'suicidal', strangers in a foreign land, friendless, because they have no patience with others; their God, nature, indifferent, neutral towards good and evil, often cruel; they themselves 'all children – as romantic as children, as irrational, often as savage', love and sex for them no more than 'a child's game'.

We may further note that Hamsun regarded man as nothing more than 'a chain of moods, constantly changing. Often without a trace of consistency'; that he watches cruel impulses 'calmly, even affectionately'; that his book *Hunger* 'is morally at odds . . . and incompatible with most European moral literature', that it 'blew much moralistic (*sic*) work of the time, like Ibsen's, apart' and that 'Hamsun liked to blow things apart'.

We observe his hatred of the bourgeoisie, in his view villainous hypocrites, profit-obsessed, materialistic, heartless, mendacious, the killers of the impulsive exuberant life he believed in; his hatred of England, in his view the embodiment of these unpleasant characteristics. He preferred always the company of the *Übermensch*, a society based on the *Führerprinzip*.

This is the outlook not of a man who becomes a Nazi by mere chance, as he might fall down an uncovered manhole, but of a man always a Nazi, or nearly so, and this by choice – if there be such a thing. This truth is hidden only from those who regard a writer's political or moral views (or lack of them) as a matter of private whim, irrelevant to his art, in no way influenced by or influencing his general outlook on life, no more important than a funny hat, chosen in an absent-minded moment, or a frightful tie given by an aunt. And many literary critics do think in this way: they are political neuters, moral eunuchs.

'Only connect!' wailed E. M. Forster. Yes, for all is connected.

Hamsun is all of a piece, one single whole man, part genius, part 'trousered ape' (C. S. Lewis's phrase, used by Duncan Williams as the title of a profound book). If he is to be exhumed, it cannot be in bits: it is all or nothing.

The connections were all established by Camus, whom Williams quotes. The rise of Nazism was attributed by Camus to the moral chaos caused by 'an awareness of the absurdity of life'. He wrote of the Nazi time: 'Eveywhere philosophies of instinct were dominant and, along with them, the spurious romanticism which prefers feeling to understanding, as if the two could separated.' Is this not Hamsun to the life?

Camus in 1944 wrote to 'a German friend', accusing him of regarding good and evil as equivalent, to be defined according to one's wishes, and of supposing that 'in the absence of any human or divine code the only values were those of the animal world.' Might this not have been written equally to 'a Norwegian friend'?

Hamsun is dead, Nazism too, at least for the moment. Yet the river of poison in which they floated still flows unchecked through Western thought and literature. Still daily are Christian liberal values mocked and smirched by irresponsible men of talent or even genius. The treason of the clerks is endless.

If the mocked values were in general held dear, or even the poison were clearly recognised for what it is, why should we worry? As it is, we must tremble as we wonder 'what rough beast, its hour come round at last, slouches towards Bethlehem to be born.'

Yeats called his poem 'The Second Coming'. There could be a third, a fourth . . .

Daily Telegraph, 8 March 1976

From Boy Scout to Myth[*]

I first met Tintin near Tildonk in Belgium in the autumn, it must have been, of 1944. We were out of the line, billeted in the mansion of a sugar tycoon who, thought to have been too sweet to the departing Germans, had departed too. It looked much like Captain Haddock's ancestral seat, Marlinspike Hall, an imposing edifice unmistakably Belgian rather than English and perhaps more like an *hôtel de ville* or *mairie* than a gentleman's château.

A slight snag here? You can easily enough translate the text into English or, as has been done, into almost every language under the sun. The utterances of Snowy (in French, Milou) are readily transposed from the original – 'wooah', 'wouah' or 'waaooouuu', the piteous howl with which the poor little dog laments his master's death. You can find acceptable substitutes for Captain Haddock's spectacular floods of bibulous ire and invective – though at least one uncomplimentary epithet, *clysopompe*, was put into his mouth by his creator Hergé without realising what it meant. What does it mean then? I'm glad you asked that question. Well, er, so far as my medical French stretches, it appears to be a dire arrangement of tubes more properly inserted into the rectum for intestinal irrigation than into a strip cartoon for children.

But the pictures can't, of course, be transplanted. For instance, walking through what is apparently a little English seaport, his face buried in a newspaper, Captain Haddock crashes smack (in French, I fancy, dzing! or dzionnng!) into one of those iron publicity pillars, so characteristic of bloody abroad yet unknown

* Review of *Hergé and Tintin, Reporters* by Philippe Goddin, translated by Michael Farr, Sundancer, 1988

CW aged sixteen at Stowe

here. The Captain's astonishment and rage are in the circumstances very understandable. But what child would ever worry about such trifling incongruities? And anyway most of Tintin's adventures take place in exotic places like Tibet or on the moon, meticulously researched, with which few children or grown-ups are familiar.

The friendly farmer and his wife next door invited me to dinner. They regaled me with the horrors of life under German occupation. Above all, the Germans had even paid such high wages to munitions workers that it was impossible to keep anyone on the land. '*Tiens!*' I cried, or words to that effect. I might have been listening to a farmer moaning at home. Monsieur went out to the cows. 'Can you read to the children while I do the dinner?' Madame asked, and handed me a Tintin book. The children wriggled with eager delight. They knew well what to expect, were my French up to it. I was captivated at once: the drawings so bright, so clear, so deceptively simple, so easy to 'read'. And the characters: never in a children's book had I bumped into grown-ups depicted with such wild humour, at once broad and sophisticated.

The Captain himself, met then or later with children of my own, more or less permanently drunk and explosively irascible, yet fundamentally generous and brave. The Professor, endlessly inventive and resourceful, stone deaf, misunderstanding all the questions, coming up with all the answers, hilariously inconsequential. Tintin dives for treasure. 'It worries me a bit,' says the Captain, 'that Tintin hasn't come up again.' 'No,' replies the Professor, 'but I was a great sportsman in my youth'. Ah me . . .

Then there are the two detectives, the moustached Thompsons, identical twins, equally and impenetrably stupid, charged to protect Tintin, themselves in constant need of protection and rescue. The Professor has invented a space-saving wall-bed. Descending to open, it inevitably crowns the Thompsons, producing multi-coloured stars and jamming their howler hats hard down over their ears. Closing again, it carries the dazed Thompsons with it into the wall. The Professor is surprised and mildly grieved: 'Between ourselves, I wouldn't have expected such childish pranks from them. They looked quite sensible – ' Looks can deceive.

Then there is Snowy himself, alert, curious, noisy, enthusiastic, all dog, present in almost every frame, inspecting, head on one side, all that goes on, intervening decisively when necessary, almost permanently attended by a large question or exclamation mark. I treasure specially a drawing, reproduced in this book, of the enormous skeleton of the prehistoric Diplodocus Gigantibus in the museum at Klow. The curator is staring in horror, a vast bone is missing from its right foreleg. We share his perplexity till we note Snowy fleeing, bone clamped firmly between his teeth.

As we read and looked at the pictures in the flickering firelight, poor old Hergé (actually Georges Remi, who reversed his initials to make his pseudonyms R.G., thus Hergé) was having rather a rough time not far away. He had insouciantly gone on appearing in a newspaper the Germans had 'stolen' and which was otherwise full of inflammatory Nazi propaganda. Come the Liberation, the paper was closed and all journalists and other contributors who had worked on it during the Occupation were banned. Hergé was arrested four times, though only for a few hours, and spent one night in a cell. His stuff became too hot to handle. Printers refused it: the journalists' union blacked him, as the Gestapo had partly blacked him before. He appears to have been outraged, and retained bitter memories of 'an experience of complete intolerance'.

To what extent, if any, had he asked for it? This book, a confusing account by various hands of the life, times and works of Hergé, is not a great help. It mentions pictures which, at the height of the war, 'featured one or other stereotype of a Jew'. It reproduces none. It pleads that their full 'tactlessness' could only be gauged when all the horrors of the Holocaust were known, as they were not known then, either to Hergé or to his detractors. Moreover, Hergé caricatured many, many stereotypes. Had Hitler massacred the blacks, would his irreverent drawings of the Congolese have appeared tactless? Perhaps so in our hypersensitive age.

The text of the book is frequently vague, evasive, abstract, at times unintelligible, though whether this is the translator's fault or the original writer's is difficult to say. What are we to make of sentences like this: 'Nevertheless at the moment where one gets ready to accuse Snowy of having rummaged in the dustbins of the Gestapo, too many pictures seemed crushing for their author'?

Hergé appears to have known Léon Degrelle, presumably the leader of the Belgian Fascists, though the book doesn't say so very explicitly. An agent of Degrelle's certainly offered Hergé during the war a job as official illustrator to the Belgian Fascist movement. He refused it. Why he was offered it, why he refused, we are not told.

What sort of chap was Hergé really? We meet him first as a Catholic boy scout, and that he seems to have remained in essence all his life. Scouting, he records, gave him 'a taste of friendship, love of nature, animals, games. It is a good school. All the better if Tintin bears the hallmark.' Scouting took him to the Pyrenees, his 'Tibet', 300 kilometres on foot. It took him walking and camping all his life. It was scouting which presumably later clapped rucksacks on to wives No 1 and 2, one wife replacing the other after an extremely muddling mental, moral and marital crisis, which wife No 2, in an unusually sensible and sympathetic memoir, effectively discounts.

The drawings from Hergé's scout period are often comic, sometimes richly romantic. A cover he did for *Le Boy-Scout Belge* in 1928 would raise any eyebrow. Is the scout depicted as a girl? Presumably not, but if he were he'd be a stunner, rather in the style of a twenties fashion-plate.

Hergé found in scouting all of Tintin, so we are told – ordered adventure, reasoned audacity, love of action, joy, the search for good, the tackling of every test. Are there perhaps also here hints and echoes of a sort of fascism, of an innocent fascism, seemingly devoid of evil and full of promise, a fascism which beguiled for a time in the thirties many ardent and restless spirits yearning for a new comradeship? Was Hergé thus beguiled? The book offers few insights, no answers.

It is a maddening book. The lay-out lads have had a field day, laying out everybody and everything in sight. Two artistic directors were let loose, advised by an artistic adviser. The result is modish chaos. In the beginning was perhaps the word: but look what happens next! The art boys have suppressed half the page numbers and detached the captions from the pictures, with only little triangular markers to tell us vaguely what they refer to. The text is cut up, packed away in confusing boxes, printed on backgrounds of different colours (all signifying something, but what?), reduced to a mere trickle or a string of puddles between the graphics, treated with no respect at all. All is for show. Even the contents pages, though pretentiously arty, are near incomprehensible.

Nor does the text, in fact, deserve much respect. Reasonably vivid and evocative at the start, it degenerates into what sounds like pompous excerpts and perorations from corporate after-dinner speeches – not wholly inappropriate, I grant, considering the extent to which Hergé dwindled from a fresh and charming genius into an invaluable corporate asset.

To crown all, a thinker called Pierre Yves Bourdil contributes an astonishing piece of gobbledegook called 'Tintin: A Myth in this Century'. The dreaded name of Sartre is invoked. Hergé's work is hailed as 'mythical': 'We use it, in a sense, like the Bible.' Tintin 'reveals to us the essential'. We are guided by him 'in a world which, without Hergé, we would find senseless.' Tintin's lunar adventure is 'much richer than reality'. A magazine confers on it 'a quasi-religious sense' and shrieks from its cover at the ascending rocket, '*Allo Allo, ici la Terre. Au nom du ciel, Tintin, repondez*!' The death of Hergé in 1983, like that of a father, 'marks the coming of our adulthood'. We must thenceforth 'judge for ourselves a world that previously we had understood through the medium of another mind'. Hergé's Tintin is a hero 'to whom the gods have given a destiny'. He lives thus in a world 'entirely meaningful'. Like Oedipus, Tintin solves riddles, 'because the gods inspire him'. 'Hergé, through the delicious music of his work, makes us participate in our century . . . ' Phew!

I struggled through this portentous cant with increasing

curiosity: who can possibly have written it? Who is M. Bourdil? Is he also a myth? Could he perhaps be a top executive in Studios Hergé who has weird visions and dreams and whom none dares tell to shut up? Or some mad metaphysician, now at work on the mythical aspects of Tom and Jerry? Be that as it may, I advise you to give him a myth.

I read him with incredulous exasperation and turned quickly back to the English version of *Red Rackham's Treasure*, as if for a breath of fresh air. On the desert island the Captain is also exasperated. 'Billions of blue blistering barnacles,' he roars. 'I've had enough!' My sentiments, exactly. He seizes an axe, brandishes it furiously. 'Leave me alone!' he thunders. 'I've got to let fly at something!' He sinks the axe furiously into the trunk of a tree. A deafening hail of coconuts falls on his unprotected head. Stars dance. 'Thousands of thundering typhoons!' He looks up apprehensively. 'That's the lot, eh?' No: one more hits him smack in the eye. Now there's a myth for you, a myth with a moral: the fruits of rage are sorrow or, watch it, nuts can hurt.

To avert the wrath of M. Bourdil, let me be quite fair. As you'd expect, the subordination of the word to the image in this book does mean page after page of marvellous pictures, not only brilliant in themselves but profoundly interesting as showing how Hergé worked. We see his drawings in all their stages, rough draft, polished up, traced, inked in, coloured, completed. We see how careful and solid and craftsmanlike his work is, everything as carefully constructed as a fine old chest of drawers, nothing skimped or left to chance. We also realise, or I did, that Hergé was an even finer draughtsman than the finished product might always suggest. Those first sketches, as also all pictures done for his own pleasure, are, like Constable's, unbelievably free, bold, fleet, wild and flowing, full of expression and movement. It would be absurd, I think, to maintain that in the long process of rendering them absolutely clear, precise and 'legible' nothing was lost at all. If this book is worth £25, it must be for the pictures alone.

The Spectator, 13 February 1988

Black Magic, White Lies

Whoever decided to prosecute *Lady Chatterley's Lover* may be proud of his handiwork. Despite his efforts the book is now in print. Apart from exposing the law to ridicule by forcing it to assess merits, literary and otherwise, which it is not qualified to assess, his achievement is solely this: to have secured for the book the maximum of publicity and a volume of clerical, academic and critical acclaim which might have astonished or embarrassed even its author, not the most modest of men nor one with any love of clergymen, dons or critics.

The Bishop of Woolwich has told us that this, in his view, is a book which Christians 'ought to read'. In it, he says, Lawrence has tried to portray sexual intercourse 'as in a real sense an act of holy communion'. Mr Norman St John-Stevas has recommended the book to every Catholic priest and moralist. It is 'undoubtedly a moral book', thinks he. Mr Richard Hoggart declares that the book is 'puritanical' – or rather puritanical in a sense which he defines: 'the proper meaning of it to an historian is somebody who belongs to the tradition of British puritanism. And the main weight of that is an intense sense of responsibility for one's conscience.' The Rector of Eastwood, Lawrence's Nottinghamshire birthplace, has suggested that the book might almost be given 'to young people about to be married as a guide in love and marriage'. Ho hum.

There must be others, neither prigs, fools, nor perverts, who have their doubts about all this; who, while conceding that *Lady Chatterley* is a work of great literary merit, indeed of dark, magical and terrible beauty, nevertheless believe it to be a profoundly immoral or even evil work. There must be others, in a word, who have *understood* it. If so, they have not yet spoken. They were not asked to at the trial. Since then they may not have dared to, such is the terror inspired by Lawrence's victorious partisans. Yet a word or two must perhaps be said, lest posterity think we were all bewitched. And I hope it may be said without denying to Lawrence either the admiration due to his genius or the sympathy due to his sickness and sufferings in mind and body.

As a guide to love and marriage *Lady Chatterley* is somewhat unorthodox, to say the least, in that the central situation is doubly adulterous. The clergymen at the trial seemed somewhat shifty about this, as well they might be.

The Bishop of Woolwich, for instance, said that the book 'portrays the love of a woman in an immoral relationship, *so far as adultery is an immoral relationship*,' but that it does not advocate 'adultery for its own sake'. The Revd Donald Tytler wriggled for some time before admitting that neither Connie nor Mellors appeared to 'regard marriage as sacred and inviolable'. He took refuge, however, in the highly arguable assertion that the book 'is a novel, not a tract'.

It seemed generally agreed that the adultery was largely incidental or irrelevant, a chance twist of the plot. It was implied, indeed, that the real meaning of the book would not have been much damaged or altered if Sir Clifford and Bertha had never existed and the two lovers had been happily married by page 120 in the Penguin edition. This, I think, is to misunderstand the main *negative* purpose of the book, which is to undermine or utterly destroy the Christian attitude to sex, love and marriage – an operation in which Lawrence could hardly have expected or even welcomed the assistance of the clergy.

Most Christians, I believe, are taught to honour sex as an essential part of love and marriage, not as an end in itself but as a means by which love may express itself and marriage be blessed with children. If Lawrence does not regard sex as an end in itself, he certainly endows it with priority not only over marriage but over love as well. For in *Lady Chatterley* the first sexual act between Connie and Mellors quite definitely precedes any love between them and, if love in any sense comes later, it cannot finally find expression in sex, because it is from sex that it first issued.

This is quite in keeping with Lawrence's general view of human relations, which seems to be that there can be no contact between people except physical, no knowledge of others except carnal knowledge, no love or responsibility without sex, no intercourse which is not largely or fundamentally sexual. Even his men are subject to this rule: they wrestle or embrace in the nude, they 'press' against each other, their love is 'perfect for a moment'. 'If I love you, and you know I love you,' Middleton Murry plaintively asked Lawrence, 'isn't that enough?' No, it wasn't, Lawrence retorted: there must be a physical mingling of their blood, an inviolable pre-Christian sacrament which should bind them together in blood-brotherhood.

It is Lawrence's point in *Lady Chatterley* that, beside sex, marriage is but an empty form, a thing meaningless in itself, and that wherever the claims of sex and marriage are in conflict those of sex must prevail. Had Connie and Mellors been free to marry at once, this point could not have been so clearly established. The adulterous nature of their union is thus an essential part of the plot, as is the disgusting nature of Mellors' marriage, and the dry vacuity of Connie's. All together, by making marriage appear ridiculous or nauseating, serve to throw pure sexuality into sharper and more admirable relief.

Marriage and love, of course, are not identical, and a book which derides the one might certainly be redeemed and ennobled by the other. Is *Lady Chatterley*, then, a book about love? One must speak here with some diffidence. One man's love may be another's lust, and it is quite possible that Lawrence wrote of what he thought was love, or of love as he knew it. If love at all, however, the love which he celebrates is certainly of a very narrow, introverted sort, in many respects remarkably akin to the masturbation which he so eloquently denounces in *Obscenity and Pornography*.

Much was made at the trial of Mellors' alleged assumption of 'responsibility' for Lady Chatterley. I have read very carefully the passage on p. 123 cited by Mr Richard Hoggart in support of this allegation. In it I find little suggestion that Mellors has willingly assumed any responsibility for anything. All I find there is a certain foreboding, vague premonitions of 'pain and doom' ahead, regret at the loss of his own privacy, a conviction that 'they' will do her in, 'no sense of wrong or sin'.

Conscience, for Mellors, is 'chiefly fear of society'. And indeed he swiftly shifts the responsibility for all that may go ill from his own shoulders on to those of society, which he knows 'by instinct to be a malevolent, partly insane beast'; on to the shoulders of 'the vast evil thing', of the 'the world of the mechanical greedy, greedy mechanism and mechanised greed' which is 'ready to destroy whatever does not conform'. The book ends, incidentally, with Connie and Mellors still undestroyed: society seems momentarily to have lost its grip.

One difficulty about Mellors assuming much responsibility for Connie is his apparent failure to assume any responsibility for any of the women he has previously bedded, including his wife and the long list of conquests of which he boasts to Connie on pp. 211–12. Admittedly his sexual experiences with these women, though varied, are uniformly unsatisfactory. Their efforts to please him awaken in Mellors no sign of sympathy, gratitude or kindliness towards them: only rage and bitterness because they failed. The lesbians were the worst, it seems: they made him 'howl in his soul, wanting to kill them'.

Thus is established another point that Lawrence wished to make: that no responsibility whatever is inherent in the sexual act as such. It is inherent only in the *perfect* sexual act. If this is an argument against promiscuity, it seems a very dubious one, since, like poor Soames Forsyte, we may wish and wish and never get it; seek and seek and never find it – the beauty and the loving in the world.

The common experience of people in requited love is to love not merely one person but, through that one person, a whole universe. Love opens the eyes and the heart, revealing the beauty in all things. In gratitude we love the God that created the beloved one. We love the sun and all it shines upon. We love even those we hate, seeing in them also for a moment our common humanity made manifest. We are one with all. Thus through earthly love even the most mundane of us may sense that unearthly love or charity which has been expressed, for instance, in our own day in the noble and joyous *passacaglia* by which Hindemith represents St Francis's hymn of praise and gratitude to God for all creation. It is this smiling, generous, and life-enhancing quality which may give even to illicit love an undeniable dignity and grace, and which makes even the strictest churchman – if he be not himself embittered or perverted – regard it as not the meanest of sins.

Of this quality there is in *Lady Chatterley* as little trace as in any novel which deals with man and woman at all. A misanthrope from the start ('oh, well, I don't like people'), Mellors' hatred of humanity becomes ever more violent and hysterical as his affair with Lady Chatterley proceeds and intensifies. His dislike of Sir Clifford is natural enough in the circumstances. Less natural is the form it takes: a bitter contempt for Clifford's impotence, brought about by a war injury: 'no balls . . . tame, and nasty with it'. This contempt finds its most vivid expression in an insult, addressed to Sir Clifford himself, of such brutal coarseness as to make the blood run cold: 'It's not for a man i' the shape you're in, Sir Clifford, to twit me for havin' a cod atween my legs.'

'Reverence for a man's balls?' 'Yes, indeed,' answered Mr Hoggart at the trial. Mellors' reverence is selective. He reveres his own balls; he does not appear to revere Sir Clifford's, or even to regret their absence.

While Mellors' love for Connie is unable to generate the slightest tenderness for any other being, his hatred for Sir Clifford and for his own wife spreads and burgeons, overwhelming all barriers, engulfing finally the whole human race. It is a constant complaint of Mellors that there are too many people around. It seems to him 'a wrong and bitter thing' to bring a child into this world. He brings one, none the less; but this is 'a side-issue', he says.

In his wild and maundering monologues it is sometimes

difficult to distinguish the misanthrope from the reformer. It is plain that he cannot tolerate anyone as they are: clumsy, ugly, deformed, money-grubbing, sexless; the middle classes, 'the mingiest set of ladylike snipe ever invented'; the working classes, 'just as priggish and half-balled and narrow-gutted', etc. In certain circumstances, indeed, the latter might be spared, provided they wear 'close red trousers, bright red, an' little short white jackets' and provided they do not 'have many children, because the world is overcrowded'. But this is a momentary weakness.

In general Mellors is 'pleased that they [the human race] hurry on towards the end'. Provided his 'cock gives its last crow', he doesn't mind. 'To contemplate the extermination of the human species and the long pause before some other species crops up' calms him 'more than anything else'. And even this gloomy contentment is untypical.

Sometimes Mellors wants to get away from it all: 'I feel the colonies aren't far enough, because even there you could look back and see the earth, dirty, beastly, unsavoury among all the stars: made foul by men.' At other times he wishes to hasten the process of depopulation by more drastic means. He wishes he had shot his wife: 'she was a doomed woman . . . I'd have shot her like I shoot a stoat. . . a raving doomed thing . . . If only I could have shot her . . . it ought to be allowed.' And not his wife alone: 'I could wish the Cliffords and Berthas all dead'; it would be 'the tenderest thing you could do for them', perhaps, 'to give them death . . . They only frustrate life . . . Death ought to be sweet to them. And I ought to be allowed to shoot them.'

It would be wrong to accuse Mellors of a total disrespect for all forms of life. But he respects only subhuman life, life without mind or soul. He can appreciate in a certain context 'the prettiness and loneliness' of the weasel, for instance, but only to show that he would have more qualms about shooting a weasel than about shooting all the Cliffords and Berthas, who 'are legion'.

'Legion' – that we may well believe: included among them, presumably, is every sad maimed, or unfulfilled person, all to be shot down like stoats. For in his Starkadder ravings poor Mellors is only feebly echoing the murderous fantasies of his own creator, whose letters and conversation breathe a bloodthirsty hatred of mankind in no way unworthy of Hitler; of the Lawrence 'who hated men', who would have liked to kill 'a million Germans – two millions', who longed for 'a deadly revolution very soon' and 'cared' only for 'the death struggle', who wanted every she-tigress to have seventy-seven whelps, each to eat 'seventy miserable featherless human birds', who wanted to have 'poison fangs and talons', who *believed* (his italics) 'in wrath and gnashing of teeth and crunching of cowards' bones' and 'in fear and pain and oh, such a lot of sorrow', who wanted to kill 'beastly disdainful bankers, industrialists, lawyers, war-makers, and schemers of all kinds', as well as, first of all, his inoffensive hostess at Taos, Mabel Luhan; of the Lawrence to whom Jesus became ever 'more *unsympatisch*' the longer he lived.

It is pity more than terror that is awakened by Lawrence's anguished flailings, by his rages and torments. And it is pity too, more than anything else, that we feel for Mellors in his loneliness and bitterness, in the eerie solitude into which, trapped himself, he lures Connie to join him, pity for a man so profoundly wretched that even love itself can bring him no more happiness or serenity than an ingrowing toe-nail.

If *Lady Chatterley* is not a book about marriage or love (or, if about love, then about a rather odd and unsatisfactory sort of love), what then is it about?

I have referred to its negative purpose: the destruction of the Christian attitude to sex, love and marriage. What is its positive purpose? In place of the Christian attitude what does it positively suggest? At this point, strange to say, we can take a hint from the Bishop of Woolwich who does seem in a muddled sort of way to have grasped that the book is not quite as simple as it looks, that there are mysterious undercurrents and undertones in it, suggestions of the supernatural. 'An act of holy communion' – yes: at this point the Bishop shows that he has both vaguely discerned and profoundly misunderstood what Lawrence was really getting at.

Hugh Kingsmill described Lawrence as 'a pseudo-mystic'. 'The pseudo-mystic,' he explained, 'whether Lawrence with an audience of thousands, or Lenin and Hitler addressing millions, appeals to the will in language borrowed from the spirit.'

Lawrence's essential credo is bluntly expressed by himself as follows:

> My great religion is a belief in the blood, the flesh, as being wiser than the intellect. We can go wrong in our minds. But what our blood feels and believes and says is always true. The intellect is only a bit and bridle . . . All I want is to answer my blood, direct, without fribbling intervention of mind, or moral, or what not . . . The real way of living is to answer to one's wants . . . 'For the living of my full flame – I want that liberty, I want that woman, I want that pound of peaches . . . '

More commonly this credo is expressed in pseudo-mystical terms: 'And God the Father, the Inscrutable, the Unknowable, we know in the Flesh, in Woman.' We are so flattered and gratified at being thus assured that the appetite for women is in fact a religious appetite that we may overlook the fact that the God thus revealed to us is not our God but Lawrence's God; not the God even of the most progressive bishop, but that 'protozoic God' which, according to Middleton Murry, Lawrence 'would if he could put us all on the rack to make us confess'.

A similar sleight of hand is attempted in *Lady Chatterley* and, to judge by the volume of clerical applause, successfully brought off.

Certainly, the book is full of religious imagery and symbolism, and in the grave simplicity and majesty of its prose it is sometimes possible to catch more than an echo of the Authorised Version. Indeed, without any obvious defiance of the author's intentions, the whole book can be read as an elaborate and blasphemous parody of the Gospels.

The first key is supplied by Tommy Dukes, whose racy,

prophetic utterances place him in the role of a sort of clubman John the Baptist. 'Our old show will come flop,' he cries. 'Our civilisation is going to fall. It's going down the bottomless pit, down the chasm. And believe me, the only bridge across the chasm will be the phallus.' On the far side, he explains, is a 'next phase', in which mankind, regenerated by the phallus, should consist of 'real, intelligent, wholesome men and wholesome nice women'. There will be 'a resurrection of the body'. At this phrase 'something echoes inside Connie'. She, like the children of Israel, is 'waiting'. In the empty incompleteness of her unregenerate life she waits for completion, for fulfilment, redemption; for the promised one, the saviour, the phallus.

Nor does she wait in vain. And when the phallus comes 'with the dark thrust of peace and a ponderous primordial tenderness', she is reborn just as the converted are re-born in Christ: 'She was gone, she was not, and she was born: a woman.' To the astonished Sir Clifford, she declares that the body, killed off by Jesus, is now 'coming really to life, it is really rising from the tomb'. 'Give me the body,' she cries. 'The life of the body is a greater reality than the life of the mind.' Rising at last to an exalted climax, she proudly proclaims that 'whatever God there is has at last wakened up in my guts . . . and is rippling so happily there, like dawn.'

In this context it is clear enough that Mellors is not indulging in any figure of speech when he addresses his own penis as 'the king of glory': he is speaking the sober truth as he sees it. Here, too, he faithfully echoes his creator, who was accustomed to view the parts of the body as endowed with separate life: endowed, in the case of Mellors' penis, not merely with a will of his own but with mastery over Mellors, 'a root in his soul'.

In this context, too, it is clear enough that when Mellors, 'with an odd intentness' and with a look of which Connie 'could not understand the meaning', wreathes his pubic hair and hers with forget-me-nots and woodruff, and winds 'a bit of creeping-jenny round his penis', this is not just innocent love play or some other questionably pretty fancy No, indeed this is the solemn moment at which the votaries ceremonially deck their idol with all the bounty of nature in token of their gratitude, dependence and self-abasement.

For this is what the book is really about: not love or marriage but the worship of the phallus. It is not a novel in the puritan tradition either as that tradition actually existed or as Mr Hoggart somewhat naïvely defines it. (For surely it is naïve to interpret puritanism as a reliance upon one's own uninstructed conscience, without reference to God's teaching as revealed in the Holy Bible? Puritanism without the Book is not merely *Hamlet* without the prince; it is *Hamlet* without Shakespeare, without its creator. Without the Book, Jomo Kenyatta is a Puritan.)

No, *Lady Chatterley* is a novel in a far older and darker tradition, in a tradition which since the coming of Christianity has been half-submerged, emerging in the West only fitfully and surreptitiously in the guise of 'the Old Religion'. *Its tradition is the tradition of witchcraft.* The orgiastic rites it celebrates bear precisely the same relationship to the Holy Communion as the Black Mass does to the true Mass. Tam O'Shanter was at least drunk when, carried away by the young witch's ample charms, he suddenly roared out, 'Weel done, Cutty-Sark!'

Nor is *Lady Chatterley* only a novel: it is a tract also. It does not merely depict: it preaches. And what it preaches is this: that mankind can only be regenerated by freeing itself from the tyranny of the intellect and the soul, from the tyranny of Jesus Christ, and by prostrating itself before its own phallus; in other words, by reducing itself almost to an animal level (almost, but not quite: for animals are mercifully incapable of the morbid cerebrations – 'sex in the head' – which alone could generate such fantasies). If this is not a doctrine calculated to deprave and corrupt, I do not know what is.

'Deprave and Corrupt' – was the jury's verdict confirmation of what many have long suspected, that these words have pretty well lost all meaning? Along with belief in original sin we seem to have discarded any belief in the original innocence which the verbs 'to deprave and to corrupt' presuppose. And certainly it is slightly ridiculous to talk of a *book* corrupting a society in which, if present tendencies are maintained, it may soon be quite usual for a schoolgirl to have an abortion before she can read.

Nor is *Lady Chatterley* likely to deprave and corrupt *many* people. It is unlikely to corrupt anyone who reads it with as little attention and understanding as that displayed by most of those who spoke up on its behalf at the trial. Nor is it likely to corrupt those millions who are now going to read it for what are laughingly called 'the wrong reasons', just skimming through looking for the dirty bits. There is nothing particularly depraving in the mere description of the sexual act, nor corrupting in a mere four-letter word, and the skimmers are unlikely to find much more in the hook than that.

No, the people it is most likely to corrupt are those few who are going to read it 'for the right reasons', the earnest ones who will read it carefully with sympathy and respect, and who have sufficient intelligence and knowledge to grasp the point. Heaven knows, it is difficult enough to keep one's sanity under the impact of Lawrence's torrential eloquence, his proud solemnity and poetic gifts. Was ever spring more tenderly or beautifully described than in this book? It is only too easy to surrender to his warlock spells and incantations, to his hallucinatory repetitions and variations, to his dithyrambic rhapsodising. Was ever book less boring? It is about as boring as the explosion of a moral H-bomb. To compel assent Lawrence has arts enough of his own. He hardly needed the full weight of clerical and academic approval to make him well-nigh irresistible.

A book which Christians *ought* to read? A book, rather, which Christians may read, or some Christians anyway – those, perhaps, with long spoons.

Encounter, February 1961

The World of William

Down memory lane we saunter, scuffed shoes kicking up the dust, laces undone, patterned stockings at half mast, the old tweed suit of knickers and jacket rent and mud-stained, pockets stuffed with string, Plasticine, nails and catapults, with whistles, whiskery sweets and treasured halfpennies and beetles in matchboxes, cap askew, tie over one shoulder, collar in revolt, grubby face contorted into a ferocious scowl, Jumble chasing butterflies or sheep ahead. We are again, as we were in childhood long ago, with our beloved hero and mentor, William, on his way down to the ole barn there to meet the Outlaws, the faithful Ginger, the angst-infested Douglas and the (comparatively) well-informed Henry: he could usually remember whether it was ole Caxton or Wat Tyler who invented the steam engine.

Enemies lurk on every side: Farmer Jenks, General Moult (whose cucumber frame is almost weekly strafed), Miss Milton, ole Markie, William's sorely tried headmaster, the Hubert Laneites led by ole Fat Face in person, all sorts of elderly female cat-lovers, other adversaries, often from the dottier periphery of the world of art, thought or letters, *New Statesman* readers every one, who appear momentarily only to be bitched, bothered, bewildered and driven triumphantly from the field. From every muddy stream and copse and wood and house to be explored, adventure beckons. And at the end looms the probability of retribution, to be exacted by irate parents, by elder brothers and sisters forever love-tormented yet always ready to strike in vengeance, or by one of those aunts, for the most part quite as scaly as the platoon of aunts which bedevilled Bertie Wooster, who play as prominent and malign a part in William's destinies as in Bertie's. Sometimes things by accident go well, and William is showered with unearned honours and rewards; more usually the story ends in disaster, often with William 'a dot on the horizon'.

Are you with me? If your childhood fell somewhere between 1922 (when the first William story appeared in a woman's magazine) and that time (1950? 1960?) when the authoress, Richmal Crompton, began to run out of steam, you probably will be. In a moment of malicious inspiration, abetted by consummate skill, Nicholas Garland based a *New Statesman* cartoon on the famous and evocative Thomas Henry illustrations, with Wilson, Callaghan, Foot and Healey as the Outlaws and Heath most memorably cast as ole Hubert Lane (Thomas Henry was really called Fisher, it seems, and apparently designed the sailor on the Players cigarette packet). The response to Garland's *jeu d'esprit* and its successors was terrific; many wrote in to ask for originals, including a whole high table of Oxford dons. Miss Crompton wrote more than thirty-five William books and must have made a bomb thereby. They went into hundreds of printings. *William the Fourth*, not a distinguished specimen, first published in 1924, had been reprinted twenty-four times by 1940. And plainly the immense and slightly guilty pleasure which these books gave lives on in countless memories, mostly male, I fancy – yet girls also warmed to William, despite his notorious yet not invariable misogyny.

What was Miss Crompton's secret? I mentioned Bertie Wooster, and certainly Wooster's world and William's have things in common. Both are more or less timeless, little private universes or happy isles from which most of the realities of life – development, pain, sorrow, passion, the struggle for survival, ageing, death and the rest – have been carefully excluded.

Yet William's world differs from Wooster's in that, while personal and private reality is kept at bay, historic reality continually intrudes and is indeed used as the peg upon which many of the stories are hung. In the twenties Bolshevism and fears thereof play a prominent part. William's elder brother Robert is drawn into a secret Bolshevist cell which bears a certain mild and muddled resemblance to that formed by the younger Verkhovensky in Dostoevsky's *Devils*. By some means this group

'The Hubert Laneites went into the village, when they did go into the village, in bands, and took flight on sight of the outlaws. They had met the outlaws in deadly combat before and had no false pride about admitting that discretion is the better part of valour.'

is to secure equal rights and equal wealth for all. Robert approaches his father to suggest, for a start, an equal division of the Brown family assets. Mr Brown, of sterner stuff than old Verkhovensky, is drily uncooperative. The junior Bolshevists, led by William, get the message. They promptly appropriate the senior Bolshevists' cigarettes, cameras, money and so forth. As Marx might have put it, the *Lumpenproletariat* dispossesses the proletariat, and the whole revolutionary movement is dissolved by its own inner contradictions.

William's flirtation with Bolshevism is in fact short-lived. He soon becomes the first to suspect that all eccentric newcomers to the district (and they are mostly very odd indeed) are Bolshevist spies or agents, to be unmasked and denounced with McCarthyite zeal and imprecision, their plans to blow up the village (or the world) to be vigorously frustrated, the captive White Princesses in their power to be set at liberty. And in the thirties, inspired by the oratory of some itinerant blackshirts and parodying the ideological gyrations of his intellectual betters, William actually starts a fascist movement, aimed at world conquest, also short-lived but a terror to the Laneites while it lasts.

Unemployment also has its impact on the Outlaws, despite their inability fully to comprehend what is wrong with having nothing to do. They try to find work for a supposedly unemployed man. The most memorable effort is that of Douglas who, by feigning insanity, hopes to induce his family to engage their protégé as a mental nurse: he is in fact given a Gregory powder.

The war comes. Evacuation gives William the opportunity, in pursuit of some other end, to impersonate a squinting and mentally handicapped evacuee with such exaggeration as to strain the credulity even of the eternally gullible adults who are his chosen butts. 'What's a cow?' he lugubriously inquires. 'What's grass?'

The war ends, involving Miss Crompton in considerable difficulties with Robert and Ethel, William's elder brother and sister who, having served in the forces, then return home, apparently totally unaltered by their experiences, to their familiar world of tennis, fêtes, amateur theatricals and flirtations. The sort of dances Robert and Ethel gave and went to were victualled by jellies, ices, cream, fruit, trifle and sausage rolls. The task of bringing them into the era of rock and roll, discotheques, pop festivals, marijuana and promiscuity may have been beyond her: at any rate, she phases them gradually out.

Even the Rent Laws, and the security of tenure which they occasionally confer upon the unworthy, offer a challenge to William's genius. His beloved Joan writes:

> Dear William, We can't come home because we let it to Miss Evesham unfurnished and we can't get her out and Mummy and I want to come home . . . and *please*, William, will you get us back again because Mummy and I are both so homesick and you're so clever I know you can. Love from Joan.

About problems of 'destatting' William has little to learn from Rachman. He soon succeeds in convincing Miss Evesham that the whole village is in the malign grip of witchcraft: his own blameless parents indeed are deeply involved in the coven. With the aid of a stuffed cat, the illusion is created of a sinister ceremony to end in the sacrifice of Miss Evesham, who swiftly flees.

Another feature which William's world has in common with Wooster's is the almost epidemic prevalence of various forms of mental illness which, whether real or feigned or incorrectly diagnosed, whether mild or severe, are never treated as matters for concern or distress but solely as means of embroiling William and his circle in ever more complex and ludicrous misunderstandings. His own attitude is cool: 'He sat and watched [Miss Polliter's hysterics] with critical enjoyment, as one might watch a firework display or an exhibition of conjuring.' In the same story which takes place by no means untypically in a clinic for nervous diseases, William finds it expedient to lose his memory; confronted by the infuriated mother of the child he is impersonating, he is forced to attribute amnesia to her too. Every angry adult is to him mad. Every high wall must in his view enclose a lunatic asylum. Many of the stories turn on William's capacity to induce two or more people to enter for his own ends into a relationship in which each or all are convinced that the other(s) is/are completely insane. Sir Roderick Glossop would have found in William's world, just as in Wooster's, ample scope for his renowned diagnostic powers.

Like Wodehouse in some respects Miss Crompton may be: but is she as good? Perhaps not; but at her best, in the twenties, the thirties and sometimes in the forties she is not that far behind: she has his tail light in view. She can write poorly. 'It was Miss Spence who voiced the prevailing sentiment about William. She did not say it out of affection for William. She had no affection for William.' As a former classics mistress, Miss Crompton should have been ready enough to see the signs of haste or slackness in that paragraph. On the whole, however, her writing does have a stylised latinate eloquence and orotund

CW (right) with friend on beach

dignity which is greatly relished by children with any love of words – she never writes down to them – and which, by stretching their vocabulary, must do them good. Beetles do not simply walk across the floor: they proceed with stately gravity. Dead, they are not just buried: 'obsequies' are 'solemnly performed'. People do not just come in through the door: they issue, emerge, materialise. Somerville and Ross also have this trick of making the trivial irresistibly comic by describing it in the pompous language of a *Times* leader.

Our parents, I remember, were terrified lest we copy too closely William's fearful accent and fractured syntax. In fact probably most of us spoke like that already, and may well have profited by noting how Miss Crompton expressed herself in the lucid and elegant passages which separate William's rambling, sub-logical, self-justificatory monologues – admirable as we felt these to be.

And many of them are admirable indeed, showing a remarkable imaginative insight, wholly unpatronising, into the semi-delinquent juvenile mind. Take for instance the noble monologue, Wagnerian in its length, prolixity and subtle variations of pace and theme, in which William tries to avert a visit to the dentist. Note how effortlessly he shifts his ground: nothing wrong with his teeth; the dentist a sadistic 'torcherer'; the pain then irrelevant, the danger to his teeth none the less acute if the roots are continuously and gratuitously disturbed; the fact that wild animals and, later, savages, do not visit dentists; the possibility of having a complete set of false teeth installed immediately, once and for all; a considerate desire not to bother Ethel, who has 'kindly' offered to accompany him. William's polemical resources are formidable, if unavailing against Mrs Brown's placid inattention.

In conclusion, may I explain that I am not (or don't think I am) one of those pathetic beings who, happily trapped in a perpetual adolescence, forever read and reread the books and mags of their youth? I enjoyed William when I was young, I enjoyed reading him to my children when they were young. And now, when the editor of the *New Statesman* suggested this piece to me, I enjoyed reading about ten of the William books for the first or second time. If you think me dotty to do so, may I ask you to test your view by reading 'Finding a School for William' in *William The Outlaw* first published in 1927 – a vintage year.

A mysterious and toothy Mr Cranthorpe-Cranborough is invited to stay. The purpose of this visit is concealed from William, whose dark suspicions, instantly aroused, are not allayed by Mr C-C's morbid interest in fractions, decimals, the dates of Queen Elizabeth and other alarming matters. Mr C-C for his part is gratified to find William apparently attentive to his every word: in fact, William is counting Mr C-C's teeth – difficult, because they move about so.

What is Mr C-C up to? He is to meet William's father for the first time that evening. William acts fast. Mr C-C is informed that William's father is stone deaf: 'You've gotta shout *awful* loud to make him hear.' This affliction is not to be mentioned to Mr Brown or any of the family: 'they're sort of sensitive about it'. Later Mr Brown is informed that Mr C-C is also stone deaf and sensitive about it. The two men meet, with William eavesdropping outside the window and Mrs Brown and Ethel listening in terror nearby.

> 'Now about this school' – yelled his father.
>
> 'Exactly,' bellowed Mr Cranthorpe-Cranborough. 'I hope to open it in the spring. I should like to include your son among the first numbers – special terms of course.'
>
> There was a pause. Then William's father spoke in a voice of thunder.
>
> 'Very good of you.'
>
> 'Not at all,' bellowed Mr Cranthorpe-Cranborough.

In the development of this ludicrous interview, and in the deft stratagem by which William finally evades a fate worse than death, Wooster might have recognised the hand of a story-teller worthy of his respect.

New Statesman, 8 November 1974

❦

A Penitent? Er, Welcome

The God of the Labour party is failing again (for the fourth time, by my count), and the usual pitiful stream of disillusioned worshippers is begging us for politico-religious asylum. Here they come, the refugees, haggard-faced, hungry, exhausted, some on crutches, pushing their few remaining possessions along in prams or little handcarts – including perhaps a well-thumbed copy of Crosland's *Future of Socialism* or Wilson's collected speeches, a Fabian tract or two, mute testimony to that moderation moderated by compassion (or vice versa) which led their possessors into error.

And we crusty old folk, who have always tried to keep ourselves nice and respectable in genteel homes in Reactionary Road, Coningsby Crescent, Petit-Bourgeois Place, Bourgeois Boulevard and Lower Middle-Class Lane, are expected to welcome this scarecrow army, to give up our beds, to double up and move over, to set up reception committees and hostels and delousing centres, to distribute blankets, tents, hot meals and drinks, injections against cholera and typhus and, above all, to listen to their interminable sordid and hair-raising tales of life in the Labour loony-bin.

It is all most exasperating. After all, they went in as voluntary patients; so why now all the fuss?

I recall the old Scotch minister who thus admonished his flock: 'Forrnicatorrs! Gamblerrs! Blasphemerrs! Drrunkarrds! Desecratorrs of the Sabbath! In the Lord's guid time ye'll all end up in Hell! And there, from the eternal torment of the flames, which burn and torture but consume not, ye'll cry up, "Oh Lord, sparre us – we didna' ken." And the Lord will luik down in his infinite maircy and thunderr, "Well, ye ken the noo." '

Exactly what I'd like to shout at all these miserable penitents – they ken the noo; but why on earth didn't they ken before?

I survey them with a mean and jaundiced eye, like an RSM inspecting a scruffy draft of new recruits. 'God bless my SOUL – HAM I hexpectcd to make Tories hout of this orrible SHOWER? Gedd up hoff of your KNEES, you frightful little MEN! Squad, squad SHUN! Right TURN! By the right, to the reheducation centre, QUICK march! Hip, hike, hip . . . '

And indeed they are an awkward squad, these penitents. They haven't the truth, so to speak, in their bones. When they were of an impressionable age, freedom did not at once enchant and grip them. No, the first thing to fill their heads and hearts was a load of pseudo-benevolent quasi-totalitarian rubbish. Thus inspired, they helped to create the hell from which they now flee. Taught by bitter experience, they discard the fraudulent passions of their youth, leaving their heads and hearts empty, ready in theory for wisdom to enter.

But alas, how difficult it is after a certain age even to be rid of familiar error, and far more difficult still to master new truths and unfamiliar wisdoms, for which much reading and thought and self-criticism is required, if not a natural predisposition – here presumably lacking – in their favour. No wonder that many ex-socialists, having lost their former daft completeness as socialists, shuffle, stalk and stare through the rest of their lives like zombies, hollow-blasted men, intellectually and emotionally dead, without vision or understanding of any kind.

Yet, Heaven knows, we should welcome them with open arms, crippled and C3 medically as they may be. Elections will not be won, nor countries saved without them, any more than wars won without the most preposterous assistance. The Austrian Emperor did not disdain the services of Schweik.

The trouble is perhaps that, like sergeant-majors, I lack charity. I have always found the parable of the prodigal son the most difficult to understand and accept. 'Joy shall be in Heaven over one sinner that repenteth more than over ninety and nine which need no repentance.' Why so, I mutter sourly. Why lay out the red carpet for that bum? And the fatted calf too – who fatted the ruddy thing? That's what I'd like to know.

The parable does indeed appear to show God in an attractively human light, almost feminine in his impulsive indulgence and capricious affection. Divine justice must be in that parable too: but I suppose I'm too mean-spirited to recognise it.

There is something in me, as certainly in the extreme doctrinaire left, as perhaps in you and in all of us, which longs not only to possess the truth but to be the only one who does possess it, or one of a very small exclusive fraternity. Part of me longs to convert; another part draws haughtily away from converts.

There was a time before the recent war when I was (or wrongly thought I was) Anton Bruckner's only English fan. (Richard Capell, our late respected music critic, was in fact another.) How apologetically and patronisingly in those far off days a solitary performance of Bruckner's 4th symphony on the BBC was introduced by some critical flunkey: 'clumsy construction . . . garrulous incompetence . . . symphonic boa constrictors . . . clodhopping scherzi . . . inexplicable halts and awkward pauses . . . tedious Teutonic solemnity . . . unctuous religiosity . . . naïvety . . . ', etc., etc.

At last the symphony was allowed to begin, not his best perhaps, but oh, that opening – a dark, shimmering forest-girt lake of strings upon which that magical horn-call glides like a swan. Who could hear it and not be lured on into endless exploration of that heavenly God-saturated Styrian landscape, with its huge mountains and valleys, its smiling villages and churches, its splendours and miseries, its tremendous crags and castles and echoing chasms, its sombre woods, its charmed magic casements, its faery lands forlorn?

For years I wandered alone and wide-eyed in this enchanted country, lost to view, forgotten or thought mad – what's become of Waring? – yet blissfully happy in my secret and solitary joy.

And now, Bruckner is a popular success, a smash hit, part of the repertory. Everyone knows him, many like him; Bernard Levin bids me rejoice in the 8th – me! He'll be advising Harold Acton not to miss Florence next, or recommending a Woburn coach trip to the Duke of Bedford!

Trippers swarm all over the 5th, the 4th has a coach park, the old difficult vertiginous mountain track up to the climax of the 8th adagio is now asphalted and signed all the way; the magnificent view from the peak of the 7th is in all the guide books; they are building a rack railway up the 9th; ski lifts and snack bars are planned even for the remote and unfamiliar 6th. The grass is all trodden down, the flowers broken or plucked, the rocks worn smooth; toffee papers litter the arpeggios, Coke tins the codas.

And am I delighted by all this, as I should be? Yes, like Wordsworth when they were threatening to build the railway to Kendal, I gibber with feeble and ungenerous rage . . . Enough! It is my turn to do the meals-on-wheels for Block 2 today.

'Ah. Lord Chalfont, how are we today? Getting our strength back? Ah yes, it must have been dreadful – all that equality! And the restrictions of liberty! It must have been worse for a nobleman like you . . . Dear me! And the *noise* and the people! . . . Glad to have you with us, sir! Must be nice to be home again . . . '

He kens the noo . . .

Daily Telegraph, 17 January 1977

*Freedom and the Rationalist Dilemma**

Is there still existing any man opposed to, or profoundly suspicious of, all the following manifestations of the *Zeitgeist*? – social justice; the Welfare State; the redistribution of wealth; nationalism; imperialism; Socialism: Conservatism; egalitarianism; untrammelled majority rule; progressive taxation; death duties; *dirigisme*; price controls; quantity restrictions; John Maynard Keynes; the present privileges of trade unions; universal old-age pensions; public relief without proof of need; state-provided health services; rent control; 'housing subsidies; agricultural subsidies: the enforced conservation of natural resources; state education; material aid to under-developed countries; inflation, whether controlled or not.

There is one man at least, and not lacking the courage to speak his mind. He is Friedrich August Hayek, author of *The Road to Serfdom* and Professor of Social and Moral Science at the University of Chicago,

He does not oppose these things out of irrational perversity, misanthropy or a reactionary temper. Rather is he reasonable, benevolent and progressive. Nor does he regard all these things as bad or wholly bad in themselves. Rather does he regard them as incompatible with the great gifts which he offers us in return: prosperity, progress and above all liberty, which last he believes to be not merely one value among others but 'the source and condition of most moral values'.

Lord Beveridge once playfully warned Bertrand de Jouvenel, who was dining with Hayek: 'Don't be convinced by him. Hayek

* Written on publication of *Agenda for a Free Society* (a symposium of essays by various hands on Kayek's *Constitution of Liberty*) by Hutchinson for the Institute of Economic Affairs.

has a continental mind: he is much too logical for us.' The British have lately become accustomed to praising in themselves a pragmatic befuddlement which is in fact nothing to be proud of. It was not always so.

We, too, have produced minds distinguished for logic, clarity, penetration, far-sightedness and the power to connect and generalise: such minds for instance as those of Milton, Hume, Adam Smith, Paley, Burke, Macaulay, Gladstone and Acton. These, as it happens, are Hayek's declared heroes and intellectual progenitors: this is the tradition in which he stands: it is sad that Britain appears no longer to produce such minds.

In a characteristically oblique double-insult, Lord Attlee, in 1945, referred to Hayek as an Austrian theorist. Austrian by that time Hayek was not: he was and remains a British subject, a British theorist, if you like.

For he has a coherent theory of society which, implicit in *The Road to Serfdom*, is made explicit in *The Constitution of Liberty* and is then applied with ruthless logic to the world we live in. The first book, brilliantly negative, cleared the ground: the second, earnestly positive, builds upon the vacant site.

Lucid but abstract, it is not easy to read, Yet Professor J. W. N. Watkins declares it 'the most important book in its field since the war'. A just tribute: yet 'in its field' – in what field? For it is the singular merit of this work that, as Professor Watkins points out, 'it organises into a system philosophical, sociological, economic, legal, historical and political views'.

This is a very continental thing to do; equally continental is Hayek's attempt to use this system 'to picture an ideal'. Yet the ideal he actually pictures is not a *state* but a *becoming*, not an arrival but a journey. He does not portray an ideal society, but rather ideal arrangements designed to permit continuous improvement towards ideals unforeseen, as yet unknown and perhaps never wholly to be attained.

Hayek's ideal is, in a word, freedom – which he defines as the absence of coercion. It is thus not an exclusive ideal but an inclusive one, freely permitting the pursuit of many other varying and conflicting ideals.

Indeed, a general progress towards a single absolute ideal is expressly precluded. The ideal society, acceptable as such to all, is neither thinkable nor attainable. For Hayek, genuine progress can be confidently expected from one source alone: from the free and spontaneous activity of society as a whole.

His reasoning starts from the fact that, outside our own small special field, we are all ignorant. Some of us may be less ignorant than others; but all of us are profoundly ignorant when our own personal stock of knowledge is measured against that possessed by society as a whole.

In our daily lives, we are able to use a vast fund of knowledge which we do not individually possess. What puts it at our disposal is civilisation – itself a harmony of interests too complicated for individual comprehension.

By continuous process of innovation and selection, moreover, which can neither be foreseen nor directed, society places more and more knowledge at our disposal. In this process any one of us may have a part to play. For this reason, to subject any one man to another's will is to rob society of that man's potential contribution. This is a grave crime: far graver is to subject the whole of society to any single directing will. This is, in effect, to substitute for the activity and knowledge of millions of minds the knowledge and activity of one mind.

Himself an unrepentant rationalist, Hayek thus poses for us the rationalist dilemma: the use of reason aims always at control and predictability; the advance of reason none the less depends on freedom and unpredictablity; society in seeking to subject itself to rational control, will destroy the spontaneous forces which make the advance of reason possible.

Does Hayek then recommend blind, unpredictable advance? To some extent: in at least one field, in my opinion, to an unwarrantable extent. For I cannot accept his application of the rules of free competition to morals. As Professor H. B. Acton points out in *Agenda for a Free Society*, Hayek's views on the modification and improvement of morality could lead via indiscriminate tolerance into moral nihilism. In doing so, they could undermine the very conditions upon which Hayek relies to make progress fruitful and beneficial.

For Hayek does not believe in *laisser faire*: indeed he pours scorn on it and considers an inactive government which does the wrong things far worse than an active one which assists the spontaneous forces of the economy.

All activities of the government, whether political, economic or any other sort, must, however, be strictly confined within the rule of law. The limits of this rule are thus, in turn, strictly defined by Hayek: that the laws must be known and certain; that they must also be general and abstract; that, wherever discrimination between classes of people is necessary, the resultant laws must be equally acceptable to those indicated and not indicated; that the laws must otherwise apply equally to all, despite the inequalities which will result in practice; that they must not be administered by those who make them, and that they must not give wide discretionary powers to those who administer them.

A close scrutiny of Hayek's aversions, listed at the beginning of this article, will show that nearly all of them directly or indirectly violate one or more of his conditions.

No government has ever submitted themselves willingly to the rule of law as Hayek defines it. What is to make them do so in future?

Hayek is a firm believer in constitutional limitation of legislative powers. For final safeguards, however, he is compelled to retreat upon 'the moral tradition of the community' – a bulwark which he himself has done something to make insecure.

Turgenev somewhere reminded reformers desirous of levelling everything to the ground around them not to forget their own legs. Hayek appears at this point, as at others, to have done something of the sort.

Yet, legs or no legs, he remains more than a match for the whole monstrous regiment of planners. His theory stands, not faultless but firm: a shining vindication of freedom and a powerful weapon against all its enemies.

Daily Telegraph, 28 August 1961

Lord Stansgate Gives Hades to the Nation

It is a great pity that P. G. Wodehouse, Lord Emsworth and Sir Roderick Glossop, all noted for their profound insight into the problems of aristocratic – well – eccentricity, are no longer with us to observe and comment on the symptoms periodically displayed by the second Lord Stansgate, alias Tony Benn.

(In parenthesis, we must deplore the fact that his incognito is presumably maintained for reasons less innocent and more disruptive than merely to preserve a noble name from being sullied by reports of drinking champagne [or in his case tea] from the buttoned bootees of *cocottes* [or in his case vivacious party entryistettes]. We may also note that a more proletarian pseudonym could easily have been formed by a simple anagram. Does not the name Stan Gates immediately suggest one of those young ambitious, polytechnic-lecturer Labour MPs whose amatory vicissitudes form the substance of so many drear novels and television plays?)

Lord Stansgate's insolent and grandiose antics invariably and variously provoke among the peasantry astonishment, hilarity, distress, envy, disbelief, horror and rage. His latest extravaganza is to throw away £320 million – no less – on a fantastic plan to 'insulate' all council dwellings and other buildings in the public sector (that is to say, in his own private sector). And this, mark well, is proposed in the interests of economy, of saving money and/or fuel! With these laudable objects it has, as any fool can see, no connection whatever, or no more than a bit of pushed string. The till is empty? We are broke? The party is over? We need to save? To tighten our belts? Then let us spend, spend, spend! Such is Lord Stansgate's haughty logic.

Let us suppose that Lord Stansgate, having inherited the ancestral pile, Stansgate Abbey in Essex, finds himself suddenly in financial straits. Not easy to suppose, I agree, unless the markets for magazines, pottery, nonsense (his own speciality) and pork products (which form the basis of his bluestocking lady's goodly inheritance from Cincinnati) all collapse simultaneously; but let us suppose it. What does he do?

In fact Stansgate Abbey is a modest enough seat. Yet in my mind's eye I picture him as at vast expense he double-glazes (with stained glass?) the cloisters, the chapel, the dorter, the refectory and privies; insulates the soaring Early English vaults, turrets, spires and aisles; engages numberless extra staff to go round switching off all the lights and stoves, dousing the flambeaux and log fires, searching vainly under the floorboards for coins, digging the grounds for treasure and diving in the nearby Blackwater for sunken galleons. His difficulties accumulate, his economy measures become ever more desperate and expensive, until at last the embarrassed nobleman sinks uncomprehending beneath the tide of ruin.

To return to reality, what will be the consequences of spending £320 million? Well, we shall be £320 million the poorer or perhaps double that, for sure. The lagging trade will be by something less the richer – lucky old lags!

We shall see the recruitment of hundreds of energy officers (local authorities have already been urged to get cracking), mostly recruited from harassed private industry, their salaries paid by the tottering taxpayer. Beneath them will swarm deputy assistant energy officers and the rest. Vast over-heated energy offices will be erected, bought or rented to house them – Energy House, Stansgate Towers. There will be numberless energy-saving limousines, with flags and personalised numberplates, energy-saving stenographers, telephones, files, bribes, expenses, lunches, forms, campaigns. Masses of information will be required from everybody, on pain of imprisonment in over-heated prisons.

And what of the vast fuel savings to be expected? Will there be any at all? Not a therm, predicts Mr N. L. Carrington, a shrewd reader.

Gone are the days when the British notoriously liked cold

showers, open bedroom windows, water freezing in the bedside carafes, fresh air. These British were anyway probably confined to one Spartanly-educated class, and that oddly enough the one from which Lord Stansgate springs. The odder his conduct, and odder still in view of his own pleasantly invigorating open-air appearance, which strongly suggests the sort of handsome fresh-faced bonehead who would frighten Bertie Wooster by inviting him for ten-mile runs before breakfast, who in pre-war comedies was always asking who was for tennis, or who in old Chilprufe advertisements, relaxed in his long-johns after squash with a pipe, a glass of sherry and a pal in the changing room.

Perhaps he was transformed by his year in the navy, a notoriously fuggy service – 40 degrees below above decks, maybe, but 90 degrees above below.

Lord Stansgate's inferiors have always liked a nice fug. They like their air like curry or winter woollies – the thicker, hotter and smellier the better, provided you can see the telly through it. Their ideal home is probably the bizarre one portrayed in the double-glazing advertisements – outside, through the vast picture window, a terrifying Wenceslas-worthy winter scene, complete with groaning conifers and snowman; inside, a family sweltering in swimming trunks and bikinis.

Insulate two million council houses and what will happen? Will the occupants turn down the heat? Not bloody likely. No, a satanic perfection will be for them a little nearer attainment – an atmosphere in which the plants wilt, the pets gasp and croak, the furniture cracks, the very cactuses shrivel and turn to dust, and all at someone else's expense!

Insulate schools, hospitals and government buildings and the present frowsy enervating torpor therein will be intensified. Learning, healing, the mighty government machine itself, will falter and expire as the public sector is turned into a sort of Aden.

The chalk drops from the fainting teacher's hand; the patient sweats half-stifled in drugged uneasy slumber; all the letters of her typewriter hit the paper together as Miss Chapman, the deputy energy officer's principal personal assistant, swoons on the keyboard; the very revenues needed for Lord Stansgate's wild plans are uncollected as the bloodsuckers are overcome by heatstroke.

The famed complexions of our womenfolk will turn to deathly waxen pallor. Doctors' surgeries, already overcrowded, will be crammed with sufferers from the head colds and sinus troubles which excessive heat engenders – and all in the name of economy!

To be sure, there are old poor people who will die of cold this winter. Very well: instead of this vast, prodigal and random expenditure, as useless in its effects as that which built the Pyramid of Cheops, why not set those energy officers to search these poor old people out? Many of them are tenants of private landlords (such tenants are on the whole poorer – yes, poorer – than council-house tenants); some are themselves landlords, often poorer even than their tenants.

None of these qualities for Lord Stansgate's eccentric munificence, though all will help perforce to pay the bill

Search these out; bring them fuel; bring them pine logs hither; stop their draughts; lag their pipes and ceilings; give them clothes; give them money, one-tenth, one-hundredth of the wasted £320 million; dry their weeping walls and eyes and noses before it is too late.

Has Lord Stansgate thought of this? Probably not: he is himself perhaps already too well insulated from the cold but invigorating draughts of reality.

23 January 1978

*Underdogs or Wolves**

This is a vast but very readable account of the much-travelled John Pilger's journalistic and pre-journalistic life, an *apologia pro vita sua*, a sort of progressive pilgrim's progress. (Yes, Pilger is of German descent, *Pilger* meaning pilgrim.) It includes material recycled from the *Daily Mirror*, *New Statesman* and other left-wing organs. I found in it, I must confess, much more to like, admire and respect than I or he (or my revered colleague Auberon Waugh, who is mentioned with a not unfriendly jest) could have expected. What? Well, admirable courage, for a start. Oh no, I don't mean that bogus courage fatuously attributed to people who express silly or unfashionable views. Some of our pilgrim's views may be silly, none are unfashionable. His sort of tosh and even mine normally entails no risk. Normally, yes, but our pilgrim was warned by the egregious Marxist journalist Wilfred Burchett that because of what he, Pilger, had written, his life would be in danger in Cambodia. The regime there had already murdered a third of its subjects, so this was no empty threat; but our pilgrim set off undaunted. Exactly where Burchett had been ambushed, so was he, so he tells us: a covered truck across the road, a hair's-breadth evasion via the verge, and the snapshot left in his mind is 'of armed men in black lying on their bellies aiming point blank at us'.

With disarming modesty, he mentions the ingrained caution or even cowardice he has to overcome. It is sufficiently repressed to permit a thorough inspection of a Cambodian 'hospital' in which plague and anthrax victims are dying untreated on stone

* Review of *Heroes* by John Pilger, Jonathan Cape, 1986

floors. It permits him to enter Czechoslovakia with a prohibited film camera under the floorboards, and to accompany a mad nocturnal Palestinian mine-laying expedition into Israeli territory. It began with the 'leader' blowing the leg off a table while inexpertly loading his automatic and ended with the leader's death amidst thunderous detonations. I could cite many other examples. Our pilgrim has been in more tight corners and tighter ones than most of us. With whatever reservations, I raise my hat to Mr Valiant-For-Truth-As-He-Sees-It .

What spurs him repeatedly into discomfort and danger? Well, pride in his craft, pride in being 'only a journalist', part of a goodly company including, for him, William Howard Russell and Robert Fisk of*The Times*, Philips Price of the *Guardian*, Ed Murrow. Martha Gellhorn and James Cameron, all proudly 'only journalists'. My hat is still half off. One must respect the respect of others, though my list of journalistic heroes would not be identical. Where we really differ is in his implication that journalism is no good where it does not challenge, 'investigate' or undermine authority, 'them' or the established view. More alien to him than to me is any idea that authority, 'them' or the established view might be right or partly so, and might legitimately on occasion expect to be defended. He thinks he is always on the side of the underdog; but some of his underdogs, the miners' pickets, for instance, look suspiciously like wolves to me. It is ideas like these which, spreading like a plague among nearly all ambitious, self-confident and *demi-savant* young journalists, have turned 'investigative journalism' into a threat to the survival of our free institutions, which do not command our pilgrim's affections.

If my hat soon comes right off again, it is because our pilgrim's pride in his craft, deformed as I may think it, does help him to write with notable force and clarity, vividly and without affectation. In this respect at least he is a true model for his peers and followers. Let them study for instance the awesome opening pages of the long chapter, 'Year Zero', which unforgettably describes the hideous and desolate remains of murdered Phnom Penh. Apart from the tendentious bits blaming America for all that went wrong, as if Chamberlain were held primarily responsible for the Final Solution, mark how our pilgrim sees and can make us see too: mark, shudder, reflect and profit. There are other passages as fine.

What fuels our pilgrim's burning prose is not only craft pride but a tremendous if sometimes forced indignation, a sense of outrage as often as of the absurd. Oh yes, my hat is still half off. Our pilgrim would be astonished to know how much of what outrages him or strikes him as blackly comic outrages also old fogies like me or creases our storm-eroded features in ghastly smiles.

I too regard the BBC's pretensions to balance as absurd, though from a different angle, and our pilgrim's suggested remedy, the election of BBC bosses by the staff, would not calm my agitation. I too am shamed by the insults and injuries inflicted on coloured people in this country, though less inclined to suppose noisy counter-demonstration the best answer: as tempers rise, peace and innocence are in danger. I too deplore the gratuitous misfortunes of the homeless in Britain and the fate of the aboriginals in Australia, though this last disgrace would make me, especially if I were an Australian as our pilgrim is, rather less censorious about South Africa's lesser sins. To call him a humbug about this would perhaps be unfair, since he apparently favours paying for Australia's guilt by giving aboriginals grotesque powers to prevent development in their ancestral territories. Ruined by Australia, they would be given in return the power to ruin Australia – *cui bono?* He is appalled by the Khmer Rouge, but so am I. It may even come more naturally to me, in that I rightly or wrongly discern in it a logical development or grim perversion of the egalitarian socialism which he cherishes and I don't. Did he oppose them before they seized power, or favour them, as he favours other aspirant monsters?

The thought of napalmed Vietnamese babies, of soil in Vietnam poisoned and sterilised by noxious chemicals, of all the cruel devastation wrought there by American bombing fills me, like our pilgrim, with grief and pity. As often, we agree about what disgusts us without agreeing wholly about its causes, consequences or even extent. Unless I err, some of the atrocities alleged against the Americans and Thieu's Saigon regime by left-wing holy writ have been proved to be false or exaggerated, while much of what was alleged against Hanoi has been retrospectively vindicated by its vicious conduct since the fall of Saigon. Our pilgrim says there was 'no bloodbath' there. Isn't this playing with words? So many are dead. Our pilgrim's reporting of united communist Vietnam is comparatively sketchy and, in the absurd sense, 'balanced'. The disappearance for 're-education' of one distinguished and fearless opponent of Thieu's (as if he were the only one to disappear!) is routinely deplored as 'Stalinist barbarity'. It is balanced by an idyllic picture of a communist orphanage. Ah, sunbeams and showers . . .

Having praised our pilgrim, however grudgingly, must I bury him? Did I presume to try, I lack the proper spade. All that may be false or misleading in his pages could only be corrected by an army of experts on the recent history of all the places his *Pilgerfahrt* has taken him to. No such expertise can I claim. Nor perhaps can he. Does he speak the requisite language? He mocks the *Daily Telegraph* for having employed as its under-correspondent in Saigon a Vietnamese army officer. But that officer could at least talk without an interpreter to the natives. Meanwhile, I can only make a few warning noises to alert readers as innocent as I.

Our pilgrim portrays Ho Chi Minh as by nature a pro-American liberal, devoted to 'life, liberty and the pursuit of happiness', who was forced into communism by American hostility and betrayals. Haven't we heard this before, about Castro? Aren't we hearing it again, from our pilgrim among others, about the Sandinistas? Doan Van Toai is a Vietnamese who escaped from what he calls 'the giant prison camp Vietnam had become' in 1978. In a recent *Commentary* article he asserts that Ho's liberal nationalism was a deception from the start. The Vietnamese communist party hid itself, its ideology and plans in the background (our pilgrim admits the Khmer Rouge did likewise, but they have forfeited his favour). It operated always in the background behind fronts offering what the Vietnamese really wanted, independence and democracy. But it always had the intention of establishing the society which now exists, with a regime 'far worse than the foreign oppressors', which maintains its power by ruthless use of starvation and blackmail, hard-labour camps and prisons – in one of which Toai spent twenty-eight months without charge. For this and other reasons our pilgrim might not regard him as a good witness. I'm sure he would have believed him when he was, to his regret, a vociferous opponent of Thieu and supporter of the NLF. Why then not now? Toai's article was called 'Vietnam: How We Deceived Ourselves'. Our pilgrim pooh-poohs nowadays the Marxism of the Sandinistas. When they hail and extol it as their guiding light, do they wink and smile at our pilgrim – only a game? Or is he deceiving himself again?

If so, he is presumably led astray by his pervasive and vision-distorting anti-Americanism, against which another warning noise seems appropriate. He seems to think America always in the wrong, her opponents always in the right. Would he in former days have had a kindly word for Hirohito, Hitler and the Kaiser? His sour denigration of American motives in Vietnam causes him to ignore many aspects of the truth and sad might-have-beens. Of course the war there was a tragic failure, though our pilgrim eccentrically accuses the Americans of having won it, in the sense of having reduced Vietnam to poverty and misery: as if that were their mad and evil purpose! He ridicules the healing American belief that it was after all 'a noble cause'. Does incompetence in execution automatically strip all causes of all nobility?

Now, if the Americans had not relied excessively on bombing; or if, relying on bombing, they had bombed immediately and effectively, rather than in gradually increasing politically restricted doses; if they had heeded earlier Robert McNamara's anguished remark about 'the crushing futility of air war'; if they had not been so terrified of conscript casualties (I agree with our pilgrim that 58,000 Americans killed out of a total of 1,300,000 dead in Vietnam is not a creditable figure); if they had not ruled out in advance any possibility of victory; if they had not sat there stoically on the 17th parallel like 'targets' (Pilger's word), not soldiers; if they had swiftly occupied North Vietnam or most of it; if they had established then in both parts of Vietnam an order more tolerable to the Vietnamese and themselves than the present tyranny; in other words, if they had won and won quickly, at acceptable cost – but from the America-hater all such benign possibilities are hidden and, if they were not, he would hate them too. The rest of us, not least the betrayed Vietnamese, contemplate them with dark regret.

The Spectator, 31 May 1986

The Man Who Took Too Much for Granted – Crosland Reconsidered

Is it too fanciful to suppose that across the last years of Mr Anthony Crosland's life, so tragically cut short, a certain shadow fell? Gone or waning was that former self-assurance and inner certainty, amounting at one time almost to arrogance. In conversation he retained at will his wit and charm. Yet a certain weariness and indifference, a growing detachment, showed itself in the increasing gladness – or at least tolerance – with which he suffered those he would once have thought fools. Was he perhaps no longer convinced of his own wisdom and good judgement? In some ways he seemed to have become more human, more fallible, more genial, more gently quizzical, even in a way more apologetic. Yet one felt – perhaps wrongly – that a spring had broken, that an inner light had gone out, that purpose and bearings had been lost, that – as once for another distinguished and clever politician – it would never be glad confident morning again.

Is it too fanciful? Perhaps; but, if not, it would be silly to search in his personal life for any cause. Just before his death he told Ivan Rowan of the *Sunday Telegraph* how he and his wife had agreed that if they were killed together (say, in a plane crash) they could have no regrets – everything had been worthwhile. He added: 'What a marvellous life it has been!' Friends all testify to his domestic happiness.

Was it the strain of high office? We may doubt whether a man so capable was ever overstretched by any of the positions he held.

Was it, then, thwarted ambition? This too we may doubt, at least in part. Indeed he must have been aware of his intellectual superiority to most of his colleagues. He may well have thought himself in particular better qualified to be chancellor than any of those who were preferred to him. He would have been a very unorthodox chancellor, perhaps, who proclaimed that 'rapid growth requires a reversal of these priorities [i.e. growth must be given a higher priority than the value of the pound and a healthy balance of payments] and a government which really *believes* [his italics] in expansion', and who proposed to hold down inflation not primarily by monetary restraint but rather by fiscal measures and direct controls. Or has bitter experience taught us by now to regard such chancellors as orthodox?

He must himself have relished the irony which placed instead at the Foreign Office a man like himself who, to judge from his published works, had little interest in international affairs, and who regarded foreign countries primarily as examples (often ill-chosen for his purpose) to us of how to conduct the domestic economic affairs which preoccupied him or, alternatively, as recipients of the lavish British aid he was always eager to dispense.

Perhaps he had higher dreams still. Certainly he never went out of his way to offend those of his colleagues who differed from him and whose support he might yet need in any eventual serious bid for the Labour leadership. (He stood last time and came bottom out of six, with only seventeen votes.) His commitment to our joining Europe, for instance, quite explicit in those massive works from which few of his colleagues could probably quote at will, became in practice at the crunch conveniently ambiguous and unimportant to him. Yet, on the other hand, he never stooped to the base intriguing and ingratiating arts by which people like Sir Harold Wilson and Mr James Callaghan became leader: his grand indolent manner and independent character probably forbade it.

A question remains, moreover. Could an intellectual of this sort, who thought so much, who wrote and achieved so much in the world of the mind, who had such influence and changed so many minds by persuasion; whose *Future of Socialism* was described by Dr William Pickles as 'the most important [book] on its subject since Eduard Bernstein published his famous work in 1898' and by Hugh Dalton as 'brilliant, original and brave . . . by far the most important book on Socialism in England since the War'; who was so refreshingly right about so many things that his works were read with approval by many who can hardly have shared, perhaps did not even notice, his general purpose; who twenty-odd years ago did so much to make socialism seem respectable, undoctrinaire and safe, clearly the most sensible and humane if not the only way of running our affairs – could such a man ever know the sheer unadulterated greed for power which obsesses men who have no other means of winning eminence? Surely not: we may think of him rather like Bishop Blougram, musing with a smile,

> I am much, you are nothing; you would be all,
> I would be merely much. You beat me there.

Yet if we do believe that some shadow fell on his last years, and if we seek a reason for it, perhaps we have already stumbled on it. Was it the shadow thrown by *The Future of Socialism* (1956) and by its lesser successor, *The Conservative Enemy* (1962), in which various of its themes are developed and varied? For this future, this 'future of socialism' was no remote millennial Utopia, to be achieved in distant years to come by the patient selfless work of generations or, if sooner, by some shattering cataclysm. No, it was the immediate, practical and attainable future, to be started at once and to be pushed rapidly and effortlessly through, bringing in its train no paradise indeed, no finite Utopia, but valuable and measurable benefits to all save the rich and wicked few, with the prospect of more to come. It was painless socialism, socialism without tears; or so it said. It is recognisably, in outline if not in detail, the socialism that has prevailed in this country, apart from the first part of Mr Edward Heath's bizarre interregnum, since 1964. Of all that this socialism has by intent done, much was explicitly or implicitly urged upon it by Mr Crosland and nothing that I can think of expressly forbidden.

Yes, even the so-called 'social contract' (Wilson's version, not Rousseau's) was his child in all but name.

> We must have a prices and incomes policy [he told trade unions in Copenhagen in 1971]. Such a policy is only possible within a framework of government policies for greater social and economic equality as a whole. It is no good simply asking the trade unions to cooperate in a prices and incomes policy against a background of reactionary social policies . . .

In other, more cynical words, the unions demand and are to get, in return for something valueless which they cannot deliver, the ruin of the nation – 'the social con-trick', as Jock Bruce-Gardyne has called it.

Mr Crosland was thus condemned to live in his own future. He saw it, and it didn't work. As a younger man he had always been shrewd and percipient, ever ready to re-examine the evidence, conspicuously unready to take old dogma on trust – his major works give short shrift to old twaddle and new, from Marx to Galbraith. Could such a man fail to notice that most of his major benign predictions had come unstuck; that what he had once taken for granted now shook and crumbled beneath his feet; that some of those people and views he had once scoffed at were beginning to look a bit wiser; that what he had advocated, wherever it had been put into effect, had produced few of the foretold blessings and many of the disastrous consequences he had pooh-poohed; and that his own reservations and hesitations, by no means few even if unemphatic, were being endowed by the grimly and inexorably unfolding future of socialism with an ever greater and sadder significance? It must have been like living in a haunted house, a place built in a sunnier season for comfort and beauty, yet infested now by the spectres of hopes blasted and dark fears crowding in.

It is true that in 1974, in essays and speeches reviewing the first Harold Wilson regime and plotting the way ahead, his understanding of what had gone wrong, the extent of it and why, seemed most imperfect. His pages abound indeed with lamentations and breast-beatings: 'nobody disputes the central failure of [Mr Wilson's] economic policy' – the performance (and I must take my share of responsibility) did not live up to the hopes which we . . . had entertained' – 'general disappointment' – 'this dismal record creates a public mood of discord and discontent' – 'the economy is in a state of semi-permanent crisis, and inflation is rampant' – 'this wretched showing, for which all of us who were in government must share responsibility' – 'the record of growth has been lamentable; the facts are dreary and familiar', and so forth. What renders these confessions and apologies sterile is his failure to examine possible connections between policies he thought good and developments he recognised to be bad. The real cause for all that went wrong for Harold Wilson was, I think, in Crosland's view 'the basic decision not to alter the exchange rate', i.e. not to devalue the pound: from this mistake all other evils flowed. And indeed, if it was a mistake, it was one for which Crosland for all his protestations could bear only nominal, formal responsibility – for he had certainly never bothered himself much about the value of the pound. Thus self-absolved, the blame shifted implicitly on to one major but inessential error, not to be repeated and not really his own, he is free to justify his own and Labour's general record.

For instance, the rise in public expenditure under Wilson from 41% to 48% of GNP, so pregnant with evil as some might think, is regarded by him as 'solid progress' . . . 'impressive' . . . 'a brave performance'. About education he is more crudely specific:

> expenditure in education rose from 4.8% of GNP in 1964 to 6.1% in 1970. As a result, all classes of the community *enjoyed significantly more education than before.*

(My italics, to emphasise the iron link in his mind between money spent and value got, as though in this case spending *equals* learning; by such standards the housewife who is continually diddled in the shops enjoys significantly more goods than the one who is not.) He quotes with approval Michael Stewart, who referred to 'a measurable improvement [*sic*] in the distribution of income' as one of Prime Minister Wilson's 'main achievements' – an 'improvement' marked by a fall in profits from 15.6% to 12.3% and by a 'large increase' in social benefits, producing 'a favourable effect'. With the same grim complacency might an alcoholic sadly review a past year of disasters, of declining health and mental powers, of mounting debts, of failure and ruin approaching inexorably, and yet conclude that the picture was not *wholly* black: after all, he had managed to keep up his alcohol intake, even to 'improve' it, a 'brave performance' in the circumstances.

The previous optimism has gone; full self-realisation is yet to come. Did it ever come? How can we know for sure? The Costa Rica lecture of 1975 denies it; it keeps up a brave front. Yet is it not a fact, apparent to us all as we grow older, that the capacity of the mind for really new thought, for constructive self-criticism, grows atrophied? We tend to repeat and develop what we once thought, modified as little as experience and disillusion will permit. Not to be envied is the man who in youth equipped himself with a *Weltanschauung* which, however imposing, does not fit the times through which he is later condemned to live. What he thought and said he thinks still and says. But his heart is not in it; the season is unpropitious, and he shivers at the nip in the air; the party is over.

But I go too fast. Let me return to the two books which made and consolidated his reputation, not least because they appeared initially in part in these *Encounter* pages.

'My political misfortune', he confessed in Costa Rica, 'is that I was born an optimist.' Despite their sometimes impatient, exasperated or even petulant tone, *The Future of Socialism* and its successor seemed at the time extremely *optimistic* books. They seem almost incredibly so now, in darker times. All problems were solved or readily soluble, all hopes securely grounded, all dangers illusory. With confidence the Captain Crosland of those days tapped the barometer, stuck at 'set fair'. In such weather it seemed to him perfectly safe to neglect all traditional precautions, to take on cargo and passengers till the

Plimsoll line was well below the surface, to run down the fuel reserves and to steer near the rocks. What was needed was boldness, 'verve and determination'; the risks were negligible. In 1956 it was clear to him that 'the British economy is behaving in a reasonably buoyant and productive manner and there is certainly no sign of imminent collapse. The present rate of growth will continue.' This being so,

> material want and poverty and deprivation of essential goods will gradually cease to be a problem. We shall increasingly need to focus attention . . . not on the economic causes of distress but on the social and psychological causes. We shall want the advice not of the economists but of psychiatrists, sociologists and social psychiatrists.

Crosland characteristically foresaw a time, 'as material standards rise, when divorce law reform will increase the sum of human welfare more than a rise in the food subsidies . . . ' The dismal science, in his own hands so far from dismal, would make way for pseudo-science, the benign rule of crackpots presiding over more and more broken homes. He noted 'a world-wide change in the economic climate'.

> The business community [he went on] accepts the fact that prosperity is here to stay, not only because full employment will be maintained but also because we have entered a period of rapid growth in personal incomes and consumption.

In these happy circumstances, he no longer regarded 'questions of growth and efficiency as being, on a long view, of primary importance to socialism. We stand, in Britain, on the threshold of mass abundance.' He took too much for granted.

By 1962 his optimism had by no means abated, though he himself in retrospect thought it had. He thought then that by 1964 prosperity, hitherto a Tory prerogative, might be taken for granted by an electorate which might thus feel itself free to vote Labour again. Perhaps it did so take it for granted; certainly he did. He mocked those Labour MPs who decried the then prevailing prosperity as 'bogus' or 'phoney', due to be 'engulfed in an inevitable slump'. They had 'no warrant' for such a view. 'Something approaching full employment will be maintained in Britain,' he assured them, 'if only because the Conservatives know that a failure here would lead to defeat at the polls.' At this point as elsewhere he displays his conviction that full employment can in all circumstances be maintained by government action, such as a 'continuing mild inflation', so swift and sure and harmless in its effects that it would be madness for any government not to take it. He thus ignores the possibility that inflation, in order to perform (or rather to strive vainly to perform) the beneficent tasks allotted to it by him and its other advocates, must become less and less mild, more and more rapid and progressive, always a little bit more than expected; for 'expected' inflation is discounted in advance and produces no effect on demand. He was fated to see an unprecedented inflation and high and rising unemployment – a combination he must have found puzzling and disquieting.

In Costa Rica he referred to 'pessimists' who 'fear the consequences for democracy of a combination of slow economic growth and rapid inflation in societies where rising expectations have developed from aspirations into fierce demands.' In this malign development he himself had played his part, by continuously inflating aspirations and expectations into *rights*, not reasonably to be withheld. Add then to the witches' brew of slow growth, inflation and 'fierce demands' a further ingredient, unemployment, and indeed those silly old pessimists might well shake in their shoes.

He further deplored, in 1962,

> a strange sad alliance between the Conservatives and the extreme 'left', both contending (falsely) that we are at the limits of taxable capacity in the mixed economy. The Conservatives . . . maintain that higher taxation would inhibit economic growth; the extreme 'left' . . . maintains that it would be incompatible with the existence of a private sector.

Turning to corporate taxation, he found also

> a united front between the apologists of business and the 'New Left', both maintaining that profits cannot be heavily taxed without catastrophic results . . . For [he is here paraphrasing the Jeremiahs of business and the Left] if taxed beyond a certain point the profit system will break down; the 'oligopolists' will refuse to invest, send their capital abroad and precipitate an economic crisis.

He scorned all such fears and hopes. Tax on, he cried; taxation is good for you. He was in no way inferior to Mr Denis Healey as a pip-squeaker. He himself conceded that 'personal taxation must at some point impinge on the supply of ability, effort and risk taking, and cause individuals either to emigrate or opt for leisure'. He saw no sign, however, 'that we in Britain are at or near this limit – with the *one possible* [my italics] exception of direct taxation on marginal earnings'. How he would have recognised that limit when it came we do not know. How hard it is to measure such impalpables as effort withheld, enterprise thwarted, hopes blasted, skills unacquired or left dormant, leisure preferred, though emigration figures are more precise! Meanwhile his words could be used to justify tax piled upon tax, like some ignorant peasant loading more and more on to a half-starved donkey till it expires – when it is too late to unload. As for profits taxes, he agreed with 'most economists' (Lord Kaldor is the one he quotes) that they 'tend in the long run to be passed on to the consumer in the form of higher margins and prices', leaving the profit system 'unaffected by the whole operation'. That is, presumably, as long as the poor old consumer goes on doing his stuff. Our consumers seem of late to have let us down.

Anyway at that time he declared that

> we have all become wearily familiar with the unending lamentations about the 'crippling' level of taxation, the 'crushing' burden of government expenditure, the alleged disincentives to growth, investment and efficiency, and so on *ad nauseam*.

In other words he proclaimed the British economy to be

fundamentally in rude health, able easily to bear not only existing burdens but others innumerable soon to be imposed upon it; indeed, that with these further burdens its health could be expected to become even ruder. All this he took for granted.

What kept him so cheerful? It was not, I fancy, any faith in any sort of socialism, his own sort or any other, though I do not question his sincerity. No, paradoxical as it may sound, it seems rather to have been an incongruous, profound and comforting faith, itself irrational, in the ability of capitalism – or at least of the late-capitalist or managerial system which he described and favoured – somehow to keep going, to maintain growth and to enhance prosperity, even when deprived of *rationale*, of all the discipline and rewards, the rules and conditions, the sticks and carrots hitherto thought essential to its success. He often derides Marx's belief in the inevitable collapse of capitalism; is his own belief in its inevitable survival any less absurd? Is it not indeed rather more absurd, in that Marx at least proposed to give the odd helpful nudge to historical processes which he thought inevitable, while Crosland does everything he can think of to render false his own more sanguine expectations?

Now take the profit motive, for instance, the mainspring of capitalism, the devil's work to all good socialists (or, since Anthony Crosland, to most). It was Crosland who first, or most memorably, suggested that profit need not be a dirty word to socialists, thus causing a widespread rearrangement of demons on the left and commending his work to all non-doctrinaire 'men of goodwill'. And indeed, as I have said, he was so refreshingly and unexpectedly right (or at least non-left) about so many things that non-left people tended to overlook his flaws. For mark now with what qualifications he defends the profit motive. Profits and the market system for which they supply the moving force are perfectly in order, yes – but only on two harsh conditions. One is that effective demand must be equalised, i.e. that incomes must be rendered more equal than the market system would supposedly have arranged unaided. As he puts it elsewhere, 'Production for use and production for profit may be taken as broadly coinciding now that working-class purchasing power is so high.'

The other condition is that profit must be retained and not distributed, the penalty for the latter crime being swingeing taxation. This continuous 'ploughing back' must, of course, have very adverse effects on the raising of capital for new firms and industries. If existing firms hang on to all they gain, where is new risk capital to be found? Crosland everywhere neglects the needs and role of *new* businesses, and seems to overlook their importance to growth and innovation. Dr Ludwig Erhard took the opposite view, and actually taxed retained German profits more than distributed profits, thus encouraging money to move rapidly about. He was wise to do so if, as there is reason to suppose, retained profits are often or usually uneconomically invested.

Now we can readily see that the profits Crosland tolerates are profits which have lost much of their purpose, in so far as that purpose was to elicit and reward skill, hard work, risk-taking. The word 'profit' remains, but the lure and the reward have disappeared. Little reward will find its way into private hands; what does will promptly be redistributed in order to ensure that production, if any, is of 'necessities' rather than of 'luxuries', i.e. is for 'use.' The greater part of these pseudo-profits will be retained and ploughed back into the business, leaving the original entrepreneurs and their successors as mere spectators of what they have set in motion – even in a sense prisoners of it. For, should they seek to escape from their ill-rewarded bondage, whether by death or by trying to realise their capital in the hope of some gain, real or illusory, for themselves or loved ones (a gain which must be greatly reduced by the incidence of the high taxes urged by Crosland on distributed profits and 'unearned' incomes), then he is waiting for them with an electric fence, dogs and machine guns at the gate. Taxation, he cries, must be made 'to *bite* more *deeply* and more *fiercely*' – my italics, yet surely the savagery of his imagery is not without significance? 'The two most important requirements are a comprehensive Capital Gains Tax and a tax on gifts *inter vivos* to restore reality to the death duties', in order to appropriate 'a proportion of all gains accruing anywhere in the economy' – of all gains, that is to say, real or, under continuing 'mild' inflation, illusory.

These measures and the like were designed by Crosland to correct an inequality or inequity (he used the terms interchangeably) in the distribution of wealth. The extent of this inequality, this 'maldistribution of property', he grossly exaggerates:

> Less than 2% of adult persons own 50% per cent of total personal net capital; 10% of persons own nearly 80%.

Polanyi and Wood (in the Institute of Economic Affairs' *How Much Inequality?)* estimate that 10% probably own about 40% of the wealth, but that if each member of that 10% has on average one dependant, then that 10% should be 20%. The 'inequity' is not then so vast. That it is to Crosland an inequity is illustrated by his contention, after arguing that '*some* differential rewards for talent and ability' are to be tolerated, that 'justice must here be tempered with efficiency'. The inference is clear: justice equals equality, and talent, ability and effort have no claim in *justice* to any differential reward whatsoever. Expediency alone secures their gain, if any, just as it is not justice but expediency which causes us to hand our watches to the mugger.

Inequality even in earned income is to him far too great, also presumably to be corrected by the increased personal taxation which he elsewhere regards as dangerous. The idea that 'just' rewards, as some might define them, could actually be more unequal still is naturally to him not worth discussing. He is everywhere concerned to preserve 'reasonable rewards', 'small and medium savings'. He cares nothing for the exceptional rewards which may be required by exceptional efforts and ability, and neglects the contribution to society of exceptional men – even of exceptionally awful men, as he and I might think them. He has little sympathy for any economic aspirations and appetites which he, as a 'normal' man, does not share. The average, the mean, the normal, the 'reasonable' (the mediocre, some might say) dominate his mind and command his allegiance. Even in the field of education he is of the view that 'we need less concentration on an educational élite and more on the average standard of attainment' – two aims of which the first and more disastrous, as we have learnt to our cost, is easier to achieve than the second.

To what extent recent heavy taxation has contributed to equality is still debatable. The poor pay taxes as well as the rich; and the tragedy of those who owned businesses now bankrupt must be measured against the tragedy of those many more thereby thrown out of work and the tragedy – more imponderable – of those who are denied the jobs which could have been provided in new enterprises which prospective entrepreneurs, surveying the odds now against them, the imbalance between risk, effort and reward, have reasonably decided not to launch. It is difficult or impossible to make the rich less rich without making the poor poorer still, and the effort may end with an Eskimo-equality in universal poverty.

Behind what Anthony Crosland urged may be discerned a failure to recognise any logical or just connection between production and distribution. They are to him quite separate phenomena. What is produced is produced: that may be taken for granted. What is produced, including profits if any, may then be freely distributed according to egalitarian or other whim. 'In the end,' as he says in another context, 'the proper division of the surplus depends simply on one's own view of the right distribution of total income.' Someone created the vineyard, you might say; someone now owns the vineyard; some toil in it; some sell the grapes; some make the wine; but someone else altogether may fitly decide on the proper division of the reward.

The logic and justice of the free market economy is indeed dauntingly complex and obscure. It must seem to ordinary people to distribute its favours and brickbats much as Ophelia distributed her flowers. Yet surely we had a right to expect from a man so clever as Crosland, often so wise, a slightly more sophisticated view of the distribution of wealth than this: that, if wealth is not strictly distributed by the government according to its own system of social priorities, then it will 'fall where *economic chance* [my italics] dictates' – that it will 'remain with those so placed in relation to the productive process that they initially receive it . . . ' As elsewhere, he speaks contemptuously of 'the accident of birth' (which is in fact only an accident to those who view the process coldly from outside, from a long way off, ignoring the chains of mutual love and inherited qualities and attitudes which normally bind parents and children together), so the free economy appears to him a mere lottery, as such also contemptible. He notes with resentment the prizes it offers; he notes with some complacency the efforts it elicits and the wealth it creates. But he does not recognise, or if he recognises does not emphasise, any link between the two. The first can safely be diminished, almost abolished, without affecting the supply of the latter. He does not see any conflict (as others do) between equality and prosperity; if he did, he would presumably choose equality.

Characteristically he regards inherited wealth as particularly and self-evidently indefensible. Certainly it is slightly more difficult to defend than wealth still in the hands of whoever created it. There seems at first glance (and Crosland is in too much of a hurry to give it two glances) little to connect an old lady living comfortably in Bournemouth with any sort of wealth creation. Yet the connection is there all right, but usually buried in the past, a whole period to which in his haste Crosland pays too little attention. Someone created wealth to ensure – perhaps *inter alia* – that this old lady should not want. She has at least as much right to part of the wealth which she in part caused to be created as Crosland or any of his proposed beneficiaries, who had nothing whatever to do with it. She is, so to speak, a retired incentive and, as such, entitled to her pension.

C. A. R. Crossland's economic sports day is thus one without prizes, or rather with only the most modest prizes, such as might be thought appropriate by some don or the like, not primarily moved by hope of gain; and these prizes are to be held only temporarily, on sufferance, like the school running cups which have to be handed back at the end of the year. To achieve any sort of durable financial success in such a world, were it possible, is to expose oneself not only to Mr Crosland's icy disapproval but, more important, to the envy and resentment of the masses – ugly and unconstructive sentiments which, so far from rebuking, he fully endorses, tries even to share, and proposes to assuage by levelling down the objects of envy. Did it not cross his mind that the greater the relative equality prevailing, the more all surviving inequalities (and he permits some) will be resented? If, moreover, greater enforced equality is accompanied by or actually causes (as many would expect) a relative or absolute decline in general prosperity, then will not envy find in economic failure its most fertile soil? Long ago Adam Smith defined a healthy society not as an equal one but as one in which most people are getting better off, or can reasonably hope to do so. In such a society equality is of little interest, envy no problem. Should Crosland perhaps have noted a profound book I must commend to all – Helmut Schoeck's study of *envy*?* Professor Schoeck contends that the progress and prosperity of the Western world has only been made possible by the suppression of envy (a suppression which we owe in part to Christian doctrine), of that envy which prevents innovation, which punishes excellence, which falsely suggests that one man may prosper only at another's expense, which prevents individuality, inequality and progress and which, wherever it rages unchecked, wherever in particular it is used as a basis for policy, produces nothing but stagnation and poverty.

If any of this be true, it is a sinister horse indeed on which Crosland rode. He did so with complacency on account of his oft-expressed contempt for the rich.

> Only a rather insignificant fraction of surtax incomes is directed towards any intellectual activities whatever; the bulk goes on expensive cars and houses, holidays in Cannes, servants, gin, hotels and restaurants, dances, lavish parties and

* *Envy: A Theory of Social Behaviour*, Secker and Warburg, 1969

> the like. Indeed Britain can perhaps claim in recent times to have had one of the most illiterate wealthy classes in history.

Private patronage, he declares, 'could hardly be said to have had a uniformly splendid record'. He chides the rich even for failing to preserve 'innumerable Georgian buildings', without bothering to reflect on who put them up in the first place or on how many have been destroyed by public activity and compulsory purchase. Beyond the first generation at least, the rich he regards as totally functionless or, if performing any function, then only one which can be performed as well or better by public authority. He scornfully remarks that

> it does not require that we preserve all our millionaires on the off chance that one of them may fight an occasional battle for freedom, any more than on the off chance that one of them may prove an enlightened patron of the arts.

Very well: but let us look at this from the other side. Are not freedom and independent art and thought in all their variety, the future of *Encounter* itself, if you like, are they not certainly in far less danger if they can rely for their protection and patronage on one or more millionaires of varied interests and tastes or better still, upon the variously cultivated members of a whole wealthy and leisured class rather than just upon the monopolistic and monopsonistic state alone, which is all that Crosland proposes to leave them?

To do him justice, even he shows signs of disquiet at the proletarianisation of culture which has followed the massive transfer of purchasing power from the educated to the uneducated. His remedy is of course to educate the uneducated – yet this somehow without imposing upon them the 'middle-class ethos' he elsewhere modishly deplores. To do him further justice, it is indeed possible that our rich have recently to some extent let us down. But he should not ignore the part which he and his envious friends, with their deep and fierce taxation, have played in bringing about this betrayal. It certainly makes more sense to drink gin at lavish parties in Cannes if you know that you can leave little or nothing to your descendants or to your pet cultural activities.

Moreover, what Crosland was light years from seeing is that even these gin-swillers perform, despite themselves, various functions. He himself refers to one important function, though without noting its full significance. He quotes Woodrow Wilson as complaining that 'nothing has spread socialistic feeling . . . more than the automobile which offers a picture of the arrogance of wealth'. Today, Mr Crosland shrewdly comments, 'Leftists wonder ruefully how rapidly it is spreading non-socialistic feeling!' Indeed, he does himself rejoice most open-heartedly and unreservedly – it is greatly to his credit – at the motors, washing-machines and other consumer durables now within easy reach of the working classes. He has little of the sour puritanism of those middle-class socialists who regard it as the function of the poor to remain poor and thus dependent, a constant object of false sympathy and self-gratifying paternalism. Yet we must ask him how many of these desirable objects would now be within the workers' reach if the rich had not existed to buy them, test them and find them good when they were novel and astronomically expensive? He notes elsewhere that education is a social good, not just a private one; it has consequences far beyond the enjoyment of the individual 'user'. Is it really absurd to regard private wealth as equally a social good, conferring unintended benefits far and wide?

For the idle worthless rich have another function still – to act as a magnet, powerfully influencing the conduct of innumerable others, less rich. There are people so base (did Tony Crosland never meet them? I have met some, and like them on the whole little better than he did, especially those prominent in Labour circles) that their creative entrepreneurial talents are elicited, and perhaps can only be elicited, by the *prospect* of drinking gin one day at lavish parties in Cannes. One might wish them otherwise, spurred on by cooperative zeal for the common good. But that is how they are – their children might be different. If society abolishes gin and parties, or puts them out of mortal reach, then it must do without the services of such people and without such growth, whether valued by Crosland or no, as they might have engendered. At one point he speculates on whether Mr Charles Clore, said to have made £47m in ten years, would 'have foregone the deals and lazed about on the Riviera, if taxation had cut this by a half or more . . . ' The answer is to him self-evident, to others less so. He has chosen an unfairly loaded example, since the public utility of Mr Clore's operations is not obvious to all. This example is used to justify heavy taxation on all capital gains many the result of vast risks taken, of successes won by great effort and indubitably to the public good. Many typical entrepreneurs take almost nothing in income out of the various ventures which they launch in succession; their sole reward comes with the capital gains, if any, on sale. These Crosland would 'cut by a half or more', boldly declaring that this would not 'inhibit efficiency or risk taking'. Why on earth should it not? Nobody is going to cut the risks by 'half or more'.

'We know too little about incentives,' he concedes at one point, 'to make firm statements' – firm statements about whether 'equality and rapid growth are hard to reconcile' and about whether 'socialist policies must necessarily slow down the rate of growth'. Such doubts would induce in other less confident men, if they valued growth as he did, an extreme caution in enforcing equality, in destroying existing incentives and in pressing ahead with socialist policies. Not so in him.

He appears throughout to proceed on the assumption that economic man is dead or dying or never lived – an assumption fair enough only in that man's motives have always been various and complex and undoubtedly include all the motives on which he prefers to lay emphasis and on which he relies to supply the energies formerly or allegedly elicited by the acquisitive instinct. Economic man, after all, was only a model – a working model, if you please. In general Crosland declares there to be

> no reason to believe that an acquisitive and individualistic pattern of behaviour is an essential condition of rapid growth . . . The fact is that advances in productivity and technical

> innovation do not come characteristically from people working competitively for individual profit, but from people working on a fixed salary in a large managerial structure.

I think that Professor Jewkes for one would not find this true; and, even if it were, can one be sure that the salaried innovators would go on innovating if it were not for the threat presented by 'people working competitively for individual profit'? I would view this 'fact' rather as another expression of Crosland's continuous bias in favour of the salaried employee as against the independent operator and in favour of large firms against small. 'Progress,' he writes, 'often demands both a scale of capital investment and an expenditure on . . . research which are beyond the resources . . . of any except large concerns . . . A system of taxation which favours large established companies is not necessarily bad for economic progress.' 'Very large companies', he declares elsewhere, 'dominate . . . the economy . . . and represent (given the inexorable increase in average size) the clear trend of the future.'

His picture of the modern manager is of an almost entirely non-economic or post-economic or pseudo-economic man. Indeed this manager may still seek to maximise profits (or nowadays to minimise losses): but to what end? Not to distribute these profits to the owners, to the shareholders, indeed, to whose claims 'many managements today are at the least indifferent and occasionally even actively hostile' – a fact noted by Crosland with approval. No, this manager maximises profits mainly

> from a mixture of psychological and social motives. He tends to identify himself closely with his firm, which comes to him to have a definite personality of its own, with interests quite separate from those of the shareholders. And not only all his corporate loyalty to the firm but all his personal motives – professional pride, desire for prestige in the business world, self-realisation, desire for power – find their fulfilment in high output and rapid growth, and hence in high profits, these being both the conventional source of business prestige and the ultimate source of business power.

Perhaps Crosland is rash to link high output, rapid growth, and high profits so tightly together: many grandiose business follies mock him. But we must certainly notice that profits are thus here reduced by him to mere tokens, Monopoly money, the symbol of other things, of prestige and power, without use in themselves except to be 'ploughed back' to produce more prestige, more power. Those who agree with Dr Johnson that a man is seldom so innocently employed as in getting money will wonder whether this emasculation and deformation of British managers is welcome, to the extent that it is real. For Crosland, to my mind, persistently overestimates the powerlessness and functionlessness of shareholders, whose power is none the less real for being so rarely exercised. He contradicts himself neatly when writing about the cooperative movement:

> Ultimate democratic control is not necessarily lost because so few attend or vote. The inactive members still retain their full democratic power in reserve; and they can exercise it at any time they choose.

Yes, and so can shareholders, as some dozy or arrogant managements have suddenly found to their cost. Shareholders can also vote with their money, by selling shares, thus reducing non-economic managers' prestige.

Yet it is undoubtedly true that, in the increasingly controlled, bureaucratised and centrally directed economy now prevailing and always favoured by Crosland, managers may well feel that they have more to fear or hope for from governments than from shareholders and adjust their conduct accordingly, as Crosland describes:

> Now perhaps most typical amongst very large firms is the company which pursues rapid growth and high profits – but subject to its 'sense of social responsibility' and its desire for good public and labour relations. Its chairman will orate on the duty of industry not to the shareholder alone, but also to the consumer, the worker and the public at large. And some at least of this talk is reflected in company policy.

Such a firm will hang on to its profits, export more than is economically justified, butter up its trade unions, never dismiss redundant workers, charge only 'fair' prices, site new plants where the government wants it to, operate expensive welfare programmes, make gifts to education, patronise the arts, and participate in local community affairs: 'Its goals are a "fair" rather than a maximum profit, reasonably rapid growth, and the warm glow which comes from a sense of public duty' – and a title doubtless for the chairman to boot.

Crosland does not altogether deny the economic waste and losses caused by such pliant and amiable policies:

> On the one hand, management becomes slothful if it is spurred on neither by a personal stake in profit nor by the pressure of shareholders; on the other hand, we have a less efficient allocation of resources if profit maximisation is abandoned and decisions are taken on non-economic criteria. I am inclined to think this is true. Yet I doubt if it is more than a small part of the explanation of our poor economic performance; and in any case it is easily outweighed, in my view, by the social gain.

By now this non-economic motivation must surely be viewed as a much greater cause of our much poorer performance. Certainly one of the joys of being rich is that one can afford to be wasteful and inefficient within reason; alas, we do not seem to have been as rich as Crosland sanguinely supposed, and the social gains are now themselves outweighed, in my view, by the resultant unemployment, stagnation and frustration of all legitimate aspirations.

Crosland thus sees managers as floating rudderless in a sort of vacuum, blown hither and thither by alternate gusts of public duty and non-economic self-interest, responsible to nobody in particular and to everyone in general. They thus become exceptionally biddable and responsive to preponderant government pressure (or 'bullying' – the word he himself uses). He refers with mixed complacency and contempt to the 'other-directed organisation-men of Shell and ICI, jellyfish where their predecessors were masterful . . . slaves to their public-relations departments', terrified of parliamentary questions, the Board of Trade, the unions, the press, a Labour government, the consumer movement, old Uncle Tom Cobbleigh and all – all of which 'counter pressures' should, according to Crosland, 'be stronger still'. Surely never was such an armoury of terrors deployed against a few other-directed jellyfish!

This contempt explains his revisionist doubt that 'the pattern of ownership will uniquely determine anything', his conviction that 'the question of ownership is of less importance than other factors', and his consequent rejection of nationalisation as a panacea for all our woes – a rejection which brought him much non-socialist acclaim and must have won many non-doctrinaire recruits for the new non-doctrinaire Labour party he appeared to represent. What indeed is the point of nationalisation if one can without it direct every jellyfish in the land by a judicious mixture of bribes, threats, arbitrary prohibitions, regulations, tax concessions, pressures and counter-pressures? His point is really a simple one: that the government is now so powerful and businessmen so wet that the former can control (or, if you please, mess up) the whole economy without owning any part of it, or certainly no part it does not already own.

Indeed he does seem to scorn not only nationalisation but also most of the other institutions and attitudes which we associate with the Labour movement. He upbraids the trade unions for becoming 'increasingly unpopular' and generating 'an unfavourable public image, some of which rubs off on to Labour'. They should look to this, and engage public-relations officers. He berates the cooperative movement for being associated with 'a drab, colourless, old-fashioned mediocrity', and for betraying 'a somewhat patronising and insulting attitude to the wants and expectations of the ordinary cooperative member'. What is required here, it seems, is 'a change of attitude'. He deplores the complacent parsimony of the left:

> The trade unions, the cooperative movement, the nationalised

> industries, local government and the Labour party itself have all been gravely weakened by the twin beliefs that all jobs can be done by laymen and amateurs, and hence that no need arises to pay adequate salaries to attract scarce expert talent – whether in top management, public relations, economics, research staff or what. We should not confuse egalitarianism with anti-professionalism; but the constant harping on managerial rewards, understandable as it is [and so it should be, to an old harper like himself], encourages us to do so.

He does not spare state education: 'In some overcrowded secondary modern schools, where the staff changes frequently, children are scarcely being educated at all. Moreover, there is no free choice' – nor does he advocate any. The behaviour of some Labour-controlled councils is to him 'the subject of anxious study'. The whole public sector falls under his lash – schools, hospitals, roads, mental homes, universities, housing. Whatever the State does it does badly, he admits; wherever it interferes the results have normally been unfortunate.

Many of us would agree with some or all of these strictures. We accordingly place ourselves at some distance from the Labour party, which seems to us to stand precisely for what is here criticised. Mr Crosland seems to see no necessary connection between the Labour party and what he deplores. He does not see all these advantages, as we do, as part of the very essence and purpose of the Labour movement, the inevitable fruits of its thoughts and actions, the price of its achievements. No, they are to him regrettable but dispensable adjuncts, inessentials, the result of 'attitudes' now to be changed, part of an 'image' no longer appropriate and accordingly to be discarded like a used paper handkerchief. Like so many other socialists, less intelligent and more extreme, he is compelled to say that his sort of socialism too is not what exists, here or anywhere else (save perhaps in a Sweden seen through rose-tinted spectacles), but something quite different and much better. What is and what should be are not connected in his mind.

A like failure to connect is evident in his oft-expressed admiration for the United States of America, for instance, and for Marks & Spencer. He is more than fair in noting what is good about these two great free enterprises. He even notes, without any apparent consciousness of irony, that the distribution of wealth in America is (allegedly but quite possibly) notably more equal than in Britain (and this surely, I must add, largely by the operation of free market forces, for nothing like the down-levelling measures which he advocates was in his day known there). What he does not note is that both America and Marks & Spencer are run on principles which are quite alien to his own, and that their virtues in consequence cannot simply be filched from them and screwed on to polities and undertakings conducted on lines harshly inimical to those virtues. He praises generously, but does not seem to reflect on or profit by it. He wants in many ways to get nearer to America: but, like the rolling English drunkard trying to get to John o'Groats, he is travelling eastwards to his destination, unlikely therefore to arrive.

About nationalisation itself his mind is similarly equivocal and ambiguous. He reviews its past without enthusiasm: 'Some of the anticipated advantages did not materialise: while certain unexpected disadvantages emerged.' Control over the nationalised public boards, moreover, is difficult to exercise. 'We now understand rather better that monopoly, even where it is public, has definite drawbacks.' (Others might say '*especially*' rather than '*even* where it is public': for a public monopoly is far more durable than a private one, protected as it normally is by statute and government interference from all change and competition.)

Crosland deplored the restriction of free choice of goods and suppliers, and had second thoughts about largeness of scale: 'Before the war it was treated as axiomatic that . . . large-scale production, especially when conducted in large-size firms and plants, results in maximum efficiency. Today we are not so sure – at least beyond a certain size.' (He later had third thoughts, commending the merger-mania of the Wilson government.) He pointed to the dangers of over-centralisation, and quoted with approval the doubts of some left-wingers: 'We cannot disguise the fact that the public corporations have not, so far, provided everything which socialists expected from nationalised industries.' 'The continuous proliferation of State monopolies' would be in Crosland's view 'economically irresponsible'. It would be bad for exports and the balance of payments: in other words we cannot afford to play the fool while foreigners are still in their right mind!

Yet nationalisation, thus firmly shown the door, soon comes clambering back in modified, but not less alarming, form through the window. It is now to be 'supple, flexible and relevant . . . to achieve certain definite socialist ends'. Vast funds would accrue to the state from that deep and fierce taxation – i.e. from the ruin of many independent businesses. These funds would be used 'generally to increase the area of public ownership' and to 'extend public investment *in any direction*' (my italics). Public boards would be set up to manage these funds and operations, at once 'independent of the government in their day-to-day operations' (a phrase we have heard before) and yet responsive to legitimate government requests, for instance, 'to play a consciously stabilising role in the [stock] market'.

Outright nationalisation itself was by no means ruled out by Crosland. The insurance industry, for instance, should be nationalised, in order to promote a more 'venturesome' investment policy and to ensure that its first duty is no longer to its policy holders – tough luck on them! Indeed by 1974 Mr Crosland had inconspicuously become a thoroughgoing nationaliser again. Encouraged by various illusory or temporary 'successes' in the public sector, he proclaims that 'public ownership . . . can now be used more freely', with land, oil, privately rented housing, and 'parts' of the construction industry at the top of his shopping list. Nationalisation is also favoured where it is necessary to force a firm to 'spend more money, or spend it differently': 'it should be a constant preoccupation of government to bully backward industries into spending more on research, investment and the developing of new products.' Old-style monopoly nationalisation would not normally be necessary:

'the object could usually be attained by selective or competitive public enterprise', by which the nationalisation of one or more individual firms 'would be expected, by the force of example and competition, to galvanise the whole industry into raising its standards of research, efficiency and innovation'.

Even from Anthony Crosland's own gloomy reflections on our institutions, we might have derived some inkling of the resultant shambles. 'A dogged resistance to change,' he wrote in 1960, 'now blankets every segment of our national life . . . Our Parliament and civil service . . . are in fact in need of drastic modernisation.' Why, then, should these bodies, outmoded and inefficient as he thinks them, be thought fit to supervise or carry through 'the galvanising of whole industries'? Has any part of private industry, without grave penalty, displayed such incompetence in the control and expenditure of funds as recently have Parliament and the Civil Service? When these have sponsored 'research and innovation', such as Concorde and arguably the advanced gas-cooled reactor, has not the resultant waste been not merely scandalous, but even gravely damaging to the nation's prosperity? And again, when have government bodies intervened to 'stabilise' anything without destabilising everything? What indeed are these boards of Crosland's but a proliferation of organised projectors and speculators, the more irresponsible for playing about with other people's money not their own, a wild bevy of Leylands, Ryders and Crown Agents, all floundering about out of their depth?

We may do well to look more closely also at the principle of 'selective competition'. These competing state firms will trade with a bounty. They will presumably have at their disposal the full contents of the taxpayer's purse (I was about to say 'bottomless purse', but that cliché now rings false). For when, if failure looks imminent, has the state ever neglected to rally to the aid of its own children? This is to say that the private firms with which the state firms compete will themselves have to finance in part, directly or indirectly, their own competitors. If the state firms compete successfully, their private competitors will lose their markets. If they compete unsuccessfully, the burdens on their successful private competitors will be by taxation increased. In either case, the prospect before private competitors looks less like any sort of galvanisation than ruin, swift or slow. They will then have 'failed the nation'. As such, they too will become candidates, more or less willing, at least resigned to their fate, for nationalisation or public aid and 'participation'.

Crosland himself mercilessly ridiculed the Labour party's frivolous and ever changing nationalisation proposals, which do indeed recall the indecision of a muddle-headed housewife in a supermarket and also, as he said, constitute a damaging, if vague, threat to the whole of private industry.

> Thus sugar and cement were in the programme in 1950, but not in 1955 or 1959. Chemicals were on the list in 1955, but not in 1950 or 1959; while insurance, meat-wholesaling, machine tools, mining machinery, aircraft and heavy electrical engineering have all made transient appearances at different times.

There was also the threat to 'the 600 largest companies'. Very well, but what comfort could private industry derive from Crosland's own approach, a bludgeon in both hands, taxation in this one, subsidised competition in that, the first ready to fall everywhere, the second anywhere, 'in any direction', setting in train a process which (unlike any one of Labour's ridiculous but relatively precise proposals taken by itself) has no limit or term till the whole economy has fallen by design or accident into the hands of the ever-swelling state?

He himself in his Costa Rica lecture declared that 'a mixed economy is essential to social democracy' and that 'complete state collectivism is without question incompatible with liberty and democracy'. A private sector is as essential to a mixed economy as milk is to white coffee. How long then can how much of the private sector survive if existing Croslandite trends are maintained? Not long, perhaps, and not much; and we may add that, if complete state collectivism is incompatible with liberty and democracy, then partial or preponderant state collectivism must be gravely dangerous to liberty and democracy. He loved them both, but put them both in mortal peril.

Have I greatly overstated the case? Had he lived, Tony Crosland could have argued so, or indeed he could have rowed back and back until in the end his proposals were more in line with the 'mixed-up variegated pattern of ownership' which he thought essential to 'guarantee personal liberty and the fragmentation of power' and which he continuously, and I am sure sincerely, favoured.

Bitterly do I regret that he is not with us to do one or other of these things, did he think fit to do so. It would not seem to me even seemly thus to argue with a recently dead man (least of all in these columns which he so often graced) from whom I personally received nothing but courtesy and kindness and whom I shall always remember with pleasure and respect, were it not for the importance of the issues involved (which he could hardly deny) and were it not for his own well-remembered joy in controversy, which he always conducted as he vainly advised his Labour colleagues to do, without rancour, malice or hatred, without personal bias or intrigue, with self-control, in a tone 'temperate and even comradely'.

On the other hand, our national experience over the past fourteen years, in which so much has gone ill in ways which should have puzzled and disturbed Crosland, does not suggest the case to be overstated; and, if it is not, then Crosland may be seen as offering willy-nilly not so much *alternative* ends to those of the extreme left as an alternative route to the *same* ends. He repeatedly (and I am sure rightly) scoffs at Marx's prediction of the inevitable crisis and collapse of capitalism, due to its own inner contradictions. Indeed, there is nothing obvious and incorrigible in capitalism itself to make such disasters inevitable. No, it is Crosland and his like who seem to me to render them likely by supplying external contradictions, from outside; they are thus anti-Marxists yoked to Marx's chariot, Marxists *malgré eux*.

He himself described the revisionism he urged as destroying

> the simplicity, the certainty and the unquestioning conviction that come from having clear-cut crusading objectives to fight for and a hated, easily identified enemy to fight against. It makes everything complicated and ambiguous . . .

His road to socialism is in exactly these ways less simple and certain than that of the left, more complicated and ambiguous, less obviously hostile to liberty and prosperity, the more insidious and ingratiating, thus all the harder to resist. It does not present itself as 'a hated, easily identified enemy to fight against'. Indeed, many non-socialists have surveyed it with a certain bemused and hesitant goodwill, thinking it perhaps more friend than foe, as truly it contains elements of both.

How could such non-socialists fail to be reassured by a man who calls not only for higher exports and old-age pensions but also for

> more open-air cafés, brighter and gayer streets at night, later closing hours for public houses, more local repertory theatres, better and more hospitable hoteliers and restaurateurs, brighter and cleaner eating houses, more riverside cafés, more pleasure-gardens on the Battersea model, more murals and pictures in public places, better designs for furniture and pottery and women's clothes, statues in the centre of new housing estates, better-designed street-lamps and telephone kiosks, and so on *ad infinitum* . . .

What an enlivening prospect: Paris rather than Moscow, more Toulouse-Lautrec than socialist realism! Yet Crosland characteristically ignores the role of private means in ensuring the survival, *ambience* and prosperity of many of these charming amenities. That riverside restaurant which we can afford to go to once in a while, on special occasions, is in fact kept going by those who can afford to eat out there often and well: no rich, alas, no restaurant.

Tony Crosland's typical neglect may in part explain the fearful contrast between the enlivening prospects he offers and the shabby, decaying slum, the haunted house, in which we have been condemned (as I argue) by his egalitarian fervour to live. All around us we see frustration, failure, hopelessness, the very soil in which alone can thrive (apart from punk rock, and whatever *that* rough beast may portend) those sour and mad fanatics whom he detested so much, whom he aimed to outflank and thwart, and for whom he has unwittingly paved the way.

Encounter, January 1979

Nicest Set of People *

'I do think the Fabians are quite the nicest set of people I ever knew.' So wrote E. Nesbit, herself a Fabian and surely a very nice person indeed, as readers of the delightful *Wouldbegoods*, *Treasure Seekers* and *Railway Children* could hardly doubt. She was married to Hubert Bland, also a Fabian but not such a nice person, though he must have had charms which time has obscured. His photograph, reproduced by Mr and Mrs MacKenzie, suggests not so much a nice person as a menacing mixture of drunken vulture, confidence trickster (complete with monocle and false moustache) and melodramatic seducer of innocent maidens. This last indeed he was: NSIT, as debs' mothers used to say – not safe in taxis. His wife kindly befriended his victims and looked after the progeny, thus becoming nicer than ever.

But what of the rest? Were they really a nice set or were Miss Nesbit's standards lowered either by charity of lack or familiarity with nicer sets still? Well, quite enough evidence to form an opinion is supplied by the MacKenzies. They are themselves nice persons, you may suppose, if fairness, narrative skill, enthusiasm, humour and an impartial interest alike in people and ideas, in gossip and ideology, in absurdities and aspirations, be any qualification.

Was H. G. Wells nice? What Bland produced in the female line, Wells later strove to seduce, much to the former's indignation. He (Bland) is said actually to have pulled his illegitimate daughter Rosamund, another Fabian, off the train in which she was to elope with Wells, leaving Wells free to put the

* Review of *The First Fabians*, Norman and Joanne MacKenzie, Weidenfield and Nicolson, 1977

Fabian daughter of another early Fabian couple in the family way, and Rosamund free to marry Clifford Sharp, yet another Fabian, first editor of the *New Statesman*, a drunken womaniser and not even in other respects a nice man at all. The Fabians sound rather like the police force, as presented in a recent recruiting advertisement: 'Dull it isn't.'

Was the fair but luckless Rosamund in fact or in part Dora or Alice of the *Wouldbegoods*? And did the Fabians' pet Russian revolutionary, Stepniak, killed in a train crash, turn up in the *Railway Children*? One can hardly help wondering – but I digress.

Was Shaw nice? Well, in a sense it is possible to view his heartless, bloodless and mostly sexless philanderings as on an even scalier moral plane than Wells's disastrous antics, which have at least the dubious dignity of being part of real life. Wells took what he wanted, as God advises the Spaniards to do, and paid for it; yes, but others paid more, far more. Shaw took a little, took it often, paid a little, and gave a lot. What woman to whom he ever wrote one of those numberless irresistibly playful, affectionate, teasing, flirtatious *billets doux* but remembered it with a smile for the rest of her life? Much anyway can be forgiven a man who – a new one to me – acidly explained Annie Besant's predisposition to martyrdom as offering the only way to become famous without ability.

Were the Webbs nice? Well, in the dictionary sense – fastidious, hard to please, precise – they were clearly very nice indeed. And I must confess to a great weakness for Sidney. Perhaps it is partly his appearance which endears, resembling in later life, though incongruously adorned with pince-nez, one of those old, indeterminate, whiskery, lumpy, scruffy, flea-ridden, smelly little dogs which have the mysterious power to engender affection even in cold fish like Beatrice. He indeed actually used to curl up on her bony lap, causing her to reflect, perhaps justly if for the wrong reason, on what a pair of old sillies they were. Certainly his preoccupations and literary productions are boring, frowsy, wrong-headed and arid. Yet he never appears in this or any other book as anything less than human, friendly, good-tempered and decent.

His courtship of the beautiful but frozen Beatrice is really touching, with elements in it of both Don Quixote and Sancho Panza. His bids her not to sacrifice all to work: 'You would have dried up warm-heartedness in order to get truth, and you would not even get truth.' He warns her 'not to crush out feelings', not to 'commit emotional suicide', 'not to settle everything too confidently by pure intellect', to recognise the claims of instinct as a motive.

These are not typically Fabian noises. The MacKenzies refer to the 'emotional poverty' of the Fabians, which 'led them to ally themselves with those who were materially impoverished'. If Sidney Webb was less impoverished than most of the others, it was perhaps because unlike them he had had a good lower-middle-class upbringing – his was 'a *happy* family', he recalled.

Most of the dominant Fabians, as the MacKenzies point out, had had to rebel against formidable or inadequate parents, to establish their place in the world by sheer will-power, to shed the social and religious assumptions of childhood. The struggle left them lonely, different, proud, conscious of superiority, reluctant to co-operate with others as equals. It also fatally flawed their thought, leading them all in different degrees to ignore or despise or even hate the family and all the human motives and affections which that institution embraces, cherishes, canalises and sanctifies. It thus turned all their good intentions to dust and evil.

Here was perhaps a bond between them; and certainly one is required to explain how such an extraordinarily disparate bunch of cranks, prim prigs, lechers, dry doctrinaires, wits, fogies, vegetarians, drunks and pedants could possibly co-operate with each other at all.

Another common link is their contempt for liberty and freedom of choice, as also for the ordinary people (average and sensual as Beatrice Webb always called them) who, given this freedom, would inevitable choose wrongly. This contempt shows itself in so many ways, long before the Webbs and Shaw finally prostrated themselves before Stalin. They had been on the read to this diabolical Damascus all their lives.

The contempt shows itself in Shaw's early conviction that society would be changed only by those with superior brains and organising skills; in Wells's absurd Samurai; in the Webbs' determination to produce a flood of economists, political scientists and administrators, of superior people to build superior societies; in the Webbs' puzzlement and horror when confronted by America, to them a chaos as distasteful as it was incomprehensible. It shows itself even in the Webbs' passion, on the face of it humble or even noble, for disinterested social research. For, to their predestination-blinkered minds, all such research, however free, could only reach one conclusion – socialism. It was not a bus which at the LSE they intended to set in motion, but a tram.

The conversion of the Webbs to Communism 'came as a surprise to many of their friends. Yet it was not the turnabout that it superficially seemed. The Soviet system touched deep-rooted elements in both their personalities – the streak of élitism and authoritarianism, intellectual dogmatism, the need for an all-embracing faith, the desire for a planned and efficient order, the belief in the rightness of the expert, the lack of sympathetic imagination for ordinary people . . . '

Such were the defects which brought the nicest set of people to worship at the feet of murderers.

The Aristocrats and the Socialists

To readers of the *Sunday Telegraph*, as to television addicts, Peregrine Worsthorne needs no introduction. Even readers of *Private Eye* will recognise, with affection, Mr Perishing Worthless.

As other noblemen have been reduced by hard times to open their stately homes to the masses, so has this patrician thrown open his stately mind. For no more than four new pence, even the humblest of us are most weeks made free of this majestic edifice, part classical, part gothic, hardly at all of our time; free to saunter through the sonorously echoing saloons and galleries; to listen to the booming belfries, some with bats; to explore the well-stocked grounds, with their thickets and fountains of eloquence; to enjoy the spacious views which open up to left as well as to right and which certainly do not neglect the romantic element of surprise; to watch the proprietor himself graciously doing his thing.

And now, for a rather larger sum, we are invited, so to speak, to stay with him. He has produced a book;* and his admirers will be delighted to see with what success the sprinter now fares in the cross-country.

A nob wrote this book, certainly; but what sort of a nob?

Not certainly of that modish adaptable sort which demeans and ingratiates itself by running restaurants or boutiques, or taking snaps of dolly-birds, or playing in pop groups, or other such excesses. Nor is he of that old-fashioned game-bagging, poacher-shooting, footpath-stopping, common-enclosing, rack-renting sort which Peacock described as an ornament to the world and a blessing to the poor.

* *The Socialist Myth*, Cassell, 1971

No: here is a man fully conscious of the dignities and duties of his class, fearlessly and shamelessly expounding views appropriate to that class in a style appropriate to the views. But it is a nineteenth-century rather than an eighteenth-century mind, this, Tory rather than Whig; moved by Shaftesbury, touched by Young England, aware of Coleridge and even of Cobbett, a bit reminiscent of the earnest young Gladstone at Oxford; feeling no contempt for the poor and humble, but rather sympathy or even a certain affinity, respectful even of their errors and prejudices.

To minds of this sort there is nothing inherently or essentially distasteful about certain aspects of socialism; nor will socialists (many, I hope) who read this book be able to dismiss it as a cheap or spiteful diatribe. The tone indeed is generous and concerned and, where pain is inflicted, regretful.

Socialists believe in a lot of government, so do Tories of Mr Worsthorne's kind. Socialists believe in bigness and in planning. So, to a surprising extent, does Mr Worsthorne – an odd lapse this into the alien modern world of pseudo-technocracy. Like socialists, he believes in social justice, though he obviously means something different by the term. Like many of them, he believes in an authoritarian paternalism, in decisions taken by an élite 'at the top'. 'I do not quarrel,' he announces for some reason at one point, 'with the Labour party's belief in the economic necessity for socialism'. With such critics, Labour might well ask, what need for admirers?

But wait: there is a snag. For the type of socialism Mr Worsthorne does not quarrel with is socialism *without equality*; i.e. socialism without what most socialists think socialism is really about. He admires the bathwater, but throws away the baby. And from the seemingly bizarre yet none the less historically respectable platform thus constructed, he launches a brilliantly exciting assault on practically everything else that Labour stands for.

What socialism needs for success is, in his view, this: a ruling class, secure in tenure, able and accustomed to command a deferential working class accustomed to obey; the pushers and the pushed around, all arranged in a hierarchical society. Socialism further needs, according to him, stable and respected institutions through which commands can flow from top to bottom; a vigorous patriotism and sense of national purpose. It needs discipline, subordination a well-defined class structure, leadership, even tradition and continuity.

What socialism needs for success, in other words, is to become Tory, to strive to preserve or recreate a distinctively Tory society. Is this ludicrous? Not really at all. In Imperial Germany, so much admired by our early bureaucratic Fabians, something like what he advocates actually existed; nor is our own history by any means devoid of Tory socialists and socialist Tories, united alike by concern for the poor and contempt for free market liberalism.

Mr Worsthorne is thus in quite distinguished company. But, alas, to his obvious distress, he is not in complete accord with the Labour party itself, which is busily destroying everything which he cherishes as necessary not only for his own well-being but also, more controversially, for its own success.

It has demoralised the work force by affluence without discipline. It scoffs at patriotism so that when it is forced to invoke it (as it often is – remember Mr Wilson and the Dunkirk spirit) it only makes itself ridiculous. It derides our traditions and institutions, and pours scorn on all authority. It desperately needs all these things: but they break in its hand. It needs leaders, too, but can produce only pigmies.

Most unforgivable to Mr Worsthorne is the damage it has done to the ruling class. By overtaxing it, by rendering it insecure, by hindering its laudable efforts to educate its children properly and to pass on to them alike its wealth and its values, it has created a disastrous vacuum at the top. This is imperfectly filled by a shifting mass of vulgar spendthrift trendy plutocrats, of dry, oppressive meritocrats and of raw intellectuals, all inept as leaders, the last by nature actively opposed to and subversive of *all* authority, whether Tory or Labour.

This is in outline, I hope, Mr Worsthorne's case, the reason why he declares that Labour government itself cannot succeed.

It digs its own grave.

Impossible for me here to make clear with what wit, verve, percipience and often profundity this case is advanced, or to describe the fascinating by-ways which he explores *en route*. Read the book and see for yourself.

I would like to heave two bricks through his windows, one possibly damaging, the other hardly less so.

First, may I doubt whether socialism would work any better with the right chaps at the top than it does with the wrong ones? If you think, as I do, that socialism is *basically* destructive, then the more efficiently and consistently it is imposed, the more damage it will do. The man from Whitehall does *not* know best: why should the man from White's (or in Mr Worsthorne's case, Boodle's) know any better?

Secondly, may I question the construction put by Mr Worsthorne on the crimes and misfortunes of Lieutenant Calley? Faithful to his class thesis he attributes all such brutalities in Vietnam to America's lack of a recognised officer class. Good gracious; does he think the old Prussian officer class (undoubtedly more correct as it was than the classless brutes who supplanted it) incapable of a My Lai? Has he never read how the Indian Mutiny was suppressed, or by whom? Was Major Renaud a working-class upstart? Does the word 'Amritsar' ring no bells?

Certainly a settled class structure must help to transmit to new generations valuable old traditions, attitudes and wisdom. But just as it passes on good things, so must it also necessarily pass on bad – arrogance, for instance, insensitivity, callousness.

We may all love a lord. But surely to imply, even for a moment inadvertently, that all top people have no vices, and bottom people no virtues, is a bit thick?

Daily Telegraph, 19 April 1971

*The Nanny**

On the dustjacket of the American edition of Sir Harold Wilson's *The Governance of Britain* are displayed some of the more deferential comments of British critics: 'unique', 'a classic', 'not . . . short of gems', 'informative', 'good humored', 'lively . . . challenging', and, from my own paper, 'Sir Harold is at his shrewdest in the comparisons he draws between the United Kingdom and United States systems of government.'

It is certainly regarded as shrewd, in a Britain rendered by Sir Harold's politics too poor or too illiterate to buy books any more, to include, however inappropriately, in all books a chapter or two designed to give them an 'American angle', and those to ensure transatlantic republication and dollar royalties. Thus, gentle reader in Grand Rapids or Great Neck, when you read of 'The Plantagenet Influence in America', 'Norman Churches in Nebraska', 'American Beefeaters', and 'Cricket in Kansas City', do not suppose the author off his head – just eager to do his bit for the balance of payments. No fool at least in baser respects, Sir Harold includes his obligatory section on 'Transatlantic Comparisons', the most striking of which is the relatively greater ease and speed with which in Britain the most ridiculous, damaging and oppressive proposals can be made law – a facility not be envied.

Sir Harold's shrewd ploy has caught the eye either of Harper or of Row, perhaps of both. It is my task, as an English reader, to guess whether their enterprise was well advised and will be richly and justly rewarded, or not.

I ask myself first: Is this the most boring book I have ever

* Review of *Memoirs, The Making of a Prime Minister, 1916–1964*, by Harold Wilson, Weidenfeld and Nicolson/Michael Joseph, 1986

read? For all Sir Harold's deserved reputation for innocent merriment, I think it might well be. For one thing, I mislaid it not once but twice – a Freudian loss? My attention wandered uncontrollably: I found myself reading bus tickets and beer-bottle labels for preference. Whole chapters slid by, presumably perused line by line, yet leaving not a wrack behind, thus to be laboriously re-read for the promised but elusive 'gems'. When I had struggled through it, making copious notes *en route*, I forgot all about it for weeks – Freud again? It really is a pulverizer.

I most now ask myself: Will the American reader find it more or less tedious than I did? Well, there are Americans, a dwindling band of pilgrims, I fancy, who regard British statecraft with a superstitious awe on account of its ripe experience, its mellow capacity for compromise, its felicitous blend of tradition and change; for these every sign of feebleness and decay is a fresh beauty. There are also hordes of academics at obscure universities who strive to impress their superiors and gain doctorates by writing unreadable monographs on minute aspects of British politics and administration. Both sorts will find gold here, the latter especially in a chapter called 'Number 10 and the Cabinet Office', full of fantastically indigestible dead matter about the machinery of government, the merging and unmerging of ministries, the proliferation of committees, ministerial and official, zzzz–zz, horizontal and vertical groups, the transfer of functions, zzzz–zz, multi-disciplinary central policy review staffs, co-ordination, zzzz–zz . . . zzzz . . .

Sir Harold regards an ability to sleep as a prime minister's biggest asset. His book helps to make Prime Ministers of us all.

Of the sparse gems, more will indeed be unfamiliar to you than to us, but more will also be quite incomprehensible, which just about cancels out. In one major respect you will find it even more boring. This is that, unless you are a quite exceptionally well-informed and disillusioned observer of the British scene, you will miss the tremendous unintentional irony which, like the smell of rotting cabbage or faulty drainage, arises from the depths to pervade the whole pompous edifice.

You may read of the prime minister's need to stand back and think about the 'longer-term strategy' of his administration. Yet the author was, in office, a grasshopper notorious for short-term expediency and dexterous improvisation, innocent of all thought for the morrow: 'a week in politics is a long time.'

You may read with wonder of the cabinet he formed in 1974, 'a trained team', 'I was not exaggerating when I called [this] the most experienced and talented cabinet this century.' Trained by whom, then, to what end? Experienced in what? Displaying what talents? Perhaps you have to have seen this seedy crew of hacks at close quarters to appreciate the full absurdity of the cardboard haloes and threadbare statesmen's robes with which they are here incongruously adorned.

You may further note that Sir Harold's economic ministers in 1974 were 'undoubtedly . . . the most highly qualified the Treasury had ever had'. Sad indeed that men of such undoubted qualifications should have to grovel, begging-bowl in hand, before the IMF!

You may marvel at Sir Harold's own prodigious and ceaseless activity, 'seven days a week, at least twelve to fourteen hours a day', his transformation of Downing Street from the 'monastery' it was under Sir Alec Douglas-Home into a 'powerhouse', his need to keep 'in close touch with the whole range of national and international issues and developments', his consequent reception of numberless deputations, his chairmanship of numberless committees, his numberless visits to industrial centres and 'work places,' his working lunches, his discussions dinners, his perusal of five hundred (*sic*) documents every weekend, his meetings with experts, his answering as prime minister of twelve thousand parliamentary questions, his indefatigable hob-nobbings with other heads of government and assorted bigwigs, three or four hundred in two years, three or four a week – I could go on indefinitely.

You may marvel, but here we most ruefully reflect, of all this hurrying and scurrying and babbling and glad-handing, how much – if not all, the greater part – was utterly barren, damaging and unnecessary. False principles of 'governance' made all this meddling and trifling activity seem essential, whether to pursue success by inappropriate means or to avert or conceal disaster. The same false principles rendered it all in vain and futile.

Sir Harold's view of governance is essentially a trivial, fidgeting one, that of a governess rather than of a governor, one might say, if it were not for the dignity and good sense displayed so often by governesses and so rarely by him.

It is perhaps with a certain relief that he descends at intervals from the stratosphere of pseudo-philosophy to such problems as Barbara Castle's laddered stockings (11 lines on page 46) and whether to allow smoking in cabinet (15 lines on page 62, together with details of where to find 'a serious discussion of this controversial item' in his *The Labour Government 1964–70: A Personal Record*. 'Frivolous curiosity about trifles,' wrote Lord Chesterfield to his son, 'and laborious attention to little objects which neither require nor deserve a moment's thought, lower a man, who from thence is thought (and not unjustly) incapable of greater matters. Cardinal de Retz very sagaciously marked out Cardinal Chigi for a little mind, from the moment he told him that he had wrote three years with the same pen, and that it was an excellent good one still.' I wonder what Cardinal de Retz would have made of Sir Harold?

National Review, 5 August 1977

Funnier Than He Knows *

'Hugh Gaitskell did not help his cause by his remoteness. While the NEC was staying at the Royal Hotel at Scarborough, Hugh and his coterie were in the Grand. They did not know that a personal friend of mine, not at all involved in the Party, was also at the Grand and was able to absorb the atmosphere.' How much pleasure and profit may be derived from contemplation of this typically sly Wilsonian revelation! 'They did not know': did they care? The word 'remoteness' really implies, contrary to Lord Wilson's intention, that Gaitskell was either a poor intriguer or not one at all. There is then Gaitskell's 'coterie', earlier described as a 'small clique of cronies', into which he increasingly 'tended to withdraw'. Among Gaitskell's 'many fine qualities' listed by Wilson earlier still was unswerving loyalty to his close band of friends'. But as the friends degenerate in Wilson's view into mere cronies, so does the quality of loyalty to them become less 'fine'. Also apparently included in the Gaitskell 'coterie' were thugs variously characterised as 'hatchet men' or 'Hugh's heavy squad'. No doubt Gaitskell had and needed friends rougher and less refined than he; but to call them a heavy squad is to import the language of *Dirty Harry* into the affairs of a Women's Institute.

In his snide analysis of Gaitskell's sinister manoeuvrings, does not Wilson impute to Gaitskell ploys and motives far more characteristic of himself? In particular, in noting Gaitskell's loyalty to his cronies, does he not damn with faint praise an

* Review of *The Governance of Britain* by Sir Harold Wilson, Harper & Row, 1977

amiable trait for which he was himself greatly liked, and less feared in office than he needed to be?

Then there is the 'personal friend' (or crony?), 'not at all involved in the Party'. Who on earth can this have been? There arc so many possibilities. Names flash before the mind's eye: Ernest Kay, Wilson's ludicrously fulsome biographer? Some member of the to-be-ennobled lavender paper mob, some personal friend involved perhaps not in the party but in activities as scaly or more so? Lord Kagan is the sort of north-country tycoon who might conceivably have been staying in the Grand anyway, just by chance, though not if he was a connoisseur of scrambled eggs – at that time there a pallid quaking cowpat, alas, in a pool of tepid water.

Or was some humble dogsbody, unknown to history, deputed to go to the Grand and 'absorb the atmosphere'? In damp rooms you can hang up an absorbent chemically treated melon-sized ball which will draw into itself all the offending moisture. After a few days you can squeeze out an amazing quantity of liquid. Did Wilson and his cronies wring out their informant into a bucket, searching for traces of blood, sweat or tears, sinister evidence of Gaitskell's intention to fight, fight and fight again, so alien to the Wilsonian fudge, fudge and fudge again? These are deep waters, Watson.

As in most Wilson books, comedy abounds, not all intended. The present volume is enlivened by many misprints, some noted by Ferdinand Mount elsewhere. The index lists 'D'Oyly Carte, Bridget *(later* Dame Dridget)', thus baffling foreigners and happily recalling for us the entry of, say, Arthur Askey in resplendent drag as Dame Dridget, on foot in a sedan-chair with no floor. Much attention is devoted to Wilson's supposed barefoot childhood. What he actually said was that at his school many boys wore clogs. He writes now of 'footware': perhaps the clogs were made of vitreous porcelain? More seriously, he writes of Bevan as Attlee's 'lock forward'. Surely Bevin was meant here, rather than the mercurial Nye?

One hilarious moment is afforded by Wilson's urgent need as new prime minister 'to make one appointment with particular speed if my plans for a technological revolution were to be given effect . . . The first evening I summoned' – recall, or wait for it! – 'Frank Cousins, and confirmed that he was to become the first Minister of Technology.' Had he summoned a Siberian mammoth, Quentin Crisp or the late Duke of Gloucester, the effect could hardly have been more ludicrous. Alas, too, memories of Stanley Holloway singing 'With 'er 'ead tooked oonderneath 'er arm' ruined for me Wilson's deferential account of how, 'after a quick lowering of the head from the neck', he was invited by the Queen, plucky as ever, to sit down. More grimly diverting too than the author can have intended are memories of the 'genial', 'happy and stimulating relationship' which united the two Harolds, Macmillan and himself. There was 'a chemistry at work which brought out the best in both of us' – how chilling to suppose this true, and to contemplate the consequences for the economy! Their 'camaraderie' did not 'mean betrayal on either side of deeply held principles'. Indeed, how could it have done? Travellers without luggage can't lose it.

Most of the merriment springs, however, from Wilson's artless, almost boundless yet endearing vanity. Who else would have called his own memoirs *The Making of a Prime Minister*? Who else would have larded them with awesome premonitions and foreshadowings of the glory to come? They echo through his pages like Wagnerian *Leitmotiven*. Particularly impressive is the prime ministerial theme itself. It is heard when the little Wilson in cap and shorts is photographed on the steps of No. 10, more wistfully when the old Wilson reflects on the 'modest circumstances' from which he rose to greatness. It thunders forth when his grandfather remarked, on Wilson's recovery from typhoid, 'That lad is being saved for something, Herbert'; again when a pompous speaker at school condescendingly declared, 'Perhaps one of these boys will one day be Prime Minister', and at many other points.

Related to the prime ministerial theme and even more often deployed are the leaping exalted themes variously characterised by analysts as the *'m'as-tu-vu'*, 'look-at-me', *Heldenleben* or *Münchhausen* motives. They accompany such passages as the

Merton tutor's surprise, at his interview, at the extent of our hero's reading, and the exultant rebuke to doubters delivered by his headmaster, after our hero had won prize after prize at Oxford: 'Will you listen to me next time?' They resound at the moment when our hero, his roommate having suffered 'a kind of apoplectic faint', 'immediately rendered first aid', 'jolly well took charge' and 'ordered people about' while 'everybody else was clucking and fussing about', They resound again when our hero's penetrating questions reduce his tutor to a helpless haven't-a-clue.

These themes also underpin congratulations received by our hero in his 'superlative' handling of Americans during the war ('my Yorks accent was a great asset and also my direct manner') and his own rehearsal of the qualities required for such diplomatic triumphs. 'In the first place, I was numerate. . . I always regarded figures as my friend, if used with care. I had a freak capacity for absorbing statistics and applying them. . . A mastery of the facts solved most problems . . . Far from being a recondite art, diplomacy appeared to be susceptible to plain speaking and getting the figures right. It held no terrors for me.' *Tarantara!* If only Benes, in his dealings with Hitler, had got his figures right!

Nobilmente themes also glorify Wilson's continuing satisfaction, absurd at the time, more so now, about his famous but empty technology speech. 'A significant turning point in Britain's social and political history', burbled some journalist known to Wilson if not to me, a speech conferring on its author 'the seal of world-leadership'. Astonishing that such guff could be written at all, let alone reproduced with a straight face more than twenty years later!

Fanfares also greet Gaitskell's delight (he and our hero were not always on bad terms) at having in Wilson an 'economic spokesman who really knew his stuff'. Gaitskell's admiration for Wilson's economic know-how was widely shared. Even retired majors of my acquaintance, who despised Wilson, hardly denied it: 'Clever chap, knows his stuff – more's the pity.'

The question poses itself: what stuff was it that Wilson really knew? Why, economics, of course – damn silly question. But no.

This book powerfully confirms what others must have guessed: that Wilson is or was fundamentally a statistician and not by inclination or training, nor by philosophy or intuition, an economist at all. Well, what's the difference? Statistics is about measurement. It quantifies what is or was, what is in consequence unalterable. Admittedly, it purports by extrapolation to predict, but only *ceteris paribus* – if other things remain as they are – which they never do. Economics by contrast struggles by establishing general rules to reduce to some sort of intelligible order an infinite variety of factors, all in constant flux. The subject matters of statistics and economics being thus as different as death from life, their effects on the minds of those who study them are apt to be as sharply contrasted

Being a statistical mind, Wilson's is economically sterile. Here, as in all his writings, you will find life of other sorts abounding, wit, fun, kindness, malice, warmth, shrewdness, cunning, but hardly ever a penetrating economic observation or judgement. He is weakest where thought strongest. Unjust? Yes, at one point. Wondering whether to abolish clothes rationing, Wilson found out that the price of clothing coupons on the black market had dropped to only a halfpenny each. He abolished them at once, a shrewd move, and based for once on an economic insight.

Wilson has recently entered Mrs Thatcher's list of approved Labour leaders, men who would never have tolerated this or that new Labour outrage, men in office long ago, never to hold it again or better still, like Gaitskell, never to have held it at all and thus never to have been rumbled. Wilson confirms his new respectability by lauding the City but not the workers, and by lamenting how far 'the Labour Party has fallen in recent years'. I wonder how long it will take a superseded Kinnock to acquire such Tory ripeness and regrets. Does a Ramsay MacDonald lurk in him too?

The Spectator, 1 November 1986

The Reluctant Hero

I was astonished, gratified and baffled to be described by Alan Watkins in the *Observer* as 'a heroic Fleet Street figure'. I have wondered since how to repay this handsome compliment with a description of Mr Watkins equally flattering and inappropriate, dithering between 'an extreme reactionary of austere elegance and unwavering seriousness', 'a rigorously scientific and donnish figure' or 'a scholar lost in silent and solitary thought'.

My son politely wondered whether 'heroic' was yet another Fleet Street euphemism, like over-tired and emotional, for drunken. It took me two glasses of Perrier to recover from this impudent suggestion.

Anyway I am delighted Mr Watkins didn't describe me as 'investigative' or 'ancillary' two words which seen recently to have acquired rather pejorative meanings. And on second thoughts I will accept the adjective 'heroic', but only in one sense, which I will try to define.

The word has often been applied to poor bemused soldiers who endured hell in the trenches because they were too frightened to leave them and who did not take to their heels partly for that reason and partly because they hadn't the foggiest idea of what was really going on. If these were heroes, then indeed I am another of that sort.

If I write nonsense, I have at least written much the same sort of nonsense, with only minor modifications, for many long years now, and this out of a truly heroic incapacity for fresh thought, for imaginative sympathy with new, exciting and obviously deft ideas, for learning new and idiotic tricks. And also I do find in myself as I grow older – don't you? – an increasingly heroic inability fully to take in and understand what the hell is going on in this country of ours.

Doubtless this is partly due to premature senility, to agues, sorrows and fatigue, to deafness, blindness, dottiness and sheer rage. That some of these infirmities, even if assumed, can be turned shrewdly to advantage I learnt some time ago from Lord Amory, whom heaven preserve.

He emerged from retirement to speak after dinner to some Conservatives. He rose. He had forgotten where he was and whom he was addressing or so he pretended; he lost his spectacles and his notes; he lost the present he was supposed to give to someone – he had forgotten to whom or why. The result was an oration of irresistible charm and exuberant inconsequence, as memorable to those who heard it as anything from Demosthenes or Lincoln.

When I referred to it on a previous occasion, Lord Amory with characteristic civility declared that he had forgotten all about it, which seems likely enough. I still have not and never will.

But truly, if our own country, for instance, does appear to us increasingly baffling, complex and inscrutable, is this really because we are all going gaga? And further, if we are all going gaga, is the cause of all this to be found entirely in ourselves? Or are external changes reducing us to a sort of uncomprehending and impotent incoherence? I wonder.

In 1945–51, when I was young, vast follies were committed, I grant – the various acts nationalising this and that, for instance. But these follies came slowly and singly, so to speak, and in a clear and definite shape, like a solemn procession of mastodons. The faulty logic which underlay each one could be discerned and exposed: there was time for that. The evils which would flow from them could he predicted and even to some extent measured in advance. They could be fought; and, even if the fight was vain, we lost a battle rather than our reason, and lived to fight another day.

But folly does not come like this nowadays, does it? It comes rather like a mighty and irresistible tide, through numberless creeks and inlets flowing. We build little dams here and there; it surges turbulently round them, washing them away from the rear and sweeping away all landmarks.

The prosperity, the culture, the very survival of our nation are now menaced, not at this one point or that, but at every point, from above, from below, from every side. They are menaced by a deep swift and swirling flood of loose and incomprehensible legislation and, worse, by the wild torrents, cross-currents, tidal races and whirlpools of folly produced by the innumerable regulations and orders, the boards and tribunals, the occult pressure and blackmail which all that legislation engenders.

Directed, usually in vain, against particular evils, often either imaginary or irremediable, each of these measures and pressures produces an infinite number of unintended evil side effects, each in their turn to be remedied by further quackeries, each quackery in its turn producing infinite further evils, and so on *ad infinitum*. Thus does chaos grow by feeding on itself.

The principles of the old free market economy were simple, its detailed workings so infinitely complex as to defeat the understanding of any single mind. Yet we did not have fully to understand it. It worked, not perfectly of course – it produced wealth without being fully understood.

Socialism by contrast looks simple alike in theory and in practice. Hence its charm for shallow and half-educated minds. Perhaps when it is complete it *will* have the simplicity the regularity and order of a prison or workhouse, of a panopticon or mental home, a Normansfield, a Gulag Archipelago or Cambodia, a Hell.

But to get to that hideous paradise we have to struggle through this present appalling and unfathomable welter, not a benign welter like freedom was but a malign welter, which will resolve itself, if at all, unless checked, in an order far worse than the disorder now prevailing.

Where is the single human mind which can survey, grasp and comprehend all this? I can't; you can't. Nor can the pitiful Callaghans and the rest who appear or pretend to direct what in fact baffles and buffets and bewilders them as much as it does us. Vainly seeking to control everything, in fact they control nothing, not even themselves. They are really but corks tossing helpless on the raging foam.

If we are now gaga, so in fact are they, though they haven't the honesty or courage or perhaps even the insight to admit it

And where is the heroic will which, having comprehended, can master and reverse this inundation of folly? Let me give an Isaac Foot answer: in no man is this true heroism at this moment to be sought . . .

Daily Telegraph, 27 November 1978

CW as Deputy Editor of the *Daily Telegraph*

So Be On Your Guard, O Vigilant Reader

Sam Goldwyn tolerated no messages in his movies. He bade his subordinates, 'If you have a message, send it by Western Union.' President Calvin Coolidge was even more taciturn. An over-keen radio reporter badgered him after an election victory: 'Have you a message, Mr President, for the American people?'

Coolidge paused in silent thought, eventually replied: 'No'

These are inspiring examples. Yet my time on the *Independent* is up, to my regret if not to yours. Surely this is a time, if ever, for valedictory messages, sombre warnings and gloomy last testaments.

Before he died, my father, first wicket down for the C of E, solemnly bade me avoid chapel preachers, Quakers and Masons, counsel I have ignored at times without disaster: my dear daughter profited greatly from her spell atThe Mount, a Quaker school at York.

My own messages to readers of the *Independent* are equally negative and suspicious. I do not need to warn you to be on your guard against the one-eyed Greek who offers for cash a half-share in a yacht now sunk in Port au Prince harbour, formerly the property of a rich widow, Senora la Zonga, and now in the hands of the Argentine bankruptcy commissioners, in return for a handsome dividend payable annually in cruzeiros. Too obvious.

But there are politicians and other chancers who offer beguiling but misleading packages, and deals less exotic in appearance but every bit as dicey.

Mistrust, for a start, all politicians and commentators who see our national economic salvation in high or low or fixed exchange rates, or in high or low interest rates, or in any succession or, still worse, combination of these intermittently fashionable nostrums. None of them is cost-free.

Mistrust all quacks who, in the field of health, regard prevention as better than cure. They really seek more power for themselves rather than good health for you; will leave you less free but not less ill.

Mistrust likewise those politicians who seek vainly for the root causes and social origins of crime rather than for its effective punishment. In the past there were more social causes but fewer crimes.

Mistrust all pawky, witty and reassuring Scottish lawyers who aspire to catch up with, say, Germany's superior welfare expenditure. As they push briskly forward they do not notice the Germans hurtling hastily back, appalled by the country's spreading paralysis and inability to compete.

Mistrust again those lawyers who, well aware of growing unemployment, promise to combat it by establishing employees' 'right' to be employed and, if sacked, to be re-employed. Such rights are absolutely worthless without the concomitant duty of others to provide employment. How else to enforce this duty except by more regulation, which will make industry more arthritic than ever and thus reduce employment?

Mistrust equally all politicians who prate of charters. These in effect seek to cure social or economic malfunctions by futile exhortation, by more unsustainable 'rights' and unenforceable duties. Their results will be transitory, disappointing, perhaps counter-productive and not renewable.

Mistrust all miracle-workers who promise to reduce the national deficit without reneging on any of the state's enormous assumed obligations. Higher taxation simply cannot do it all, not least because, by suppressing enterprise, it brings in less and less revenue.

Mistrust all the public men, mostly Tories, who loudly echo John Stuart Mill on the deleterious effect of over-government on the character of the people, and who then ignore the effects of their prophecies come true. According to these pundits, our government has turned us all into delinquent sheep or patients in intensive care. Very well, but can you suddenly here, like the Khmer Rouge in Cambodia, wrench away the life-support of those poor zombies and turn them all out, unable to fend for themselves, into the jungle?

Beware also those other pundits who find our economic salvation in applied science. They hold that scientists are simultaneously underpaid and in short supply – something wrong here? They normally expect vast financial dividends from inflated scientific education. Beware, they are paid in cruzeiros!

Mistrust not least those who continuously proclaim that the Cold War is over and defence therefore unnecessary, its entire cost to be safely squandered in a peace dividend. The Cold War has *not* ended. The form of it may change, the protagonists, too. But it remains the natural state of fallen mankind, to end, if at all, only in a hot war, which is worse.

On a different and darker plane, mistrust all those social workers who find satanic child abuse everywhere. But mistrust, too – more difficult – those bluff, sensible chaps who pooh-pooh the very idea that such unnatural and monstrous crimes can occur in our godless age. Evil is endlessly inventive. Everything is possible.

Mistrust those Tories who credit the follies of our government entirely to the damaging machinations of Brussels. We generate plenty of follies of our own. The European Community was designed, perhaps ill-designed, to secure the safety and prosperity of all Europe. It must be turned back to its noble origins, not just destroyed. What has to be destroyed is Monsieur Delors' oppressive *dirigiste* idea of Europe, which repels the wise, enchants only fools and bids fair to wreck the lot.

I myself fell passionately in love with Europe in the winter of 1944–5. The old beauty was not at her best. Corpses everywhere, human and animal, hideously swollen, the unforgettable stench, sour and sweet, of death over all, of death and of sewers bombed open to the sky. The great cathedrals shattered and desecrated. Germany's beautiful cities reduced to rubble, with crippled survivors shuffling and stumbling about, their faces grey with shame, lost hopes and hunger.

The effects of all this on us invading liberators were various. Some of us, disgusted, couldn't wait to get home and stay there. Others, profoundly moved, vowed to ensure that this would never happen again.

Mistrust, if you like, whoever, especially in Labour and Liberal ranks, is drawn towards Europe for bureaucratic or social reasons. Be kind and patient, however, if you can, to those of us who once saw clearly into hell and remain faithful to the glorious vision of a united Europe. We try always to see in Europe, ugly as it may momentarily appear, what Disraeli saw in the British working man: the angel in the marble. Farewell, and try to do likewise.

Independent, 20 September 1993